The Spirit of Father Damien

JAN DE VOLDER

The Spirit of Father Damien

The Leper Priest—A Saint for Our Times

Translated by John Steffen

With a Foreword by John L. Allen Jr.

IGNATIUS PRESS   SAN FRANCISCO

Cover photograph of Father Damien © KADOC, KU-Leuven

Cover design by Roxanne Lum

Archive Photographs © Picpus Fathers Archive

©2010 Ignatius Press, San Francisco
All rights reserved
ISBN 978-1-58617-487-3
Library of Congress Control Number 2010927114
Printed in the United States of America ∞

CONTENTS

FOREWORD

Joseph De Veuster, a nineteenth-century Belgian Catholic missionary better known to the world as Father Damien, the Leper Priest
of Molokai, was the prototype for a distinctly modern phenomenon we might call the "celebrity saint". Whatever his religious or
philosophical convictions, the celebrity saint is someone whose moral
heroism makes him a media sensation and fires the imagination of
the world. Others would follow, from Albert Schweitzer and
Mahatma Gandhi to Martin Luther King and Mother Teresa, but
Saint Damien of Molokai was the original.

   In this marvelous introduction to Damien's life and legacy, Belgian author Jan De Volder observes that a century and a half of
water under the bridge since his countryman's death in 1889, at
the age of forty-nine, has done little to diminish Damien's appeal.

   I can offer a small bit of personal testimony to the point, because
I happened to be in Rome for the canonization of Saint Damien of
Molokai in October 2009. While I have covered any number of
similar events over the years, this canonization was unique in the
wildly improbable cultural fusion it produced. Leading up to the
October 11 ceremony, the streets and restaurants of Rome, espe-
cially around the Vatican, seemed to swarm with two groups: kindly,
but somewhat prim, Belgians; and far-more-relaxed and boisterous
Hawaiians. The surreal yet charming result could be expressed as
"Hercule Poirot meets Don Ho."

   It is difficult to imagine any other figure, living or dead, who
could draw precisely the same crowd.

   For another measure, consider that Father Damien was voted the
"Greatest Belgian" of all time in a national poll in 2005. Belgium
is today a thoroughly secularized society in which traditional def-
erence to the Catholic Church has all but vanished, sometimes
replaced by suspicion or even open hostility. I write these lines in
the summer of 2010, not long after a spectacular series of police
raids on Church properties in Belgium that took place as part of a

sexual abuse probe. Most controversially, the raids included drilling holes in the tombs of two former archbishops of Brussels in search of secret documents that, according to someone's overheated imagination, might have been hidden inside.

In that cultural milieu, the notion that Belgians might lift up a Catholic missionary and priest as their greatest countryman is, to say the least, interesting. (It also invites a bit of wistfulness about the past glories of Belgian Catholicism, in comparison to its present state, but that is a matter for another time.)

Naturally, there were lots of famous saints before Damien, including some who achieved renown in their own lifetime. In the early Church, Saint Simeon Stylites reportedly had such a reputation for sanctity that he lived atop a pillar for thirty-seven years to escape the throngs of devotees. In the thirteenth century, Francis of Assisi's embrace of "Lady Poverty" was legendary to such an extent that Pope Gregory IX declared him a saint just two years after his death in 1226.

Yet Damien was nonetheless the first celebrity saint, because the category of "celebrity" is itself an artifact of the modern world that came into being only in the second half of the nineteenth century.

In the same historical moment that Damien was embracing his vocation in far-flung Hawaii, back in Europe and North America the inventions of plate photography, offset printing, and the telegraph were creating a new global media industry, which required a steady supply of celebrities and their vicissitudes to galvanize audiences. When Damien departed Belgium in 1863, he understood himself to be leaving the "world" behind; propelled by the communications revolution of the late nineteenth century, however, the "world" caught up with Damien, even in Molokai, and made him a star.

The physiognomy of celebrity sainthood can perhaps be defined in terms of four characteristics:

- Intense coverage in the mass media
- Acclaim across religious and ideological lines
- An ambivalent relationship with authority figures
- Scandal or purported exposé, which generates a vigorous defense

All four were clearly part of the life story of Saint Damien of Molokai.

To begin, the newly born mass media of the late nineteenth century fell in love with the story of the Leper Priest, all the more so because of its exotic locale. Newspapers and mass circulation periodicals published lengthy accounts of Damien's life, which were usually one part hagiography, one part travel writing, and one part action-adventure story. Photos documenting the impact of leprosy upon Damien's ruddy peasant face and body, including a famous shot taken just after his death, also drew huge interest around the world.

Damien's admirers certainly included all types. One example is the American travel writer Charles Warren Stoddard—a onetime secretary to Mark Twain, an open homosexual, and (improbably enough) a convert to Catholicism. Stoddard penned the small book *The Lepers of Molokai* in 1884, which first propelled Damien to fame in the English-speaking world. Without intending to do so, Damien also became an ecumenical pioneer, developing strong friendships with other Christians in Hawaii and attracting strong international support from Anglicans in particular.

Like many charismatic figures who have to make their way in a heavily institutional Church, Damien sometimes had a tense relationship with ecclesiastical authorities. He chafed against what he perceived as a lack of understanding, while his superiors often saw him as a stubborn crank, drunk on his own fame, and so fixated on the welfare of "his lepers" as to be incapable of seeing the bigger political and ecclesiastical picture. (It is one of the great mysteries of Catholic life that the Church recognizes this dynamic only in hindsight, so that things never seem to get any easier for the saints-in-making in the here and now.)

Perhaps the final proof of Damien's celebrity, in the modern sense of the term, is that his reputation was briefly clouded by a sex scandal. When Damien died in 1889, a Presbyterian minister in Hawaii named Hyde published a letter asserting, among other things, that Damien had contracted leprosy through sexual dalliances with native women. (At the time, it was widely believed that leprosy was an advanced stage of syphilis, so lepers were often assumed to have brought the disease upon themselves.) In response, a much better-known Scottish Presbyterian, Robert Louis Stevenson of

Treasure Island fame, traveled to Molokai to interview eyewitnesses to Damien's life and then published a ringing defense of the priest's virtue. Stevenson correctly predicted that Damien's reputation would flourish, while Hyde would be remembered only for his fruitless attack upon it.

De Volder manages to present these episodes with both economy of expression and depth, which is never an easy combination. Taken together, they also provide the raw material for an explanation as to why Damien's fame seems undimmed by the passage of time, while so many other erstwhile celebrities have fallen into obscurity.

First, Damien exemplifies a perennial Christian option for the marginalized and forgotten—though, admittedly, few Christians ever live that option quite as radically as he did. There are, of course, obvious parallels between how leprosy was viewed in the nineteenth century and how HIV/AIDS is seen today, which makes Damien an important source of inspiration for Christians involved in the struggle against that disease. Yet even assuming that the day comes, God willing, when HIV/AIDS is no longer a global pandemic, there will still be pockets of people who are isolated—by poverty, by disease, by ethnic or religious profile, or by some other force. As a result, Damien's identification with the least of the world has no expiration date; it will always seem fresh.

Second, Damien of Molokai can be regarded, at least informally, as a patron saint of a globalized world. He was a European who chose to live on the cusp of Asia, among an indigenous population put at risk by the broader social and political currents of the day. Damien's life brought him into contact with the broadest possible cross section of humanity (including a number of Americans, who became important figures in his story). To be sure, Damien lived and died in Hawaii as a Catholic missionary, and there was a time not so long ago when that alone disqualified him as a role model. In some circles, both inside and outside the Catholic Church, the very idea of "mission", in the sense of an explicit invitation to conversion, came to be seen as an expression of Western colonialism. Today, however, when the mixing of peoples of all sorts is regarded as the natural byproduct of a globalized economy and culture, Damien looms instead as a positive model of encounter.

Third, Damien embodies a "warts and all" sanctity ideally suited to a voyeuristic postmodern age, in which no one's foibles remain hidden for very long. Damien certainly was not, in the words of Belgian cardinal Godfried Danneels, a "porcelain saint". As De Volder presents him, Damien could be brittle and given to self-pity. He had a history of up-and-down relationships with the people closest to him, which cannot be entirely explained as their fault. Damien was also shrewd, willing to play his fame like a trump card when it suited his purposes. None of that tarnishes his halo; instead, it makes him a recognizable human being, with whom flawed men and women of every age can feel at home.

Pope Benedict XVI once observed that in the end, Christianity has only two arguments to make for itself: the great art it has fostered and the great saints it has produced.[1] This highly engaging book by De Volder demonstrates that the story of Damien of Molokai, the original celebrity saint, has lost none of that evangelical punch. Damien thus illustrates a truth that applies even in our secular, postmodern cultural milieu, and one that deserves to be a cornerstone of any serious reflection on Catholic apologetics and evangelization in the twenty-first century: sanctity, like sex, always "sells".

---

[1] Joseph Cardinal Ratzinger and Vittorio Messori, *Ratzinger Report: An Exclusive Interview on the State of the Church* (San Francisco: Ignatius Press, 1985), p. 129.

SOURCES, BIBLIOGRAPHY, AND ACKNOWLEDGMENTS

The unpublished *Le père Damien De Veuster: Vie et documents*, compiled by Odile Van Gestel, SS.CC., with 212 letters of Father Damien and other documents about him, remains the primary source for any work on Damien. The present work also relied on the source material collected during the beatification process and put together in the various Vatican *positiones*: *Positio super causae introductione* (Rome, 1954); *Positio super virtutibus* (Rome, 1966); *Disquisitio de quibusdam quaestionibus vitam servi dei spectantibus* (Rome, 1974). The recent *Positio super miraculo* (Rome, 2008) brings together the documents on the miracle required for canonization. A number of additional documents were found in the archives of the Congregation of the Sacred Hearts in Rome and Louvain. Exhaustive new source research, however, fell outside of the purview of this work.

Further, this work relied on the many published biographies of Damien De Veuster, in particular John Farrow, *Damien the Leper* (1937, republished in 1998); Gavan Daws, *Holy Man: Father Damien of Molokai* (New York, 1973); Steven Debroey, *Wij melaatsen* (Averbode, 1989); Hilde Eynikel, *Damiaan: De definitieve biografie* (Leuven, 1999); and Richard Stewart, *Leper Priest of Molokai: The Father Damien Story* (Honolulu, 2000). Also very useful was the recent biography of Damien's fellow priest and successor, *Lambert Louis Conrardy*, by Werner Promper (Louvain-la-Neuve, 2009). For the history of the leprosy colony on Molokai, I refer partially to the recent work of John Taymans, *The Colony: The Harrowing True Story of the Exiles of Molokai* (2006); and for the history of the Belgian missions, to Edouard de Moreau, *Les missionaires belges de 1804 jusqu'à nos jours* (Brussels, 1944), and AA.VV., *Rond Damiaan: Handelingen van het colloquium n. a. v. de honderdste verjaardag van het overlijden van pater Damiaan 9–10 maart 1989*, KADOC-studies 7 (Leuven, 1989). When yet other studies are referred to, bibliographical references are provided in the endnotes.

Many people have contributed to the realization of this book, and I wish to thank them. Several fathers of the Sacred Hearts of Jesus and Mary have been helpful to me in one way or another: postulator Alfred Bell; Edouard Brion; Frits Gorissen; archivist Jean-Louis Schuester; and Felix Vandebroek, pastor of Kalaupapa.

Patrik Jaspers, staff member of the Louvain Damien Center, and Professors Francesco Dante, Jean-Pierre Delville, and Leon Lemmens always willingly answered my questions. Any mistakes and the interpretation of Damien's life and spirituality, however, remain my responsibility.

I am grateful to Archbishop Raymond L. Burke, prefect of the Apostolic Signatura, who has been inspired by Father Damien from his childhood and who encouraged me to have this book translated into English. I thank John Steffen; his wife, Lieve; and his friend Brad Gregory, who made this translation with love and passion. I thank Father Joseph Fessio, S.J., of Ignatius Press, who was favorably disposed to publish the English version.

Thanks to the loving support of my wife, Hilde, and daughter, Lena, the project of this book could be finished on time. Finally, I thank my friends of the Community of Sant'Egidio, who in "Kamiano", its restaurant for the homeless in Antwerp and Brussels, make concrete Damien's spirit of free service to the outcasts of our time. I am grateful that I was able to accompany to Molokai, at the end of 2008, Diederik Vekeman, cofounder and director of Kamiano, on the unforgettable last pilgrimage of his life. To Diederik I happily dedicate this book.

INTRODUCTION

Father Damien has been canonized, 120 years after his death. Already during his lifetime, the Belgian priest enjoyed world renown for his holiness. The extraordinary witness of his voluntary banishment with the lepers of Molokai spoke to the nineteenth-century imagination. When news of his death came on April 15, 1889, the *Times* of London demanded that the world not have to wait forty years for his beatification. Yet it took more than a century for the formal process of his beatification and canonization to be completed. The Catholic Church prefers to take her time, and Father Damien's temperament did not correspond perfectly to the traditional image of a "pious and holy" life. He indeed was no "porcelain saint",[1] as Belgium's Cardinal Godfried Danneels has put it. It is probably due to the tireless advocacy of Mother Teresa of Calcutta, who has meanwhile been beatified herself, that Damien's canonization happened at all.

The canonization Mass, celebrated by Pope Benedict XVI on October 11, 2009, in Saint Peter's Basilica, was attended by thousands of pilgrims from around the world, including King Albert II and Queen Paola of Belgium; Herman Van Rompuy, then the Belgian prime minister and soon to be elected the first president of the Council of the European Union; and several cabinet ministers. U.S. president Barack Obama sent a presidential delegation that was headed by the U.S. ambassador to the Holy See and included the bishop of Honolulu and a U.S. senator from Hawaii. Also in attendance were leprosy patients from Molokai. The procession to place Damien's relic on the altar included the Hawaiian woman whose recovery from cancer a decade earlier was attributed by the Vatican to Damien's miraculous intercession.[2]

In his homily, the pope said that Father Damien's missionary activity, which gave him so much joy, reached its peak in charity. "Let us remember before this noble figure that it is charity which makes unity, brings it forth and makes it desirable. Following in St

Paul's footsteps, St Damien prompts us to choose the good warfare, not the kind that brings division but the kind that gathers people together. He invites us to open our eyes to the forms of leprosy that disfigure the humanity of our brethren and still today call for the charity of presence as servants, beyond that of our generosity." [3] Following the Eucharistic celebration, the pope went out into Saint Peter's Square to greet some forty thousand additional faithful who could not fit inside the basilica. He urged them to pray and help those involved in the battle against leprosy and "other forms of leprosy that are due to lack of love because of ignorance and cowardice". [4]

A lot is known about that noble figure and his missionary activity. Damien left behind 212 letters, which already in the first year after his death were collected together. Every time period has shown interest in him, right up until today. Countless biographies in numerous languages have been published, while theater performances and films about his life have been made. Is there anything new to say about him?

Perhaps there is. In this book we go in search of the spirit behind Father Damien's extraordinary life. We seek to understand why today, at the start of the twenty-first century, he remains so appealing. In 1936, when his body was returned to Louvain, Belgium, via San Francisco and Antwerp, his appeal was understandable. During the five days that Damien's body reposed in San Francisco's cathedral, a steady flow of visitors paid homage, while in Belgium unprecedented crowds witnessed the transfer of his body to his native land. The immense popular interest fit seamlessly into the Catholic mass culture of the time in Europe and suited the nationalist feeling that wanted Belgium's own hero to rest on the country's own soil. Afterward the transfer drew a lot of criticism. Did Damien not belong to the Hawaiians? Or to all the earth's lepers?

But with time, Damien's star has not faded. His witness seems to have become even more powerful. How did he survive the secularization of the West? Is that perhaps not the greatest miracle of his life?

Why did Belgians, who in the past few decades have in large numbers stopped practicing their traditional Christian faith, nonetheless choose Damien as their "Greatest Belgian" in 2005? Is that not remarkable for a man who, other than a big heart and great faith, did not have a lot going for him, whether intellectually or in his appearance?

What is there in his life that speaks so deeply to our contemporaries? Not just to people in Belgium and the United States, but across all national borders? Not just to Christians, but also to people of other faiths and of no faith? Damien's popularity transcends many boundaries. What is it in his life that strikes a universal chord?

Perhaps his life speaks to us because it confronts postmodern men with their flaws and weaknesses. Damien was a man who was all of a piece. How starkly does that contrast with the often-fragmented existence of our contemporaries? Damien was a man who made decisive choices and remained faithful to them until the end. What a contrast with our indecisiveness. Contemporary men want to try a bit of everything, to have as many experiences and get as many kicks as possible. What does Damien's self-giving to the outcasts of humanity teach us about what makes a human life worth living? Damien was a doer, someone who was not afraid to get his hands dirty: he built churches, houses, and schools and cared for the lepers with his own hands. But most of all, he built up the community of God amid the poorest. Perhaps that also speaks to the heart of our contemporary Church, which all too often, especially in the West, has become a Church obsessed by administration.

Damien was through and through a child of his age. He shared the missionary dreams of the Church of his time as well as the civilizing work carried out by the expanding Western world. After decolonization, that strong missionary tradition was criticized. For was the missionary not the spiritual accomplice of the colonizer, trampling—often with the best intentions—valuable local cultures? Was the missionary's approach not paternalistic and thus condescending?

In some cases there might indeed be something to such accusations. Yet simplistic critiques have a way of dying down again. Our contemporaries appear to be a little more open to the incredible adventure that induced ordinary young men and women to sacrifice their lives for people on the other side of the world. One sees that many missionaries, in their loving approach, did not regard their flocks as savages but as fellow human beings whom they often deeply loved. More than just the gaining of souls, their mission also focused on the full well-being of the local population. Damien was a pioneer in this regard, or rather a real missionary with his heart in the right place. Moreover, he evolved: if at the start of his mission he had aimed mostly at winning as many souls as possible for the true Catholic faith, gradually his compassion and love for all men grew, including for those who ultimately did not embrace his faith.

Damien's dedication to the outcasts of Molokai, his efforts to introduce new medical techniques, showed that he deeply valued the material side of life and bodily health. Yet he was more than a development worker. He shared his very life with those pariahs on the margins of the world, treating them with his own hands, not hesitating to touch them with love, until finally he became a leper himself and died from the disease.

With his life, and the celebrity that came his way, he put leprosy on the map. His contribution has been important in generating the energy needed to conquer the disease and eradicate it—a battle that still has not been entirely won. Above all, it showed something universal, something essential in Christianity: namely, that in love for the poorest, lived as self-giving until death, lies a road to salvation. Neither Islam nor Buddhism produces this kind of saint.

The Christian martyr contrasts sharply with the martyrs exhibited in various extremist religious movements today. The latter look with contempt on their own lives in order to destroy the lives of others and bring them down into the grave with them. The Christian martyr gives his own life in order to save the lives of others. It is a testimony that depends not only on events, on context—it is a universal testimony that withstands the ravages of time and transcends space.

For that reason, it is perhaps a good thing that Rome waited more than a century for Father Damien's beatification and canonization. For his extraordinary witness has become even more powerful as the historical context of his life has become further removed from us. Father Damien was a man of his time. With his canonization he becomes a universal example, a saint for our time.

1. From Jef De Veuster to Damien

One always has to be rather careful with stories about the child-hood and adolescence of a saint. Such accounts are often colored retrospectively by the saint's later life. It is noteworthy that in his letters, Damien referred little to his childhood. He probably con-sidered it unexceptional and considered his real life in Christ to have begun on the day of his solemn profession in Paris or his priestly ordination in Honolulu. His early years were bathed in the cultural setting of traditional Catholic Flanders and the spiri-tual revival of nineteenth-century Europe. His youth differed little from that of many other boys of his time and place. Though Damien's parents were devout Catholics, they had envisioned a dif-ferent life for him. As the second youngest of eight children, Damien was inspired by the examples of two of his sisters, who entered the convent, and his older brother, who became a priest. The opportu-nity to follow that same path offered itself to him only in due time, but when it did he grasped it with both hands. This character trait of seizing opportunities that presented themselves was typical of the later Damien.

Youth stories

Joseph De Veuster was born on January 3, 1840, the seventh child and fourth son of Frans De Veuster and Anne-Catherine "Cato" Wouters. Little "Jef" was baptized on the day of his birth—not only because his godfather, Jacques Govaerts, an Antwerp grain merchant, was in a hurry to return to his business, but also because infant mortality was very real in Flanders at the time. Though life expectancy was rising slowly, one-fifth of infants in the first half of the nineteenth century still did not survive their first year.

Damien's birthplace and childhood home, circa 1895.

The De Veuster family lived in Ninde, a hamlet between Tremelo and Werchter in the province of Brabant, about six miles from Louvain. His parents had known one another since childhood and had married in the summer of 1829. They were not entirely uneducated, as it is known that they had to flee from the boarding schools they were attending at the time of the Battle of Waterloo in 1815. At the time of their marriage, Frans recognized the two daughters already born to Cato. In that era, Christian circles also saw out-of-wedlock births; marriages followed if and when financial means permitted. During the first years of their marriage, the couple lived with Frans' parents, his father a merchant and his mother an innkeeper. Frans too was more a merchant than a farmer, regularly away from home seeking buyers for his agricultural produce. Soon their income enabled them to afford a house of their own, the first brick house in the hamlet. That parental house, which they built with their own hands and in which Joseph was born, serves today as the Damien Museum. One can still view the room in which Damien was born.

Tremelo was a village consisting of some ten hamlets, laced with woods and meadows. The inhabitants were known as poor, diligent workers with unrefined manners, who could let loose only at the occasion of the *kermis*, the local fair. In this rural setting, between the Nete and Dijle rivers, Jef De Veuster grew up, a child as vivacious as he was devout. This is clear from the many anecdotes gleaned from the testimonies of family members, neighbors, and friends, recorded much later in the context of the beatification process. Damien's brother Auguste (or Father Pamphile), two years older than he, was an important source of information about his childhood. There is the story that Damien went missing as a four-year-old in the commotion of a *kermis*, until he was found in church praying before the altar. Another story has him nearly falling through thin ice while skating, and yet another failing to avoid an oncoming horse and buggy, an incident from which he sustained some lasting injuries. Cautiousness was not his strong suit.

Generosity and helpfulness, on the other hand, were. Numerous stories attest to how, as a child and adolescent, he was always ready to assist others, staying through the night with a neighbour woman's sick cow or giving away his sandwich to a schoolmate who looked hungry—or who pretended to be.

Jef De Veuster attended elementary school in Werchter. He was certainly not a top student, but he did have a good teacher, Mr. Bols, who instilled discipline and a sense of fairness in him. The boy's innate interest was geared more toward manual work. He enjoyed spending his spare time around carpenters, from whom he learned at a young age the tricks of the trade, which would serve him so well in his missionary work.

Liberal and Catholic

The world in which Damien grew up still exhibited the outward features of rural life as it had existed for centuries. Below the surface, however, nineteenth-century modernity was budding, following the Industrial Revolution and the political upheavals that ended the ancien régime in both France and Belgium. Damien's world was on the brink of the "great acceleration" that characterized the second half of the nineteenth century. Most people still traveled by foot, the wealthy classes by horse and buggy. But five years before Damien's birth, a railway line was constructed between Brussels and Mechelen, the first on the Continent. The line was not far from where the De Veusters lived, and perhaps Damien's parents also stood by to watch the first steam engine, a symbol of progress. Belgium was a young, dynamic nation, and the Industrial Revolution quickly left its mark on the country's societal life. The result was a growing entrepreneurial spirit, which also was not unknown to the De Veusters.

Living conditions slowly improved. The importation and wide-ranging spread of the potato led to the gradual end of chronic hunger in poor Flanders. During Damien's childhood, however, a serious famine caused by the potato blight affected large areas of Europe from 1845 to 1849. In the famine's wake, many immigrated to the New World. To make matters worse, a cholera epidemic claimed many victims, including the youngest De Veuster child, Marie, who died of the disease when she was four.

Damien's time was one of sweeping change, which saw major scientific and technological innovations: photography (1839), the telegraph (1843), the telephone (1876), and the electric light bulb

(1880) were all invented or further developed during his lifetime. Though he himself barely came into contact with them in his life as a missionary, Damien was delighted by them.[1] He was immersed in the spirit of the era, which was one of increasing, progressive optimism and the belief that the future would be better than the present.

The Catholic Church played along with the changing world. After having lost many of her traditional privileges with the demise of the ancien régime, the Church sought ways to carry on her mission in a new era. That was not so simple, for much Catholic blood had been shed during the French Revolution, and even Napoleon's concordat with the Church in 1801, for example, prohibited the contemplative religious orders from recruiting young people. It was a difficult period for the Church, which after the Battle of Waterloo and the Congress of Vienna (1815) often placed her hope in the Europe of the antiliberal forces of the Restoration. Yet there were countervailing voices in the Christian world. French thinkers like de Lamennais and Montalembert argued that Christianity and democratic liberalism could work together. The Belgian Revolution of 1830 put that theory into practice: liberals and Catholics formed an alliance against the regime of William I, the king of the Netherlands. The Belgian constitution of 1831, which recognized multiple freedoms, including freedom of the press, of assembly, and of expression, was the most liberal of its time. The new nation was internationally significant as the laboratory par excellence of cooperation between Catholicism and liberalism.

In Rome and elsewhere in the Catholic world, critical voices were heard: would so much freedom not encourage undesirable ideas and practices more than anything else? However, Belgian Church leaders persuaded the pope and the critics of the advantages of this constitution for the Church as well. It gave a great deal of freedom to citizens, but the Church too was entirely free. She could name bishops and priests without state interference; she could establish schools and hospitals anywhere; and religious congregations could be founded and developed without restriction. Moreover, the state provided the money for religious education and paid the salaries of priests. What more could the Church have hoped for?

Around 1840, the year of Damien's birth, Belgium was known not only as the most liberal state of Europe but also as the most Catholic country north of the Alps. Travelers to Belgium were amazed by the wide range of activities that the Church could foster in this liberal context and were surprised by how respectfully the clergy was treated in public places such as train stations.[2]

The Church in Belgium experienced an impressive revival following the difficult decades of transition from the ancien régime to liberal democracy. Active religious orders and apostolic works sprang up everywhere, launching educational and other social initiatives. These deeply social forms of religious life were genuinely modern, harmonizing with the dynamic and the spirit of private initiative and entrepreneurship that characterized the economy and social life.

Religious vocation

The De Veuster family was barely aware of this historical framework yet was fully immersed in it. Religious education was rooted in the countryside of Catholic Flanders, but through the grain trade the family also encountered traveling merchants and ideas from elsewhere. At one point Frans De Veuster even set up a trade in leeches, which brought him to Germany—exposing the family to a world with shifting frontiers, a world that was growing ever larger.[3]

The De Veuster children received the faith from earliest childhood, especially from their devout mother. Yet Cato was not an easy woman and could also be quite harsh with her children. One of the few books in the house was a large volume with stories of saints and martyrs, written in Old Flemish and printed in gothic letters. Several witnesses later mentioned this. Cato regularly read from this book, which the children enjoyed. Jef would have had a preference for the story of Cosmas and Damian, the brother physicians who died as martyrs in 303. The *Legends of the Saints*,[4] which at the time was popular throughout Flanders, observes regarding these two saints: "They became excellent medical doctors, curing many people, more through divine than through human skill. Their eyes were not fixed on temporal gain, and they did not cure for money, but only for the mercy and love of

God, through whose power they cured." [5] If young Jef had heard these words, it is entirely possible that they left a deep mark on him.

Did his child's heart already begin to long for a great and holy life? In any case, it is known that Jef once arrived late to school with three of his brothers and sisters because they had stopped in the woods along the way to pray like real hermits.

Yet initially Jef did not seem destined for the religious life. Several of his brothers and sisters had already followed this path. His eldest sister, Eugénie, entered an Ursuline convent when Damien was only two years old. His brother Auguste, two years older than he, with whom he had a good relationship but who got much better grades in school, left Tremelo to become a novice in the French Congregation of the Sacred Hearts of Jesus and Mary. Jef was then thirteen, the age at which he, the less able student, was taken out of school to help on the farm. Some of the children had to ensure the future of the small family business. This was the life that seemed to be in store for the strong, broadly built, healthy youngster.

When Jef was fourteen, his sister Eugénie died of typhus in the convent. She had contracted the disease while preparing a sick girl for her confirmation. This was the second sister whose death he had known, following the death of his youngest sister, Marie. Illness and death were part of young Jef's life. He also saw how his favorite sister, Pauline, reacted to Eugénie's death: she immediately offered to take her place in the convent. The example of his sisters must have made an impression on the boy: in his heart too the desire grew to devote his life to the sick and to take their yoke on his shoulders.

When Jef was seventeen, his favorite brother, Auguste, entered the novitiate of the Congregation of the Sacred Hearts, also called the Picpus Fathers. Thereafter he was known as Pamphile.

Joseph remained on the farm for five more years. His sturdy, powerful body seemed tireless, and the demanding work did not exhaust him. He did not want to pamper his body, preferring to sleep on a hard board rather than on his softer bed of straw, as his mother once discovered. Spiritually, Joseph was restless; farm life failed to satisfy him. His heart longed for a different life, with deeper meaning and a wider horizon. But how could he rise beyond the humble life that appeared to be laid out for him without disappointing his parents?

The opportunity came when he was eighteen. In the spring of 1858 his parents sent him temporarily to a boarding school in Braine-le-Comte to improve his poor knowledge of the French language. That would be useful later in life, his father believed, and definitely in business. In the new state of Belgium, in the years following its independence in 1830, knowledge of French was indispensable for advancement in life. Much of social, political, and commercial life in then-bilingual Flanders was carried out in French. Joseph studied hard. Too often he had been frustrated due to his ignorance, when he could not understand conversations in French. If he did not want to spend his life as a farmer and a businessman, he had to seize this opportunity. That seemed to be a constant in his life: Joseph De Veuster was someone with a nose for *kairos*, or the opportune moment. He seized this opportunity with both hands. Had he not done so, we probably never would have heard of him. His first, undated letter home makes clear both his desire to learn and his passionate character: "All of the Walloons that laugh at me, I smack them with my ruler." [6]

The distance from home afforded him the chance to reflect on his future. He was strongly attracted by the example of his brother Auguste, now Brother Pamphile, who was well on his way to living the life of a missionary priest, and that of his sister Pauline, who was about to take her vows. In a letter to his parents, he wrote that Pauline had had "the happy advantage" to take upon herself "the most difficult task one can fulfill on earth". He continued, in words that were restrained for the ardent soul he was, "I hope that when my turn comes, I will be able to choose the path I must follow. Would it be impossible for me to follow in the footsteps of my brother Pamphile?" [7]

In the summer of 1858 Joseph stayed with Pamphile in Louvain. Pamphile enjoyed teaching his inquisitive younger brother, helping him further improve his French, a language with which the Fleming was never really comfortable. Yet it gave Joseph the opportunity to talk a great deal with his brother, whom he admired and with whom he liked to compare himself. In the autumn he was back in Braine-le-Comte, where he heard a priest speak in a way that set his heart on fire. He was now convinced of his own vocation. Night after night he prayed at length. Coupling his penchant for arduous physical labor with his desire for mortification, self-denial, and solitude, he thought for a while of becoming a Trappist monk. He also inquired into the possibility of studying at the American College in Louvain, where, from 1857, European priests were formed with an eye toward missionizing the vast regions of America. According to one source, he was refused entrance because of his rudeness in manner and lack of languages.[8] Naturally, he discussed his vocation with Pamphile, who recommended his own Congregation of the Sacred Hearts with such enthusiasm that Joseph chose it without a problem.

Joining the Sacred Hearts

Joseph had made his choice. The remaining problem was to convince his parents, especially his father, who had placed so much hope in him for the future of his business. "But do you not have to obey God more than men?"[9] That strong sense of obedience—not so much in the everyday sense of "being submissive" but understood in a religious way—more than once played an important role in the fundamental decisions and turns in his life. Otherwise he would never have become the person he became. Joseph was convinced he had to go his own way: not according to his own feelings and ideas, but according to the vocation that God had given him. In a letter to his parents written on Christmas Day 1858, he revealed his choice for religious life and requested their permission: "Most beloved parents, I ask you once more whether you would be content about this matter, because without your approval I would not dare to enter into such a state, since it is God's commandment to obey your parents in your years of reason as well as in your childhood years." But then he added, more strongly and with the passion and impatience so characteristic of him, "In forbidding your child to follow God's will in choosing a state of life, you would show yourself to be very ungrateful to God, who could punish you for it in a terrible way."[10]

Joseph was to an extent pushed along by Pamphile, who let him know that sooner rather than later a conversation with the superior in Louvain was advisable regarding immediate entrance into the novitiate. Joseph lost no time. At the beginning of 1859 he traveled from Braine-le-Comte to Louvain, without visiting his family in Tremelo. His father sought him out in Louvain, but he realized he could not hold back his son.

Joseph was accepted into the congregation as a postulant, but initially the superior did not see him as a candidate for the priesthood, for which his education was too limited. His French was still insufficient, his Latin and Greek nonexistent. So he was assigned to the choir brothers, whose responsibilities included perpetual adoration of the Blessed Sacrament, teaching in the colleges of the congregation, and care of the chapel.[11] Was this not an excellent choice for the practically inclined young man?

On February 2, 1859, Joseph received the habit as Brother Damien. To what extent his religious name was his own choice is unclear from the documents. But without question it was prophetic. "Damien" referred to one of the brothers Cosmas and Damian, the physician-missionaries about whom he was told in his childhood. Damien certainly thought of himself in terms of the younger brother, who walked in the footsteps of the older brother. Yet he did not see himself as a hanger-on or a follower; on the contrary, much in his life should be seen as a kind of holy competition with Pamphile, who helped him to strive for ever greater holiness and willingness to serve. Saint Francis of Assisi too had converted when praying before the crucified Christ in the church of San Damiano, which was the beginning of a road that led him both to rebuild that crumbling, humble church and to show love to lepers along the way. The extent to which Brother Damien was aware of this is unclear. What is clear is that the name "Damien" perfectly suited him: how much of his life revolved around sickness and health, lepers, the building of churches, and the founding of a community?

More than anything, the name change indicated that Joseph De Veuster was no longer Jef, destined to dedicate his life to his father's farming business. He had cut himself loose from that destiny and had become Damien. Henceforth he strove for higher goals. God's call had not been in vain.

The Picpus Fathers

The Congregation of the Sacred Hearts of Jesus and Mary was founded in 1800 in Poitiers, France, by the diocesan priest Pierre Coudrin and a noble lady, Henriette Aymer de la Chevalerie. From the start the congregation had a male and a female branch. Priests of the congregation were soon called Picpus Fathers, from the location of the motherhouse in Paris on the rue de Picpus.

Their purpose is to practice and propagate devotion to the Hearts of Jesus and Mary, and equally to make Christ's love present in the world. The congregation was one of the new forms of religious life in postrevolutionary France working on the revival of Catholicism. From 1827 onward the congregation also sent missionaries to remote regions in the Pacific Ocean. The papal congregation Propaganda fide entrusted those largely unexplored areas to the young congregation.

Around the year of Damien's birth, 1840, the founders of the congregation died, and a struggle ensued between the followers of the style of the initial period and others who thought that an adaptation to changing circumstances was required. In 1853 Rome put an end to the conflict: the new superior generals of the congregation's two branches restored the lost unity and promoted the recovery of the spirituality of and obedience to the rule. The congregation got its second wind, which went hand in hand with the extension of its activities, both in Europe and in the mission territories. Hence Cor Rademaker, a Dutch Picpus Father and a historian, could write: "That way Joseph De Veuster ended up in a religious community that breathed an atmosphere, on the one hand, of renewed spiritual depth and, on the other hand, of missionary expansion." [12]

In the congregation, Damien came in contact with some outstanding clergymen who had a lasting influence on him. Among those were certainly the novice master, Father Caprais Verhaege, and the superior of the Louvain community, Father Wenceslas Vincke, two dazzling personalities with robust spirituality. The then superior general in Paris, Father Euthyme Rouchouze, however, had the deepest influence on Damien, who never forgot the lessons of Father Euthyme's conferences about the founders of the congregation, the spirituality of the Sacred Hearts, and the obligatory fidelity to the rule. Once in the missions, Damien wrote to him, in conformity with the rule, a yearly letter. These letters radiate the warm affection of the pupil for his master.

Damien devoted himself in a serious way to the spirituality and the rule of the Fathers of the Sacred Hearts: he was a community man and always desired to have a confrere with him, including during his mission. When that appeared not possible during the most difficult moments of his life on Molokai, he wrote that the loneliness was harder on him than the disease.

When he was alone, Damien also remained loyal to the succession of prayers and moments of reflection prescribed by the order. That appears from his personal notes preserved from his time on Molokai. At no time did his isolation undermine his loyal bond with his congregation, not even when he was confronted with much incomprehension from his direct superiors.

The congregation's full name is the Congregation of the Sacred Hearts of Jesus and Mary and of the Perpetual Adoration of the Most Blessed Sacrament of the Altar. This Eucharistic piety and adoration of the Blessed Sacrament were important in the spiritual life of Damien; in these he found support and consolation.

When the disease had manifested itself all over Damien's body, he was happy that his hands remained good enough to keep consecrating the Eucharist. However, the more devotional aspects with which the love for the Sacred Hearts was lived in his congregation were not all-determining of his spirituality. For Damien, love was first and foremost a verb. That love manifested itself in the love for the poorest and most vulnerable, for whom he did not spare himself.

On his deathbed he said: "How sweet it is to die a child of the Sacred Hearts." [13]

2. Who will go in my name?

Damien was resolved to dedicate his life to God. Exactly what form his life would take, he did not know. That depended on the congregation he had joined.

In school he had never been a high achiever. If one of the De Veusters was an intellectual, it was Pamphile. The younger brother compensated for this shortcoming through his boundless energy, dedication, and eagerness to learn. From the beginning he wanted to become a priest, like his brother. When Pamphile suggested to him that he learn some Latin during his postulancy, he agreed to the proposal with such enthusiasm and progressed so rapidly that his superior quickly changed his status to "brother" and allowed him to study for the priesthood.

The path ahead of him was clear: following his postulancy, there would be a novitiate of a year and a half, part of which would take place in France. He would take his vows in the motherhouse in Paris, after which he would return to Louvain to study philosophy and theology. Only after these studies were completed would he be ordained a priest and given an assignment.

Damien was well liked by his fellow students, as he was friendly, humble, and fond of laughing. And he earned their respect because, despite his deficient basic formation, he managed to master the academic program through intensive study. Being mainly interested in what could be put into practice, he was not one for theoretical discussions. His intellect needed things to be concrete. After a conference, he once carved into his wooden bench the key words "silence, recollection, presence of God". That insight, which today can still be viewed in the house in which he was born and raised, now the Damien Museum, resulted in a rare scolding.

His physical strength was striking, but so was his ascetic zeal, which suited his temperament and the religious formation he received. Various stories about his ascetic side were recorded after

Shortly before Damien's departure for Hawaii. The 23-year-old strikes the pose of his great model, Saint Francis Xavier.

his death. He usually chose the difficult time from two to three o'clock in the morning to do his weekly hour of nightly adoration, making it a point of honor not to return to bed afterward. He often slept on the floor rather than in his bed and tried to eat moderately, regularly abstaining from meat. His time at prayer in the chapel, including at night, exceeded the prescribed amount. Occasionally the typical student talk of his fellow novices irritated him. He thought such talk "unworthy" of future servants of the Sacred Hearts and made this explicitly clear.

Dying to your old life

Damien's novitiate, first in Louvain and later in France, at Issy, came to an end in the autumn of 1860. He was twenty-one and ready to take the solemn step toward full membership in the congregation. His profession took place on October 7 in the rue de Picpus in Paris. The ceremony of transition, in which the professed dies to his old life, closely resembled the funeral rite. Together with his fellow novices Damien prostrated himself before the altar and was covered with a black pall; the celebrant sprinkled him with holy water. Lying dead to his past world and old self, he was reborn into a new life of service to God. Damien later often thought back on that moment.

The rite of solemn profession corresponded well with Damien's deepest intuitions. He was keenly aware of the brevity of life. In accord with the thinking of his day, he understood our short time on earth as a period for gaining the salvation of our souls. That thought recurs again and again in his correspondence. A few quotations from his 1861 letters to his parents suffice as examples. The thought of mortality must cause "sharp pangs in the heart" for non-Christians, so he wrote, but not so for Christians or religious believers like Damien, "who regard ourselves as exiles in this world, and who yearn for the moment of the dissolution of our body so we can enter our true home".[1]

At Easter Damien received word of the death of his *mamère*, his paternal grandmother, with whom he had been close. Distraught by the news, received while at table, he could not eat another bite and wanted to leave the refectory. His initial reaction was replaced by joy when he reflected that his grandmother was now in heaven. "And to obtain that blessing, dear parents, we must begin today preparing ourselves for a good death; let's not waste another moment of the brief time we have left in this life."[2]

In the ideas of the soon-to-be priest, there was undeniably an element of zealous diligence, which belonged to the enthusiasm of youth and certainly was not tempered by his formation. In this vein, at the start of the harvest season, he recommended to his father that he worry less about the yield of the earth than about his soul. "I believe it would be better for your present life and the future if you would detach yourself a little from worldly anxieties, in order to give yourself to the important matter of your salvation, the only thing absolutely necessary."[3] And he continued: "Dear Father, I think I am allowed, as the youngest son, to offer a small bit of advice: receive the sacraments, pray day and night, do everything for the greater glory of God, meditate on his great love, on the seriousness of sin, on death and the Last Judgment."[4] That constant awareness of the hereafter is far removed from our contemporary attitude toward life, which focuses so intensely on the here and now. Even Christian life today is lived less from the perspective of death and the next life. Yet it would be wrong to think that Damien saw his life solely as a "sacrifice", as a "preparation". On the contrary, all of his choices revealed a strong desire to make something of his present life—hence his dream to leave the family farm and become a religious, a missionary, and so leave Europe, dedicating himself to the poorest of the poor, giving himself completely to the lepers of Molokai. Behind those choices was a passionate aspiration not to waste his life on meaningless matters but to spend it on the one thing that matters.

New worlds are beckoning

Little is known about the sixteen months Damien spent in Paris, from the beginning of 1860 until September 1861. The big city made an impression on the country boy on his arrival, but it did not appeal to him. He found it a bit dreary and certainly all too worldly. These were eventful years for France, with Napoleon III coming to power and attempting to breathe new life into the memory of the empire of his famous great-uncle, whose name he shared. In Paris the chief civic planner, Georges-Eugène Haussmann, oversaw the construction of wide, impressive boulevards. Internationally too, these were times of sweeping change. In 1860 the largest part of the Papal States was seized by the armies of the House of Savoy. The future of the papacy concerned Catholics the world over. Damien's own interest, however, lay elsewhere. It is remarkable that nowhere in his letters does he make any mention of current events.

He might not have been charmed by the metropolis of Paris, but he was enthusiastic about other aspects of nineteenth-century modernity. At that time vast and still-unexplored worlds were opening up. Technological innovations such as the steamboat and steam locomotive made it possible to cross enormous distances more rapidly. A radiantly self-confident Europe was on the threshold of a new era of major expansion, a globalization *avant la lettre*.

Christian culture shared fully in that spirit of the times. With the opening of the new worlds, the missionary idea received a new impulse, both among Catholics and Protestants. The idea of bringing civilization to unexplored regions, of bringing the Gospel to non-Christian peoples, spoke to the hearts of many young people. It was a way of life that was not banal but on the contrary was a grand adventure. Although that nineteenth-century missionary idea was later criticized for its overt paternalism and sense of superiority, it was undeniably part of modernity.

Damien's passion was to live this missionary life. During his studies, he prayed daily before an image of Saint Francis Xavier, apostle of the Far East, his great exemplar. The most distant coasts and unexplored areas spoke most to his imagination. In Paris he once heard Bishop Tepano Jaussen, apostolic vicar of Tahiti, speak about the needs of the mission in Polynesia. Those words touched him and kept him under their spell. Without delay he tested his parents' view: "Probably he will take a few of us along. Would you be pleased if I went along?" [5] In September 1861 Damien left Paris and returned to Louvain, a trip he made together with Jaussen. He probably heard many stories about those exotic lands. Again and again throughout history, God asks the same question he once asked the prophet Isaiah: "Who will go in my name?" Damien was bursting with eagerness to be able to answer: "Here I am, Lord. Send me!"[6]

What he desired so ardently was given instead to his older brother. The Congregation of the Sacred Hearts was seeking reinforcements for its mission on the Hawaiian Islands in the Pacific Ocean. Pamphile, who meanwhile was ordained a priest, was chosen for this voyage. Tickets were booked for a ship that would bring him, together with five fellow priests and brothers and ten sisters of the same congregation, from the German city of Bremen to the Hawaiian capital of Honolulu. Damien must have been consumed with envy, while his brother himself showed little enthusiasm for his upcoming departure. Fate was kind to Damien. A typhus epidemic had broken out in Louvain, and Pamphile, who regularly visited the sick, was also infected. The disease was not mortal, but departing was excluded. The impulsive Damien saw his chance. Did not his sister Pauline take the place of Eugénie?

There was no time to waste. Damien immediately wrote to the superior general in the Picpus headquarters in Paris, bypassing his local superior in Louvain: "Send me!" Damien had always gotten along well with Father Euthyme Rouchouze, then the superior general. The approval of Paris followed quickly, to the anger of the local superior, who regarded Damien, not yet ordained a priest, as too green for the mission. Not the least bothered, Damien rushed to his brother's sickbed and proclaimed jubilantly: "I am to go instead of you! I am to go instead of you!"[7]

There was just enough time for a brief, final meeting with his mother. Those who left for the missions did so in the knowledge that they likely would not return. The short farewell took place at the Marian shrine in nearby Scherpenheuvel, where, together with her, he prayed for the opportunity to stay "twelve years" in the mission. Their good-bye was not sentimental, at least not on Damien's part. There was in young Damien a religious fervor that rendered him insensitive to anything that came across as a worldly concern. In that, however, he was not at all exceptional for his time: countless young men and women made the radical choice of saying good-bye forever to their families, friends, and homelands.

Damien then left for Paris for a three-day retreat. In Paris he made use for the first time of the new technology of photography. The portrait shows a strong young man, looking somewhat bewildered, wearing small glasses, the Bible in the background, and in his left hand, held straight up, the cross of Christ. One need not search long for the model for this photo: Francis Xavier was portrayed exactly this way in the image in front of which Damien had so often prayed. A last letter to his parents dating from immediately after his departure testifies to a rock-solid faith and a vision of life that seems stripped of every doubt, perhaps also to a youthful drive that more often characterizes candidate-priests prior to their ordination: "Adieu, dear parents, adieu! Be sure always to live as devout Christians. Never allow the least mortal sin to stain your soul. Always walk on the straight path. That's the last thing that I ask of you. Promise me this, and then I will be assured, as far as you are concerned, to see you again in our heavenly homeland. Adieu!" [8]

The trip from Bremerhaven to Honolulu took five months, from October 23, 1863, until March 19, 1864. The ship, the *R. W. Wood*, did not stop in any port along the way. Christmas was celebrated on board, in the middle of the Atlantic Ocean, just south of the equator. Damien, not yet a priest, made the trip with five fellow brothers and ten women religious of the Sacred Hearts. On board they led the life of their religious order: they followed their rule, prayed and celebrated the Eucharist at the prescribed times, made time for study and relaxation, and obeyed their superior, Father Chrétien, the only priest in the group. Damien mainly made use of the long sea journey to study English intensively.

We learn from his letters that he was occasionally seasick, something from which he also suffered later on. He was far from the only one. What he regarded as his greatest ordeal was living in close quarters with Protestants, whom he, in conformity with the times, called "heretics" and nonbelievers.[9] The missionary life and the misery on Molokai would gradually bring him to think differently about fellow Christians outside the Catholic Church.

Three weeks into the new year the ship rounded Cape Horn and started the dangerous passage through the South Pacific. Twenty years earlier, in that same area, a ship carrying twenty-four Sacred Hearts missionaries had sunk, with everyone perishing. Damien's ship also sailed through a violent storm, and towering waves toyed with the ship for days. After ten days the weather calmed down, and the rest of the journey passed well.

Honolulu

On March 19, 1864, Damien disembarked in the harbor of Honolulu, capital of the Hawaiian Islands. About sixty thousand native inhabitants were spread throughout the eight largest islands. There was also a Chinese presence, but the Western influence was increasing rapidly, in the economic as well as in the political and religious realms. Politically, Hawaii was an independent kingdom, but it was foreseeable already then that it would fall to one of the Western nations gaining influence. Damien had little interest in geopolitics; he arrived with the heart, soul, dreams, and hands of a missionary. "Impossible to express how immensely happy a missionary is", he wrote to his parents after his arrival, "when he sees the new land that he must water with his sweat to gain uncivilized souls for God." [10]

At the time of Damien's arrival a third of the indigenous population was already Catholic. The Sacred Hearts Fathers had been active there for more than thirty-five years. Protestant missionaries, who had arrived seven years earlier, were also active in the region. By 1850 the Mormons arrived, and in 1862 the Christian missionary competition was pushed to its apex with the foundation of an Anglican diocese.

Thus it was an urgent matter for the Catholic Church to send more workers into the field. Bishop Louis Maigret, apostolic vicar of Honolulu, wasted no time. Damien was ordained a subdeacon after one week on the island, then a deacon, and on May 21 a priest, barely two months after his arrival. He was twenty-four years old when his ordination was celebrated in Honolulu's small cathedral. Today, surrounded by skyscrapers, the cathedral contains the relic of a foot bone, transferred there shortly after his canonization, and many other references to Damien, for example, in its stained glass.

The new priest was happy and wrote to Pamphile about the differences between their ordinations: "You had family and acquaintances and fellow brothers among you who were all practicing, while my believers consisted of all new Christians.... My heart seemed to melt like wax when, for the first time, I distributed the consecrated bread to about a hundred people here. I actually thought that many of the people whom I saw before me, dressed in white and quietly proceeding to the communion rail, had perhaps previously fallen to their knees before idols." [11]

Damien becomes Kamiano

Maigret appointed Damien and another new missionary to the east coast of the island of Hawaii, the largest of the archipelago. It was rough, volcanic territory, with the active volcano Kilauea already attracting tourists. His confrere Clément Evrard was assigned to the Kohala-Hamakua district, Damien to the smaller Puna. Damien's district counted at most 350 Catholics, who moreover lived far apart from each other. Damien was immediately thrown into the missionary's existence, which differed greatly from his life as a novice: "Instead of a tranquil and hidden life, one has to get used here to traveling over land and sea, by horse and by foot", he remarked at the end of 1864 in his annual letter to his superior general. "Instead of strict observance of the rule of silence, one has to learn to speak a variety of languages with a variety of people; instead of being directed, one has to direct others; and most difficult of all is to maintain, amid a hundred and one miseries and trials, the spirit of meditation and prayer." [12] Damien had discerned correctly that the last of these would prove to be his greatest inner struggle throughout his life as a missionary.

Physically, Damien could handle that life well, unlike his confrere Clément, who had a much weaker makeup. As early as the spring of 1865, less than a year after their appointments, their superior agreed to switch the two men. Damien became active in Kohala-Hamakua, a much larger area, ninety miles long and thirty miles wide. He compared it to the vastness of the Archdiocese of Mechelen. For eight years he lived in Kohala-Hamakua, where there were perhaps three thousand Hawaiians, half of whom were Catholic. He had a little wooden church and a rectory with a thatched roof, but in reality he was nearly always traveling. He carried the church on his back, as he said: four poles to set in the ground, a board to put on top, and an altar cloth formed his traveling altar. The faithful were called to Mass with a conch shell.

Traveling through that inhospitable territory was not easy. Along the way he always happily accepted the invitations of the local population, both to eat and to spend the night. Damien built several churches with his own hands: he himself did the heaviest work, but he also involved the local population. That involvement would increase their love for their own church, so he hoped.

Damien's superiors were pleased by his unrelenting dedication, though at times they considered him too driven. He made quick decisions, went on baptizing and building, and sometimes made his superiors feel that he outpaced them. The continuous need for funds, which had to keep pace with the young missionary's zeal to build, was not always met. "Father Damien is a *vir desideriorum*. His visit here was so short that we barely had time to get a good look at his noble figure brimming with health", provincial Modeste Favens wrote about him.[13] "In the letter that I write to him today, I tell him that you have to want to do good with moderation, because it is easy to set up projects for good causes; but it's not so easy to implement them, especially if you have to free up the necessary funds." The admonition was formulated with fatherly empathy. Yet it would not be the first time that Damien's fervent enthusiasm would clash with the more sedate rhythms of his superiors, who had to keep in mind the mission in its entirety and had to monitor the cash flow.

Damien learned the local language of the Kanaks, as the indigenous population of Hawaii was called. That meant learning yet another foreign language, having already zealously applied himself to learning English during the long journey to Hawaii. As with his other languages, his Hawaiian was far from perfect, but he could manage to get by with it. Fortunately, Hawaiian is a very simple and sonorous language: the alphabet consists of only twelve letters; a word never ends with a consonant; two consonants never follow in a row; and the plural is formed by repeating the word twice.

Hawaiian lacks the dental consonants *d* and *t*. So Damien's name became "Kamiano". It was his second name change, and this time he did not choose it himself. But that did not make his new name less dear to him. Quite the contrary. He wrote to his parents in March 1865: "Our poor islanders rejoice when they see Kamiano coming, and I, for my part, love them very much and would willingly give my life for them, like our Divine Savior."[14]

Kamiano did not mind sharing the simple life of the Hawaiians: he was not keen on comfort, and without difficulty sat cross-legged with the local inhabitants to eat of the *poi*, the local food, with his hands. His approach was anything but aloof.

Like most Catholic missionaries of that time, he saw his mission in intense competition with that of the Protestant "heretics", who did not kneel while praying and who distributed the local *kalo*, made of taro root, instead of bread for communion and even water instead of wine. Damien thought that with relentless dedication he could win most inhabitants for his Church.

In the initial years of his mission, Damien saw the rivalry with Protestants almost as a game: for instance, in a letter to Pamphile, he mentioned full of pride that he had scaled a two-thousand-foot-high mountain in three quarters of an hour, while it took the Protestants' best climber at least two hours.[15]

He noted the flaws of the Protestant missionaries: they let anyone preach ("even the women") and charged money for attending services. "Once they become very rich, most of them resign and go into business."[16]

As he became better acquainted with the indigenous lifestyle, he also discerned its weakness more clearly. He had already been warned, during his formation and upon his arrival on the island, about the loose lifestyle and sexual mores. Many Kanaks did not take marital vows too seriously. A priest had to be on his guard not to be led into temptation.

A few times Damien had to guard himself. Damien, who constantly traveled as part of his pastoral work, was frequently invited by the hospitable inhabitants to spend the night in their homes. He often accepted, but if he was not entirely sure of the female company or himself, he preferred to spend the night outside, which he did more than once. He spoke about this at the end of his life with Joseph Dutton.

Earlier on, Damien had already had opportunities to see how easily he could rouse the enthusiasm of the Kanaks, for instance, when he called on them to help build a church. Then they were enthusiastic in an almost childlike way. But, like stubborn children, they could be equally unmanageable, unreasonable, and unteachable.

Damien was especially exasperated by traditional Hawaiian medicine, in which the Kanaks continued to place their trust—as if it produced the same results as Western medicine, and as if they could find in it as much consolation and support as they could in the prayers and sacraments of the Catholic Church. Though it rarely helped them, they invariably turned to a *kahuna*,[17] or healer, when they became ill. And there were plenty of pathogens on the islands.

The leprosy epidemic continued to spread on the islands, with the mortality rate rising. According to official health policy, victims of the epidemic had to be quarantined. To accomplish this goal, a colony for leprosy sufferers was founded in 1866 in Kalawao, on the island of Molokai. Damien had witnessed a couple of his parishioners being sent there. He looked on the effects of the disease with sadness. The population was steadily declining. If things kept evolving this way, the Kanak population would be threatened with extinction. It troubled Damien that he so often arrived too late to give the last sacraments, perhaps depriving his faithful of the opportunity to safeguard their souls. But above all he witnessed the tragedy of forced segregation, which tore many families apart.

Meanwhile, the loneliness on his vast and inhospitable mission post weighed heavily on him. The Catholic mission was struggling with understaffing. The twenty active Picpus Fathers were responsible for four islands. Their number increased, but not very fast. On the largest island, Hawaii, where Damien's mission post was situated, six missionaries were responsible for an area of 2,300 square miles, which moreover was especially inhospitable.

The island was regularly hit by heavy natural disasters. More than once, volcanic eruptions and the earthquakes that followed brought death and destruction. On April 2, 1868, Good Friday, one such event occurred, along with a devastating tsunami. Forty inhabitants were killed, with churches and houses left in ruins. The bells of the newly built Church of Saint Louis were found two hundred yards away. The missionaries would have to start building all over again.

He seldom saw a confrere. A visit from Bishop Maigret, who even in his old age traveled long distances by horse, was a rare opportunity to have priestly companionship. Daily life was marked mostly by loneliness. Sometimes for months on end he saw no one else but his Hawaiians, which led him to have dark thoughts. "While the missionary feels God's assistance in a special way, still the heart calls for a kind of external assistance from a confrere to drive away the black thoughts you acquire through daily contact with a fallen world."[18]

He insisted that his superior send him a confrere. Did the rule of the Sacred Hearts not say that a priest should not be alone? He thought about his brother Pamphile. Could he not come and join him on the island? Was he not a missionary? He suggested the idea in a letter to his superiors at Honolulu. They did not agree. The truth was that the intellectual Pamphile also showed little enthusiasm for the existence of a missionary: Damien's letters, in which he excitedly described the primitiveness of his existence, might have even contributed to that. Meanwhile, Pamphile had begun a doctorate in theology and had started to teach. Damien in his letters liked to make fun of his brother's tidy life as a professor, while he himself was working up a sweat and getting his hands dirty on the other side of the world. "Instead of being a poor missionary among the savages, there you are climbing another rung of the career ladder",[19] he scoffed.

In the end, he got the longed-for confrere: Gulstan Ropert was a new missionary from Brittany, the same age as Damien. He was considerate enough to wear the cassock that was meant for Damien's brother. On the inside the name "Pamphile" was embroidered into it. "Vox quidem, vox Gulstani, sed manus, manus sunt Pamphilii" (The voice is Gulstan's, but the hands are Pamphile's), Damien joked in Latin.[20] It was an allusion to the biblical story of Jacob and Esau, in which the younger brother obtained the right of the firstborn and the blessing of his father, Isaac, via a ruse. The allusion was not accidental: Damien recognized himself in that younger brother who outdid the older one.

Damien had a cordial relationship with Father Gulstan, who after Damien's death became the apostolic vicar of Honolulu. Damien derived a lot of strength from the monthly contact with his confrere and from the opportunity to confess his sins. They had fun together and laughed heartily. "Afterward we feel stronger, able again to dedicate ourselves to our holy work of service."[21]

Damien himself did not escape the pathogens that were present everywhere. At one time in 1870 he had so much fever that he became "all skin and bone".[22] He was only thirty-two years old when he wrote: "When I become sick I rejoice that my end approaches."[23] Fortunately, he recovered and without trouble regained his old weight of 175 pounds. But the disease afforded him the opportunity to reflect on his life and vocation. He was already six years on the island, and the challenge was somewhat gone. "Soon the *kanaka* will be as civilized as the Europeans",[24] he wrote ironically. Was he also influenced by the news of the Franco-Prussian War and the shocking murder of seven confreres during the Commune uprising in Paris? While his brothers in Paris were dying the death of a martyr, he was leading an all-in-all quiet missionary existence. But Damien rarely wrote about the political events in a restless world. He also hardly wrote about the First Vatican Council, which proclaimed papal infallibility and had to be broken off in dramatic circumstances due to the invasion by Italian troops of the papal city of Rome.[25] His attention was focused on the mission post entrusted to him.

Damien was to stay another three years in Kohala, in good relations with Gulstan. But his heart was yearning for a greater challenge. The opportunity came in the spring of 1873: on a rare occasion Damien left his post to join his confreres and Bishop Maigret for the consecration of a large church on the island of Maui. There he heard Maigret speak about the wretched conditions in the leprosy colony of Kalawao on the island of Molokai, where there was no permanent priest. A few days each year a priest visited from Maui, and the previous year a missionary had built a small church dedicated to Saint Philomena. Invariably the returning priest had pleaded passionately for a permanent priestly presence in Kalawao, but up to then it had not happened. Nonetheless, the pressure to take that step increased, and not only within the congregation. In mid-April 1873 the newspaper *Nuhou* of Honolulu dedicated a much-noticed article to the miserable conditions in the leprosy colony. The newspaper was of the opinion that the recently crowned king of Hawaii, William Lunalilo, should visit Kalawao to console and inspire his exiled subjects. "And if", so the article continued, "a noble Christian priest, preacher or sister should be inspired to go and sacrifice a life to console these poor wretches, that would be a royal soul to shine forever on a throne reared by human love." [26]

Father Aubert Bouillon, who had been to the leprosy colony many times, adamantly insisted on the need for a permanent priest. He himself was a candidate, but Maigret thought his health too weak.

The apostolic vicar was cognizant of the pastoral need, but he did not dare to permanently charge a priest with that assignment. Was that not too much of a risk and too cruel? For that reason he asked of the missionaries themselves: Who wanted to go, in rotation, to Molokai, each time for a period of three months? Four candidates quickly volunteered: Gulstan Ropert, Boniface Schäffer, Rupert Lauter, and Damien De Veuster. Who would be the first to go? Damien was chosen. The reason for this choice is unknown.

This decision would be a decisive turn in Damien's life. It was a happy coincidence that he had traveled to Maui for the consecration of the church, but his willingness to volunteer was not coincidental. His heart was open to the *kairos*, the opportune moment, when it offered itself. At thirty-three years of age, he was as old as Jesus at the time of his passion, and what had he done with his life? "Who will go in my name?" Damien was ready, more than ever. "Lord, send me!"

The nineteenth-century missionary movement

The story of the life and vocation of Damien De Veuster cannot be understood apart from the history of the Christian missionary movement that got under way in the nineteenth century and lasted well until into the twentieth. That missionary impulse characterized the whole of Western Christianity—Roman Catholic, Anglican, and Protestant. To an extent, it went along with the Western urge to expand and colonize, but it by no means entirely coincided with it.

The missionary movement was part of the large-scale religious revival that followed the excessive rationalism of eighteenth-century Enlightenment thinking and the bloody *tabula rasa* that the French Revolution tried to make with regard to the Christian heritage.

It was no coincidence that the first and strongest impulses of the Catholic missionary movement were found in heavily afflicted France. Nor was it strange, then, that Damien De Veuster ended up in a French congregation.

Damien belonged to the founding generation of Belgian missionaries. The life story of "the Apostle of the Lepers", together with that of others like Pieter-Jan De Smet, "the Apostle of the Indians", inspired countless men and women to follow in their footsteps.

Belgium quickly assumed an important place in the Catholic missionary landscape. The enormous number of missionaries from Belgium testifies to the dynamism that the Catholic Church developed there and to the generosity of her faithful. A comparison may suffice to illustrate that dynamism: in the year 1927 Belgium counted more active missionaries abroad than any other country in the world, with the lone exception of France.

Until the beginning of the nineteenth century, the overseas mission was the terrain of the older, established religious orders and congregations, such as the Jesuits and Redemptorists. Typical for the nineteenth century, however, was the arrival on the scene of numerous new missionary groups.

Originally it was the men's and women's congregations established with a local aim that directed their activity also to foreign missions, such as Damien's own Congregation of the Sacred Hearts (founded in 1800, active in Oceania since 1826), the Oblates of Mary (founded in 1816, active among the Eskimos in Canada since 1841), and the Society of Mary (the Marists, founded in 1816, active in the western Pacific since 1836). The 1840 encyclical *Probe nostis*, in which Pope Gregory XVI emphasized the Church's obligation to continue her missionary activity, gave the signal for the foundation of pure missionary congregations: the Missionaries of the Sacred Heart of Jesus (1854) in France, the Congregation of the Immaculate Heart of Mary (the Scheut Fathers, 1862) in Belgium, the Comboni Missionaries (1867) in Italy, the Missionaries of Africa (the White Fathers, 1868) in French Algeria, the Saint

Joseph's Missionary Society (the Mill Hill Missionaries, 1873) in England, the Divine Word Missionaries (the Steyl Missionaries, 1875) in the Netherlands, and so on. Moreover, many sister and brother congregations were active in foreign missions, such as the Brothers of Charity, founded in Belgium in 1807. Although the missionary impulse waned in the second half of the twentieth century, these orders and congregations still exist and now get most of their vocations from the mission regions themselves.

Although their founders, their specific spiritualities, and their fields of action differ, nineteenth-century missionaries have a number of characteristics in common. They were characterized by a real pioneer spirit, a longing for unknown regions and for the discovery of new peoples, languages, and cultures. The missionaries' contribution to cartography and the knowledge of indigenous languages is invaluable.

At the same time, they were convinced of the holy urgency of their task, believing that all who died unbaptized risked forever being deprived of divine mercy. So one had to hurry with the proclaiming and baptizing, in the interest of those to be evangelized, who had to abandon their idol worship and come to know the true God. Usually, nineteenth-century missionaries were willing to give their own lives for that proclamation, and many aspired to the "grace of martyrdom". At the same time, the missionaries were imbued, whether consciously or unconsciously, with the sense of superiority of Western culture, which in their eyes was synonymous with Christian civilization. The native populations were often seen as "savages" or "barbarians", to whom not only the true religion had to be taught but also a higher form of civilization.

In the twentieth century greater attention was given to the necessary respect for local cultures and even for certain positive dimensions of other beliefs and religions. Criticism of the "proselytism" and condescending paternalism of the missionaries grew louder in the twentieth century, both inside and outside the Church. In the context of decolonization, and supported by Marxist interpretative schemes, missionaries were seen as accomplices of the oppressive structures of exploitation.

That criticism still often resounds in today's secularized West-ern culture. But as the period of colonization and the nineteenth-century form of missionary activity recedes from us, space has opened up for a more nuanced judgment. It cannot be denied that in Africa, Asia, and America, some missionaries acted bluntly, narrow-mindedly, or arrogantly. On the one hand, this held the risk of trampling local cultures; on the other hand, missionary work aimed at saving those local cultures from destruction. For the missionaries also brought, with all their human shortcom-ings, the Gospel message that all the peoples of the world can share in the love of God, who especially loved the poorest of the poor. For many cultures, this was an unprecedented message of equality and liberation, of which many peoples have since taken advantage. Finally, one cannot but be impressed with the bound-less generosity of spirit of entire generations of Western Chris-tians from that time. In the heart of nineteenth-century culture, which has often been described as the dawning of the age of individualism, the missionary movement formed an impressive counterculture of gratuitous self-giving for the foreign "other".

Brief history of Hawaii

Hawaii consists of a total of 137 volcanic islands in the middle of the Pacific Ocean, with eight main islands. They were inhabited from the fifth century by Polynesian population groups. Possibly the Spanish landed already in the sixteenth century, but the famous eighteenth-century explorer James Cook counts as the official European discoverer. He called the archipelago the Sandwich Islands. In 1779 he died on the islands in a hand-to-hand fight with the natives.

In 1810 all of the inhabited islands were subjugated under a sin-gle ruler, King Kamehameha I (1758–1819). Despite its strategic location, its increasing immigration, and the expansion politics of the great powers, the kingdom managed to remain an indepen-dent state for most of the nineteenth century. Gradually the native Hawaiian population became a minority on the archipelago.

David Kalakaua became king in 1874. In 1879 he began construction of the luxurious Iolani palace in Honolulu. In 1888 the Constitution of the Kingdom of Hawaii considerably limited the power of the monarchy, at the demand of a number of American sugar plantation owners. Because the 1887 constitution was signed under threat of violence, it is commonly known as the "Bayonet Constitution".

Following his death, Kalakaua was succeeded in 1891 by his sister Liliuokalani. A coup d'etat of 1893 led to the end of the Hawaiian kingdom and opened the door to American annexation. When the strategic group of islands came into the hands of the United States, it established there a deepwater naval base, Pearl Harbor, which served as the home of the U.S. Pacific fleet. In 1959 Hawaii became the fiftieth state of the United States of America. The new state was allowed to immortalize two national figures in Statuary Hall at the U.S. Capitol in Washington, D.C. The first choice was almost unanimously for a non-Hawaiian: Father Damien. The cubist design of the New York artist Marisol Escobar was selected and unveiled on April 15, 1969, the eightieth anniversary of the death of the missionary.

Father Damien at age 33, the year he landed on Molokai.

3.The lepers: To isolate or to touch?

Damien landed at the leprosy colony of Molokai on Saturday, May 10, 1873. More than a century later, that date was chosen as his feast day in the Church calendar. He was thirty-three years old at the time. Bishop Louis Maigret sailed with him. The *Kilauea* also carried about fifty lepers, departing forever for their place of exile. Like the family and friends they left behind, they knew that they would not return. Leprosy was incurable. One went to Molokai to die.

Damien was a strange passenger on board. He was healthy and young and chose to live among and serve these diseased outcasts. To what extent did Damien realize that this could cost him his life? He was familiar enough with the disease to know that it was contagious. In any case, he wrote in his letters that, already before being chosen to go to Molokai, he had a strong feeling that he "never again would depart from there".[1]

The stench of death

Molokai is one of the eight larger Hawaiian Islands, located between the island of Oahu, where the capital, Honolulu, lies, and the island of Maui. From the eastern and southern sides of Molokai, you can see the neighboring islands. The leprosy colony did not cover the whole of Molokai but only a small northern peninsula. It was named Kalaupapa after the landing place, but the largest village was then Kalawao. The peninsula was a well-chosen place of isolation: on three sides it was surrounded by a turbulent ocean; on the land side, it was cut off from the rest of the island by a towering cliff called a *pali*. This cliff rose up as a two-thousand-foot-high wall. For much of the day it blocked the sunlight from Kalawao, as though

that part of the peninsula was in the shadow of death. It was possible to go by land from the peninsula to the rest of Molokai. You
had to climb the steep and often-slippery slope along a hacked
zigzagging path. That was not a problem for a strong person like
Damien, but for the sick it was impossible. For those with leprosy,
the colony was a natural prison from which no escape was possible.

The tropical climate made the place muggy and humid. Molokai
might be a beautiful paradise, with palm trees, beaches, and a deep-
blue ocean with a magnificent foamy, white surf; but for the sick,
abandoned, and isolated inhabitants of the leprosy colony, it was
more of a hell—the "sick paradise",[2] as one of Damien's biographers has aptly described it.

Damien had prepared for the worst, but his first encounter with
the leprosy colony was even more shocking than anticipated. The
five hundred lepers in the colony were in very bad condition. Many
were in the final stages of leprosy, their hands, feet, and faces hor-
ribly maimed. The festering sores and lumps caused by the disease
emitted an unbearable stench. Every day, someone died of the disease. The body of the unfortunate victim was wrapped in the equally
foul blanket on which the person had been lying. The wrapped
body was hung from a pole and carried away by a few chosen
lepers who still had sufficient strength. Often it happened that the
dead were not buried deeply enough, and at night wild pigs would
dig open the graves and eat the rotting flesh. Even the graves that
were not ripped open spread a suffocating odor.

Practical and down-to-earth as he was, Damien, with the inven-
tiveness of love, found a way to control his disgust at the stench of
the sick. Looking back years later, he recalled these first days: "Many
a time in fulfilling my priestly duties at their domiciles I have been
obliged, not only to close my nostrils, but to remain outside to
breathe fresh air.... As an antidote to counteract the bad smell I
got myself accustomed to the use of tobacco, whereupon the smell
of the pipe preserved me somewhat from carrying in my clothes
the obnoxious odor of our lepers."[3]

When Damien arrived, the odor of death pervaded Kalawao. Several times he compared it with the smell of the corpse of Lazarus
in his grave: *iam foetet* (he smells already).[4] Even those not yet in
the final stage of the disease were locked in the grip of death. The

hopelessness of their fate was overpowering. A great moral permissiveness resulted: many of the sick turned to drink, opium, and sexual orgies. What meaning did their wretched lives have, after all? Better to forget everything and seek as much pleasure as possible.

How did this horrific place of perdition come to be on the island of Molokai? Beginning in the 1860s, leprosy spread rapidly through the archipelago of Hawaii. The causes of the disease were unknown, but that the disease was contagious and incurable was clear. Initially, the patients were cared for in a specially created department of the general hospital in Honolulu. But one doctor and nurse after another caught the disease there, and the visiting family members as well were responsible for a further spread of the leprosy bacillus. A drastic solution was called for. In 1866 the Board of Health proposed that the peninsula on Molokai become a quarantine site. Those who contracted the disease were asked to turn themselves in, or they were tracked down. Exile was not only the letter of the law; it was also considered an act of citizenship. Many tried desperately to escape the diagnosis, which not only was a death sentence but also meant strict segregation. One patient wounded a doctor with a gun; others ran away or hid. Again and again heartbreaking farewell scenes played out on the quay, where the boats with the exiles departed. The mandatory segregation policy was harsh, but there was no alternative.

At that time it was believed that if you dealt with the patients in too lax a way or allowed exceptions to the segregation policy, eventually all of Hawaii would become a leprosy colony and be threatened with extinction. That was not such an outlandish idea: despite a high birth rate and the stringent health policy, the population kept declining. Between 1866, the year of the colony's foundation, and 1873, the year of Damien's arrival, the Hawaiian population decreased by 6,000 souls. Estimates by the Hawaiian Evangelical Association had 57,000 inhabitants in the archipelago in 1873, of whom 49,000 were native Hawaiians, 3,000 were whites, and 2,500 were of mixed ethnicity.

When the Hawaiian Evangelical Association held its annual meeting in 1873, it expressed its despair as follows: "Our Hawaiian people will become in a very few years, *a nation of lepers.* Do we consider what this means? It means the disorganization and total destruction of civilization, property values and industry, of our churches, our contributions, our Hawaiian Board and its work of Missions. It means shame, and defeat and disgraceful overthrow to all that is promising and fair in the nation. We are on the brink of a horrible pit, full of loathsomeness, into which our feet are rapidly sliding." [5]

The churches supported the severe segregation policy. Protestants, traditionally well versed in the Bible, knew of the segregation measures for contagious patients as set out in Leviticus: "The leper who has the disease shall wear torn clothes and let the hair of his head hang loose, and he shall cover his upper lip and cry, 'Unclean, unclean.' He shall remain unclean as long as he has the disease; he is unclean; he shall dwell alone in a habitation outside the camp." [6] Forced segregation and quarantine had been the fate of lepers for centuries. It was no different on the archipelago in the Pacific Ocean in the middle of the nineteenth century.

Touch

Christians could have read further in their Bibles. In the New Testament, Jesus regularly meets those suffering from leprosy. He does not avoid contact with them; quite the contrary.

"Do not touch them. Do not allow them to touch you. Do not eat with them." This was the advice that Damien had received from his superiors as a rule of conduct among the lepers. The hygienic precautions were based on common sense. Doctors and health care workers who came in contact with leprosy patients applied the rule as much as possible. Otherwise, the danger of contagion was real. But it was not so simple for a priest to keep his distance. Even Louis Maigret, who accompanied Damien on May 10, understood that in that place it was impossible to avoid all contact if you did not want to offend the inhabitants of the colony. How could Damien follow that rule? How could he give the dying the last sacraments without touching them? How could he give his parishioners communion? How could he pass on to those outcasts his love and the love of the heavenly Father, if he always had to keep a physical distance?

Damien understood from his first day on Molokai that that would be impossible. Despite his aversion to the repulsive wounds and mutilations, despite the unbearable stench, he blessed the dying, he embraced the sick, he ate with them from the same pot, he even shared his pipe with them. Loving them meant letting go of an attitude of distance and instead being physically close to them. Had not his Lord Jesus Christ done this when he touched victims of leprosy? Damien had so often read in the Scriptures: "While he was in one of the cities, there came a man full of leprosy; and when he saw Jesus, he fell on his face and begged him, 'Lord, if you will, you can make me clean.' And he stretched out his hand, and touched him, saying: 'I will; be clean.' And immediately the leprosy left him." [7] Was not every healing of Jesus coupled with a touch and a word? Of course, Jesus' disciples did not always have the healing power of their master, to Damien's regret. Still, is loving closeness not always curative? That was the spirit of Damien. It had nothing to do with a progressive or conservative interpretation of the Scriptures. It had to do with the imitation of Christ, the loving self-giving for the least of his brothers.

Was Damien knowingly careless? That question was often raised during and after his life, as well as during the canonization process. Damien certainly did not want to contract leprosy. He prayed for God's protection and that of the Holy Virgin's. But he also did not want to keep his distance. From the beginning, even long before he had contracted the disease, he spoke to its victims with the famous words: "We lepers".[8] He felt like one of them. But he clearly realized he was in danger: "So far, my health is very good, despite daily exposure to the infection", he wrote in 1876 to two nephews, whom he urged to come help him.[9]

Gavan Daws rightly suggests that "with a priest like Damien, in whom belief was unaffectedly incarnate, faith was made physical. To mortify the body, to die to himself, to risk physical leprosy in order to cure moral leprosy—this was to be a good priest. If it meant touching the untouchable, then that was what had to be done. The touch of the priest was the indispensable connection between parishioner and church, sinner and salvation." [10]

For Damien the overcoming of his revulsion—a long and difficult struggle—was part of his conversion. He had the experience of Saint Francis, who on the roads of Assisi had met a man suffering from leprosy. Despite the disgust he felt, the young Francis

Top: A view of Kalaupapa.

Bottom: Church of Saint Philomena in Kalawao, rebuilt and restored several times by Damien.

embraced and kissed the man. "When I was in sin the sight of lepers was too bitter for me. And the Lord himself led me among them, and I pitied and helped them. And when I left them I discovered that what had seemed bitter to me was changed into sweetness in my soul and body",[11] Francis wrote in his Testament.

Although there is much that distinguishes Damien and Francis, Damien had that same experience on Kalawao. What instinctively filled him with disgust quickly became for him a life task. In those mutilated bodies, he saw the suffering Lord. "As you did it to one of the least of these my brethren, you did it to me."[12] And who was less than the nearly dead, those exiles from the land of the living? Even that first week, Damien decided that he would remain on Molokai. He let his superior, Modeste Favens, know by letter: "I send you this letter via the schooner *Waniki* to let you know that from now on there has to be a permanent priest in this place. Boats loaded with the sick arrive here; many die. I sleep under the *puhala* while I wait for the wood to build a rectory to your approval. Please send me.... You know my availability; I would like to sacrifice myself for the poor lepers. The harvest seems ripe here."[13]

Credibility

Damien's choice to go voluntarily to live with the leprosy sufferers on Molokai immediately became the talk of the town in Honolulu. Everyone spoke about it. Walter Gibson, the ambitious publisher of the *Nuhou* newspaper and a future politician, saw that his call to send a priest to Molokai had been answered. The "Christian hero" was found. The next day, he published an enthusiastic opinion piece: "The good Father ... volunteered to live with them and for them. Father Damien formed this resolution at the time and was left ashore among the lepers, without a home or a change of clothing except such as the lepers offer. We care not what this man's theology may be, he is surely a Christian hero."[14]

The Catholic mission on the island was pleased with the positive press attention Damien received. But there were also petty reactions. Even within the Catholic missionary community, there were mixed feelings. Did the other missionaries of the Sacred Hearts not do good work too? Had not others also offered to go to Molokai? During the following years, with Damien's growing popularity and the stream of money that it brought, such sentiments would only increase.

On the Protestant side as well, many did not share Gibson's enthusiasm for the work of the Catholic priest. Not that they had no respect for him, but they found a different, structural approach, such as the quarantine laws, preferable. Gavan Daws aptly describes how people such as the Protestant pastor Charles McEwen Hyde passed a heavy moral judgment on the sick. Did they not have their own permissive behavior to thank for their disease? Consequently, he chose distance over closeness.[15]

On the other hand, there were many heartwarming reactions. Damien's generous choice quickly awakened the generosity of others. When the news started to spread, the Protestant governor of the island of Oahu, John Dominis, organized a small collection in his congregation and brought the proceeds to Bishop Maigret. These were ecumenical gestures that were far ahead of their time. Damien was instantly a local celebrity. And more than that: within the month, European and American newspapers also reported on the "leper priest". From the outset, his example appealed to people's imagination. "Father Damien" became a famous name, although he himself was barely aware of it there in his place of exile.

The reactions to Damien's choice are interesting. They are relevant to many discussions today, including those in Christian and Catholic circles, where structural assistance in the form of advocating a better policy is considered to be more efficient than personal acts of loving one's neighbor. From this point of view, *caritas* is dismissed as paternalistic and outdated. But a personal relationship with the poor gives Christian testimony credibility. Damien was not opposed to a structural improvement of the lot of the exiles. But he understood that this solution could be authentic only if it was combined with altruistic self-giving. For personal testimony touches the heart far more than an aloof discourse, no matter how correct the latter is. Time would show how Damien's nonconformist choice also became the engine behind the improvement of living conditions in this place of exile.

Growth of a community

Kamiano's first work on Molokai was the burial of the dead, a special work of mercy in this place where the funerals had been unworthy of human beings. From the beginning, he himself built the coffins and oversaw the digging of the graves so they would be deep enough. That was no easy task in the hard, rocky, volcanic ground of Molokai. He also ordered wood to build a fence around the cemetery by the church, to keep the pigs away. That was not merely a matter of hygiene but also of human and Christian dignity. Damien taught his community how important it was to pay last respects to the dead body.

Damien baptized, celebrated the Eucharist, heard confession, and gave the last sacraments. The administration of the sacraments belongs to the core tasks of a Catholic priest. How great a need there was for this, and how much consolation the sick took from it became clear from the rapid success of his mission. Many asked to be baptized, and the number of Catholics quickly increased.

Naturally, this led initially to some concern in the other Christian communities: present in the leprosy colony were also an Evangelical and a Mormon church. These were served by pastors who were themselves exiled. However, from the start, the inter-Christian relations were better than they were at Damien's previous post. Of course, he still hoped to bring the lost sheep to the true faith of Catholicism, but he did not insist on this too much. Friendly attentiveness to those who were suffering was the focal point. When Damien made a successful clothing collection elsewhere in Hawaii, the proceeds did not go only to his parishioners, which would have been normal given the custom of that time. He distributed the clothing to all of the needy of the colony, regardless of their church or religion.

With the wood his superiors gave him, Damien built a house for himself near the Church of Saint Philomena. The presence of the missionary had great attractive power. He could report many baptisms to the provincial. Maigret was also pleased. Although it weighed heavily on him, he knew he had made a good choice in permitting Damien to remain there. "According to latest reports, he performed thirty-five baptisms, and on the Feast of Corpus Christi our poor locked-away people got to have their procession", he wrote.

"A procession of lepers, leper cantors, leper musicians, probably the likes of which had never been seen before. Perhaps God is more revered by those unfortunates, whom society has excluded, than by others who enjoy all the benefits of health and life." [16]

Soon the tiny Church of Saint Philomena could no longer hold the growing Catholic community. Even on weekdays some were forced to attend Mass outside the door or by the windows on the sides.

Damien, the only priest residing on Molokai, was also responsible for the rest of the island. Once a month he visited the communities on topside. Bishop Maigret asked him to build a chapel in Kaluaaha. Damien had his doubts: he could visit the rest of the island, but a long absence would mean leaving the sick and dying in the lurch. According to him, the needs in the leprosy colony were more pressing. Not only did the Church of Saint Philomena urgently have to be expanded, but in Kalaupapa he wanted to build a meeting hall. He estimated that half of the colony's population was, or wanted to be, Catholic. He therefore requested that a second missionary be sent. Would Father Aubert, who had offered, not be a good choice? [17]

In his yearly letter to the superior general, now Marcellin Bousquet, Damien described at length the circumstances in which he had ended up. He had gotten the chance to follow Christ by offering consolation to lepers. Even if he could not heal the physical leprosy, it was yet possible for him to cure the leprosy of their souls. He had his hands full with the four hundred Catholics in the leprosy colony and the additional two hundred outside of it. He insisted that Bousquet send assistance.

In the first months of his stay on Molokai, Damien twice went to Honolulu. That afforded him the opportunity not only to make his confession and to consult with his superiors but also to thank the sisters for the assistance they had sent, especially in the form of clothing for the lepers. The Board of Health disapproved of these trips. Damien had broken the quarantine law. No exceptions could be allowed. The missionary was explicitly forbidden to leave the island again. Damien, a nonleper, had become de facto an exile with the exiles. "We lepers" had acquired a new meaning.

That the Board of Health was serious became quickly apparent. Provincial Modeste Favens, who wanted to visit Damien, was denied permission to go ashore. As Damien approached in a boat, the command was shouted out that he not board. There was nothing else for him to do but to shout his confession in French from his boat. Absolution followed from a distance.[18]

Father Aubert was concerned about the isolation of his beloved confrere. During a visit to the other side of Molokai, he decided to visit Damien. He changed out of his clerical clothes and came down the *pali* in the middle of the night. He remained a full day with Damien, who was delighted by this unannounced act of fraternity. Early the next morning, Aubert climbed the *pali* again. His visit, however, had not gone unnoticed. Shortly afterward a complaint was also filed against him for violating the segregation laws.

Maigret could not accept this. It was unprecedented for the authorities to treat ministers of religion in this way. With the help of the French consul and Doctor Trousseau, a member of the Board of Health, he succeeded in restoring Damien's freedom shortly afterward. The Board of Health was prepared to make an exception for physicians and ministers of religion. Maigret showed that, with diplomacy and perseverance inspired by pastoral concern, it was possible to work with the authorities. This was in stark contrast with the attitude his successor would later adopt toward Damien in a similar situation.

Damien received more good news. The superior general let him know that he had found a confrere to come and assist him. This was the Dutchman André Burgerman, who had experience with the mission in Tahiti. Initially, for Damien, this was a relief. To be alone was not his vocation. However, as we will see later, the relationship with Burgerman did not always go smoothly.

By the end of the year 1873, his first on Molokai, Damien wrote a reassuring letter to his parents and brothers. "I live in a small house and have an old man to do my cooking. My food consists of meat and rice, sometimes a little bread—and milk—luckily every day a good cup of coffee. Although this cruel leper disease of my spiritual children—or parishioners—is contagious, my health remains the same",[19] he let them know.

And he closed his letter with the sentence that today can be read on his tomb in the Louvain crypt: "I find my greatest happiness in serving the Lord in his poor and sick children—who are rejected by others."[20]

Leprosy

Leprosy is an infectious disease caused by the leprosy bacillus (*Mycobacterium leprae*). The bacterium was discovered in 1873, the very year Damian set foot on Molokai, by the Norwegian physician Gerhard Armauer Hansen. In the Anglo-Saxon world leprosy is also known as Hansen's disease.

Leprosy is transmissible but is not nearly as contagious as previously thought. The bacillus is transmitted through breathing, coughing, and sneezing and is absorbed through the respiratory tract or skin wounds. The risk of contamination by contact with skin or objects is low. Simple hygiene, such as washing hands, reduces the risk considerably. Recently it was shown that the vast majority of people are naturally immune to leprosy.

Because the bacteria multiply slowly, the incubation period is very long, anywhere from three to seven years.

Infection is manifested first by colored lumps or spots on areas with many bacilli. Eventually, the nerves are affected and numbness occurs. Untreated wounds start to fester and can lead to disfigurement. Leprosy bacilli concentrate in the cool extremities of the body, such as the ears and nose. Blindness is also common because the patient can no longer close his eyes.

In the course of the twentieth century, many organizations joined the fight against the disease as well as the stigma and segregation traditionally associated with it. Many invoke the legacy of Damien De Veuster. Scientific discoveries and progress in medicine gradually pushed back the centuries-old disease. Treatment became possible at the end of the 1940s, thanks to the introduction of dapsone.

In the 1980s an effective cocktail of drugs (dapsone, clofazimine, and rifampicin, among others) has been developed. Today leprosy is easily treated, but the problem remains of diagnosing the disease early enough, before deformity and disability occur.

The disease has been eradicated in more and more countries. Still, in 2007 the World Health Organization registered 254,525 new cases. The disease has persisted to the present in India, Brazil, and some African countries.

4. A father makes the difference: Paternalism or fatherliness?

Damien had entered a house of death. From the moment he arrived at the leprosy settlement, his faith and his intellect intuitively knew that this was the challenge for which his huge missionary's heart was longing. Amid these biblical outcasts, who were not only utterly rejected but also radically disfigured, he understood that his presence could make a difference. These poor unfortunates were like sheep in need of a shepherd, children yearning for a father's love. "They are repugnant to look at, but they also have a soul redeemed at the price of the precious blood of our Divine Savior", he wrote to his superior. "He too in his divine love consoled lepers. If I cannot heal them, as he could, at least I can offer them comfort." [1] That was Damien's choice: to look at the lepers with the loving eyes of Jesus.

That love manifested itself in concrete action, for how could you transmit divine love and salvation if you did not keep before your eyes the concrete needs of those entrusted to you? Did the Apostle James not write: "If a brother or sister is poorly clothed and in lack of daily food, and one of you says to them, 'Go in peace, be warmed and filled,' without giving them the things needed for the body, what does it profit? So faith by itself, if it has no works, is dead." [2] Damien took care of all the material needs of his people: the food and water supplies, clothing, and housing, for which his carpentry skills came in extremely handy. And, although assisting the dying and burying the dead were his daily tasks, he was also profoundly concerned with the suffering bodies of the sick. For instance, he actively sought out the latest medicines and therapies, which, while not offering a cure, did provide some mitigation of the suffering.

Music was one expression of the joy of life that, despite everything, Damien brought into the colony.

Damien with his orphan boys in Kalawao. The signs of leprosy were clearly visible.

Damien not only cared for the sick; he also gave them back their human dignity and self-respect by pointing out their own responsibility. Despair and self-neglect often occur in patients with terminal diseases—all the more so in exiled leprosy patients. Those suffering with illness also need the medicine of human contact and friendship. Together with his sick companions, Damien entered the battle against meaninglessness, emptiness, and despair. He made sure that they did not waste their lives by surrendering to idleness, drunkenness, and an unrestrained lifestyle. If necessary, he could become very angry. But he also offered them alternatives: he taught them to take better care of themselves and of others. He reconciled them, not only with one another, but with God. Through his pastoral work, his sermons, the liturgies at which he presided, and the sacraments he administered, he taught his flock that each one of them was valuable in the eyes of God. He also taught them that their lives did not come to an end with death, which gave meaning to their lives and deaths.

In a missionary priest like Damien, one cannot draw a line between the spiritual and the material. Not only are both aspects present all the time; they cannot be separated. His spiritual attitude toward the lepers helped him to see, as Jesus did, more in the sick than the disease and decay: he read their desire for life and love. He believed that they could become "better" in every respect. A missionary is more than a development aid worker: he has the well-being of the entire person in mind. In order to achieve that goal, Damien did not spare himself.

His physical efforts were sustained by great spiritual discipline. Damien was serious in his religious life, his own fidelity to the sacraments and spiritual formation, an indication of which is found in his "Personal Rule", the daily schedule he drew up for himself. Without that spiritual support, such sustained self-giving service is unthinkable.

Damien lived among the lepers for sixteen years. Those years made an enormous difference to the settlement. He helped transform a lawless and unloved group of condemned outcasts into a dignified community. Of course, this did not happen effortlessly: the process was beset with setbacks, resistance, and failures. Nor did Damien do it single-handedly: there were the civil authorities and members of the Board of Health as well as benefactors far away and co-workers on the spot. But Damien was the one who made the difference. He did not give something; he gave himself. In recent times much criticism has been made of the so-called paternalism of the missionaries. Damien, the prototype of the missionary, demonstrates that often it was not a matter of humiliating paternalism but of a fatherliness that founded a family.

Providing the necessities of life

Damien's endeavor to improve concretely the living conditions in the colony is one of the best known aspects of his life's work. Today, when the motives of the Catholic missionary match less well the spirit of the times, emphasis is more often placed on Damien as practical problem solver. It is the story of the many occupations of Damien, who was at the same time carpenter, plumber, gravedigger, teacher, judge, and so on. That material concern was undeniably essential in Damien's daily existence, which is clear from his correspondence and his activity.

An interesting document providing insight into his achievements in this area is a report he drafted in 1886 at the request of the president of the Board of Health, Walter Gibson.[3] At the time, Damien had already been on Molokai for thirteen years and had three years left to live. There is little chance that in his report he exaggerated the improvement in the colony out of hagiology. For Damien, aware of the sensitivities of the Board of Health, knew to minimize his own role and accentuate that of the civil authorities. But precisely for that reason it is an interesting document, which additionally does away with the notion that Damien was an illiterate peasant who only worked well with his hands and operated without much consultation. Following a description of the miserable situation he found on his arrival, he zoomed in on the various aspects and the current situation. When he arrived, the situation was so miserable "that it only deserved the nickname the 'living graveyard'", he wrote. "Today that name no longer suits our institution",[4] he concluded with satisfaction.

Regarding the food supply, Damien pointed to the importance of *poi*, the cooked form of taro, the local vegetable of Hawaii and of most other islands in the Pacific Ocean. In the leprosy settlement, it was imported from the other part of Molokai. That basic food was essential to the lepers' diet, Damien surmised. Other food staples, such as rice and sweet potatoes, were insufficient substitutes. Once, due to a scarcity of *poi* for three straight months, there were several more deaths to regret, he recalled. He further pointed out that the supply of fresh milk was inadequate, as the few dairy cows were frequently slaughtered for their meat. A mere 10 percent of the residents received a small daily supply. Damien proposed to the Board of Health that it increase the herd to a thousand head of cattle to satisfy the need for milk and meat. According to him, the meadowland on the peninsula could support that number. That was the farmer's son speaking.

The water supply was an absolute disaster when he arrived. The only fresh, drinkable water was found in small quantities near Kalawao at the foot of the mountain. The inhabitants had to transport this as best they could in oil cans, either by foot or by horse. According to Damien, this water shortage explained the filthiness of bodies and clothing he found on his arrival. The year he came, Damien built a water system with pipes and a reservoir, which normally supplied enough water for the eight hundred to one thousand inhabitants. At Kalaupapa, on the other side of the island, the water supply was still problematic in 1886, with the inhabitants relying on rain or standing water. According to Damien, that was the main reason that Kalaupapa did not really develop as a settlement and that most people continued to live in Kalawao. He insisted on a speedy solution to this problem and offered a concrete proposal. He would take care of the work and the manpower, while the Board of Health would provide the pipes. That could not cost that much.

The chief problem in the initial years following his arrival, however, was shelter. With the exception of a few dwellings of some richer leprosy patients, there were no wooden houses. Most lived in simple huts covered with local grasses or sugar cane leaves. In the winter of 1873–1874 fierce winds blew away the wretched shacks, leaving many to sleep outdoors exposed to the wind and rain, with their drenched clothes and blankets.

Damien insisted that more wood be delivered from the government as well as from private donors, which he obtained. Wealthier inhabitants hired their own carpenters, but "for those without the means," he added laconically, "the priest, with his leper boys, did the work of erecting a good many small houses." [5]

Damien was an industrious worker and skilled carpenter. Not only did he prove this with his churches and chapels, of which he built one per year on average; he also readily lent his skill to those in need of it. "I'm not ashamed to be a manual laborer for the glory of God", he wrote to his mother. "The work habits I developed at home are of immense use to me here." [6]

The improvement in housing was spectacular. Just a few years after Damien's arrival, Kalawao and the smaller Kalaupapa formed two attractive villages. "I estimate the number of houses at present, both large and small, somewhat over three hundred, nearly all whitewashed and, so far, clean and neat", he reported with satisfaction in 1886. The reduction in the number of deaths, according to him, was to a great extent due to the improved housing. Still, he noted a problem: a number of houses "[were] not yet provided with good windows".[7] Damien would not have been Damien had he not immediately insisted on this improvement with the Board of Health.

Another major material problem was deficient clothing. Kalawao could be very cold and damp, especially in the winter. As their disease progressed, the leprosy patients' blood circulation decreased, causing them to become cold very quickly. Only the wealthier inhabitants, or those who could count on outside help, possessed enough warm clothes. The others were literally covered in rags. That problem too was dealt with in time. A small store was started where, among other things, clothing was sold. Damien commended the authorities for this improvement—adding immediately that the yearly voucher of six dollars was quite insufficient for the poorest. He arranged to have additional clothing sent through Christian charity. He did not report this to the Board of Health, but the superior of the Sacred Hearts Sisters in Honolulu was especially active in this regard. Also, Queen Kapiolani had organized a clothing collection. She visited the colony together with Liliuokalani in July 1884.

Self-respect and responsibility

From the beginning, Damien's care for the leprosy victims went beyond helping supply their basic material needs. His fatherly presence was also aimed at teaching them self-respect and a sense of responsibility. The condition he found in 1873 among the eight hundred lepers was one of great lawlessness and unrestrained behavior. Such lawlessness was the only rule of this place of exile: "*Aole kanawai ma keia wahi*—In this place there is no law." New exiles were welcomed with that telling axiom as they disembarked. The authorities, who at the beginning were represented by an underpaid and unmotivated superintendent, realized that they were powerless: with what could one threaten those poor wretches, who realized that they never again could get away from their place of exile and who had only a short time left to live?

Besides, there was little ambition to do anything about it: let those unfortunates have a good time, for they have nothing else, was the underlying defeatist philosophy.

For Damien such laxity was intolerable. Not only did it clash with his moral standards, but he also realized that an uninhibited life, almost animal-like, also affected the human dignity of the common life in the settlement.

"In their primitive dwellings, these wretched outcasts lived in the most revolting promiscuity, without distinction of age or sex, whether old or new cases, all more or less strangers to one another. They filled their time with card playing, hula dancing, drinking fermented *ki*-root beer, and with all that follows from this", he remembered many years later.[8] Discretion kept him from going into more detail, but it was clear that promiscuity and sexual orgies were rampant.

In any case, Hawaiian culture was already very sensual. The population had little modesty when it came to sexuality. Precisely that sensuality, according to many, especially in Western missionary circles, was at the basis of the leprosy epidemic. As Gavan Daws, the Hawaiian historian and biographer of Damien, put it: "They insisted that the root of the Hawaiians' disastrous condition was indigenous. This root they identified as the endless and endlessly renewed sexuality of the culture. The Hawaiian view of life was permeated by the generative principle. Sex was the expression, the ultimate incarnation, of the beauty and power of the forces of existence, something to be celebrated—privately, publicly, ritually." [9]

On Molokai Damien fought against both alcoholism and the sexual excesses that resulted from it. That was no easy task. It was not for nothing that Kalawao had the nickname "village of fools". For when the residents started drinking their "disgusting liquor", a distillate based on cooked and fermented *ki* root, they lost all inhibition. "They used to run criss-cross, without clothes, and they behaved like possessed people", Damien wrote. And then tactfully: "It is easier to imagine the consequences of those orgies than to describe them." [10]

The missionary did not shy away from acting harshly to eradicate the problem. A vivid, probably embellished, account was provided by Ambrose Hutchison, who arrived in the settlement in January 1879 and was the superintendent from 1883 to 1887: "Armed with a stout cane which a friend gave him," Hutchison wrote in his memoir, "wherever he went on his daily survey of the leper village of Kalawao he was attracted by the rattling noise of an *uli-uli*", a musical instrument used in the performance of the hula dance honoring the goddess Laka. But when the miscreants were warned in time, they fled through the back door. Damien then found nothing but the calabash gourds or other drinking vessels as silent witnesses of the orgy. Making a quick survey of the interior of the hut, he gave the calabash a "cracking whack with his big stick, spilling the contents on the mat covered floor". [11]

Hutchison felt sorry for Damien, writing that it was "a dramatic sight to see a Catholic priest in action to crush the evil for love of righteousness and the happiness of the isolated outcasts, people among whom his lot was cast to render helpful service and uplift them to the higher and better things of life". [12]

Damien would never completely win this battle. He had little cooperation from most of the administrators and the other pastors who succeeded one another in the leprosy settlement. In addition, his action did not exactly make him popular with those who wanted no limits on their freedom. Hutchison, however, noted admiringly that he never knew of a leper attacking Damien.

The missionary felt a deep compassion for the women and children who were used and abused by the men, and left afterward like human rags. "Many an unfortunate woman had to become a prostitute to obtain friends who would take care of her, and the children, when well and strong, were used as servants. When once the disease prostrated them, such women and children were cast out and had to find some other shelter; sometimes they were laid behind a stone wall and left there to die, and at other times a hired hand would carry them to the hospital." Damien concluded bitterly: "The so-much-praised *aloha*—hospitality—of the natives was entirely lacking here, at least in this respect." [13]

Damien also understood that many men surrendered to licentious behavior and violence out of sorrow and loneliness. That was certainly the case during his first years on Molokai, when married persons were often separated permanently when the illness affected one of them. "In many cases the separation was more unbearable than the pains of the disease itself." [14] For this reason Damien was delighted with the government's measure allowing uninfected men and women to follow their spouses to the place of exile.

Among those in the leprosy settlement who were single, he promoted, as much as possible, an openness to marriage, which he was pleased to consecrate. More than once he got into trouble with his superiors, who thought he did not check diligently enough whether the persons concerned were still validly married somewhere else. [15]

Damien further opposed the arrival of nonleper helpers, or *kokuas*, who pretended to come to help the lepers but in reality were a source of idling and licentious sexual behavior.

Damien also understood that in his moral battle he could not use the stick alone. He had to offer those unfortunates, who were condemned to end their lives on that small patch of land, something worthwhile to do. He was pleased when Kalaupapa also started to develop as a village. As a result, many regularly walked up and down the roughly two and a half miles between Kalawao and Kalaupapa, which stimulated blood circulation and was a wholesome activity, Damien thought.

But he was especially proud of the small arable fields that were laid out at the foot of the mountain, where the leprosy patients themselves could grow sweet potatoes or other crops on a small scale. "To go there by foot or horse and work the land is the healthiest occupation for our lepers." He recorded with pleasure in his report of 1886 that at that time 90 percent of the inhabitants devoted themselves to this activity, whereas previously only a small minority did so. "Probably there cannot be found in the whole world a leper asylum that equals ours and encourages the victims to do this kind of daily occupation, which has such a beneficial effect",[16] he concluded.

Moreover, in times of lack of supply of *poi* or other provisions, the lepers could sell their potatoes to the government and earn some money. "That was a great encouragement for everyone."[17]

It must have pained him when he realized that a number of lepers also found a way to distill a harmful intoxicating beverage out of the homegrown sweet potatoes.

Let the children come to me

Damien did not direct his attention only to the adults but also gave special attention to the orphans. Every year, ten to twenty children, between eight and fifteen years of age, landed in Kalaupapa unaccompanied by their parents. Damien knew that they were especially vulnerable to neglect and sexual abuse. In 1879 he built a shelter for twelve orphans. A healthy male *kokua* was responsible for the food, with the support of the Board of Health. Very quickly the facility was so attractive to the other boys in the settlement that he decided to build a second, bigger dormitory. The girl orphans were likewise entitled to protection and guidance. For them too he built an orphanage with the support of the Board of Health. He wrote to Pamphile, not without satisfaction:

> For some years I have had a small orphanage for young leper girls. An old widow, not a leper herself, serves as their mother and cook. Though their orphanages are at some distance, we have meals in common and share our rations. We each receive seven pounds of beef and twenty-one pounds of taro per week; with that we think we're well fed. We also have planted a large field of sweet potatoes, which we keep in reserve in case the ordinary deliveries do not reach us on time. There is in the leprosarium a large store where those who have money can buy clothes and other items. From time to time I receive large bundles of clothes for the poor and my numerous children, which come to me thanks to the superior of our sisters in Honolulu.[18]

With the support of the Board of Health, Damien also built two schools, one for girls and one for boys. He did not obtain permission, however, to teach the Catholic religion in these institutions, which were financed with public money. He resigned himself to that decision.

Damien's care for the children was undoubtedly one of his most beautiful achievements. In the view of Arthur Mouritz, the resident physician in the settlement from 1885 to 1887, it was "one of the finest works that this priest undertook and carried out".[19] Mother Marianne also later testified that the love with which Damien surrounded the children was one of his greatest gifts. A well-known photo shows Damien, already ill with leprosy, seated between his orphans.

Damien's loving concern made a lasting impression on the children themselves. That appears from the testimonies collected at the end of the 1930s in the context of the beatification process. For instance, the leper witness Joseph Manu, who then had lived already forty-five years in the settlement, remembered the following: "I was myself a naughty boy, and often Damien acted as if he would pull my ear or give me a kick, but immediately afterward he gave me candy. He behaved likewise with the other kids, but they were not as naughty as I was. That is why Damien loved me more, and he kept me alive for a long time."[20]

From "living cemetery" to dignified leprosy settlement

The impressive enumeration of Damien's service work should not let us forget that his attention was mostly geared to the spiritual care and assistance of the sick and dying. Also, whenever Damien was building a house, so Hutchison wrote, "he never neglected his priestly duties, visiting the sick and dying, and if there was an immediate call for him while hard at work, he would drop his tool, pull off his work clothes and put on his cassock and his stole in hand, hastened to the dying [to] administer the last rite of the church."[21]

Each year the small colony of seven to eight hundred people witnessed some 150 to 200 deaths, a shockingly high number.

Certainly, during the early years the conditions in which the dying gasped their final breath were utterly gruesome. Hutchison, who himself would reach old age despite his leprosy, described many years later what he had seen in Kalawao the day after he arrived on January 4, 1879. A man, whose face was covered below the eyes with a handkerchief, was pushing a wheelbarrow loaded with a bundle that Hutchison mistook for rags. He stopped by a small, windowless hut. "The man half turned over the wheelbarrow and shook it. The bundle (instead of rags, it was a human being) rolled out on the ground with an agonized groan. The fellow turned the wheelbarrow around and wheeled it away, leaving the sick man lying there helpless. After a while, the dying man raised and pushed himself in the doorway; with his body in and his leg stretched out, he lay there face down." Later the horrified Hutchison learned that that hut of death, where all dying patients were removed from the hospital to die unattended, had the reputation and name of *Hoopau keaho*, which means "the end of life".[22]

On that same spot Hutchison, for the first time, also met Damien, who was visiting the sick and dying. He characterized the Belgian missionary as he was: "A well knit stocky man of medium height, dark hair, prominent straight line nose, plump round smooth face and wearing gold rimmed spectacles, garbed in a black cassock with a rope girdle of the same color around his waist, on his head a black stiff brimmed hat held by four bands on the crown. His right hand held the curved end of a stout cane and the other hand held his folded stole."[23]

Damien did not limit his pastoral visits to Catholics. "Most of the lepers upon their arrival here are not Catholics but before death become so", he wrote to Pamphile.[24] Not infrequently someone wanted to be baptized at the last moment in order to be able to receive the last sacraments. Wholly in line with the pastoral practice of the time, Damien was also glad to be able to save that soul. "One starts to recognize the tree from the fruit, because most of the Protestants hardly care for the spiritual salvation of the lepers. Most of the dying also call on the Catholic priest to prepare themselves for the great crossing. I even have a large number of Calvinist leaders baptized *in periculo mortis* [in danger of death]."[25]

Although Damien regarded his most important task as a priest and shepherd of souls to be that of guaranteeing his sick a Christian death and thus ensuring the road to eternal life, he did not at all neglect the sick body.

When he had just arrived on Molokai, the sick were wholly abandoned to their fate, deprived of the most elementary care. Apparently that was the way it had been since the institution of the quarantine in 1866. "You often saw lepers on the roads who were covered with dreadful wounds. Because of the lack of bandages or salve, those wounds were exposed to dust, flies, and worms", Damien recollected. "Not only were those wounds not treated, but whoever got fever, diarrhea, or another ailment died from it because of the lack of a simple remedy." [26]

The situation improved beginning in 1873, from which point basic care was provided by a leprosy patient with some medical experience. Damien assisted him as much as he could, both inside and outside Kalawao's small hospital. From 1878 on, basic care improved when the Board of Health made certain that a physician resided permanently in the settlement. In the mideighties Damien could report that the settlement was no longer a "living cemetery".[27]

While Damien was no doctor and did not want to become one—indeed, he criticized his confrere André Burgerman precisely because he wanted to be more a doctor than a priest—he demonstrated an active interest in medicine and the various treatments. He ardently hoped for a scientific breakthrough that would cure leprosy. As long as a cure was not available, he focused on medicines that could mitigate the consequences of the disease or slow its progression.

For instance, in a letter to his superior general, he inquired about a Chinese medicine called Hoang Nan, which he had learned about through a Dominican from Trinidad. He promptly ordered large quantities of the medicine.[28] When the powder arrived, he experimented with it. He divided patients with varying stages of leprosy into two groups. In one group he replaced the medicine with a substitute. He then carefully recorded the changes in the symptoms in the two groups. As Hilde Eynikel remarks: "Without ever claiming credit for this, he had invented the well-known placebo experiment." [29]

In November 1879 he reported enthusiastically: "It has pro-
longed the life of quite a few of our sick; it has given back new
strength and normal appearances.... After three months the various effects were clearly perceptible in favor of Hoang Nan."[30]
Damien hoped that the Board of Health would be willing to invest
in the expensive medicine.

Damien later showed equally keen interest in the so-called Goto
method, named for the Japanese leprologist Shobun Goto. The treatment used herbal baths, in which leprosy patients were immersed
on a daily basis. Damien, who at the time was already suffering
from the disease himself, traveled to Honolulu for this treatment
and introduced the method in Kalawao. He wanted to build a hospital suited for this purpose, but the Board of Health found it too
expensive and dropped it. That obstacle too he overcame with the
imagination and creativity that love inspired in him. He purchased
large, empty trunks that could serve as tubs; and because there was
little fuel in Kalawao, he had the Hawaiians cut trees for firewood
in order to heat the kettles to the required temperature.

Despite Damien's desire for, if not curative, then at least mitigating, treatments, the reality on Molokai was that of omnipresent death.
Owing to the continuous arrival of new patients, the number of inhabitants in the colony fluctuated between six hundred and eight hundred. "The only thing that really grows here is the cemetery", Damien
sighed. "The pews in the church are somewhat emptier, while in the
cemetery there is hardly room left to dig the graves",[31] he wrote to
his brother at the beginning of 1880. He was annoyed that they had
even begun digging a grave on the spot he had long reserved for himself, next to the Church of Saint Philomena with a view of the ocean.
He insisted that they keep his favorite place empty.

Sometimes that ever-victorious death was difficult for him to
cope with. In the same letter, he wrote: "When I returned home
yesterday evening after an absence of six days, I found one of my
orphan girls dying. She begged me to bring her the holy viaticum
immediately. She had barely finished saying her prayers when she
gave up her soul to the Lord, whom she had just received. I made
her coffin myself and dug her grave. After the funeral Mass this
morning I was informed of the death of two more of my Christians. That makes three burials today."[32] Such things were very

hard on Damien; he also reported the incident that same day to his mother.

In the leprosy settlement, with its fast-growing cemetery, one lived as much among the dead as among the living. Damien liked to spend time there praying and meditating: "Because the cemetery, the church, and the rectory form one park, at night I am the lone keeper of this garden of the dead—all spiritual children of mine—I take delight in saying my rosary there. . . . I confess to you, my dear brother, that the cemetery and the cage of my dying people are my most beautiful meditation books, both to nourish my own heart and to prepare my teachings." [33]

Building a vibrant community

Damien accomplished a lot among the lepers. The greatest gift he gave them was to succeed in transforming an orderless throng into a living community around Christ, where they learned to care for one another.

It required a lot of dedication on the part of the missionary to visit and talk with the sick, a daily practice for Damien. Each week, he visited every house. From the beginning he learned to adapt his words to the situation. "A lot of good is to be done with those visits at home", he remarked at the outset. "In almost every house I have to change my tone. Sometimes I use soft words in order to console. Sometimes I add some vinegar, in order to make them understand the situation they are in. From time to time a real storm breaks loose. Then I threaten them with terrible punishments, whenever they would not change their heart." [34]

Damien's fire-and-brimstone sermons fit naturally in the theology and pastoral approach of his time, but the harrowing situation in which many lepers were withering away also called for someone of Damien's caliber.

In any case, his approach did not harm his popularity. To the contrary, the lepers felt that the Belgian missionary, in his angry outbursts, was genuinely concerned about them. After all, he gratuitously and voluntarily gave his life for them. Many converted to Catholicism because of him. "The number of my Christians has risen considerably. I was obliged to enlarge my main church by more than half. It now consists of a cross shape with a beautiful bell tower", he wrote to his superior general on April 24, 1877.[35]

Each year, he reported the numbers of baptisms and conversions. "Our two churches are very busy", he recorded with satisfaction in 1879. "Last year we baptized 110, out of which 27 were from outside the leprosarium. The great majority of the patients are not Catholic when they arrive, but they die Catholic."[36]

Damien cared not only about numbers but also about the quality and intensity of the religious life in his community. For instance, he formed two organizations, one of men and one of women, who visited and helped the sick. "I hope that their diligence and dedication bring much good to the Christian community", he wrote.[37] Most members themselves probably suffered from leprosy. In this Damien turned a basic Gospel principle into reality: the happiness of each person, poor or rich, sick or healthy, old or young, consists in giving to others. "It is more blessed to give than to receive."[38]

That sort of initiative fundamentally enhanced life together and solidarity among the lepers. Damien also established perpetual adoration of the Blessed Sacrament among the lepers, a prayer practice to which his Congregation of the Sacred Hearts particularly dedicated itself. "Because of their illness it is not always easy for them to fulfill their half hour of perpetual adoration at the assigned times. But if they can't come, I'm often pleased to see them at the set times in adoration on their sickbed in their miserable huts."[39]

Damien and his community took the greatest pleasure in the children's choir, which took shape over the course of the years. With practice their voices had started to sound in harmony together: the choir reflected the growing harmony in the community. Some also played instruments. Piano pieces meant for one person were played by two girls because of their mutilated hands—a moving deux mains.

The rare visitors to the island were often surprised by the music and the joyfulness that, in spite of everything, went hand in hand with it and was present in the settlement. George Woods, a physician who visited the colony in July 1876, described how one evening about twelve children of Damien's orphanage came marching over the grass field while blowing on homemade flutes. It was U.S.

Independence Day. Two flag bearers were carrying a Hawaiian and an American flag.

"Permit me, *monsieur le docteur*, to present my boys", Damien said to Woods. "They have come to welcome you and to thank you for coming so far to inquire after them, and see if anything can be done to cure them."

Damien handed the doctor one of the instruments, "made of old oil cans, fashioned by himself on which he had patiently taught the boys to play by ear", the visitor later wrote. "The harmony and musical character was perfect, though very strange and peculiar." [40]

He was rightly proud of his choir. "During Sunday High Mass my children sing like really great musicians." [41] But great love also meant pain when yet again illness and death tore one of them away. He added sadly: "Recently my choir has indeed sunk away somewhat by the death of the most beautiful voices and the illness of others."

Damien himself remained cheerful of heart and tried to be everyone's friend. According to many witnesses, humor and joy marked his apostolate. After six years in the settlement he wrote to his superior general in Paris: "I am still happy and content among my beloved lepers of Molokai." [42]

Spiritual life

None of this would have been possible if Damien had not had a strong faith supported by a regular prayer life, celebration of the Eucharist, and the sacraments.

That made a great impression on the children. Joseph Manu, who often accompanied Damien as his "boy" on his boat trips to other parts of the island, remembered vividly many years later: "Father Damien prayed very often. Frequently I saw him pray. He regularly called the children to pray and showed them how to do it. Before he came in my boat, he usually said a prayer; and when we came ashore, he always knelt down to pray." [43]

Damien's daily schedule reveals how intensive his prayer life was. When he celebrated the Eucharist at six in the morning, he had already spent three quarters of an hour on morning prayer and meditation. After his breakfast, he tried to keep his mornings free for prayer, reading his breviary, and studying Scripture. In the evening, after visiting the sick, he prayed vespers, and after the evening meal his rosary and breviary. If he was not overcome by sleep at ten o'clock, he would read in the New Testament.

For someone with the reputation of a man of action, that was an intensive spiritual program. Of course, his days often passed differently, whenever he was called away on urgent matters. One also reads how it cost him an inner battle to avoid distraction, not to let himself be seduced by always responding to new demands. But Damien did wage that fight with himself.

Also interesting are resolutions he wrote down for himself following a retreat in the summer of 1877. He resolved to be less occupied with the material needs of the lepers—he knew that danger was lurking there. To be more orderly in his life, to be friendly toward everyone, and to waste no time with useless conversations were other points of attention.

He engaged in a continuous struggle against his own weaknesses and sins. "Be strict with yourself and forgiving toward others. Scrupulously honor God in prayer, meditation, Mass, and the administration of the sacraments." [44]

It is further clear how seriously he lived the three vows of poverty, chastity, and obedience: "Everything you own is not your property and cannot be used for personal satisfaction. Carnal pleasure: chastity makes you equal to an angel, while sex makes a priest into a devil. No sensuality and no search for the sources [of material goods]. Let your superiors do with you what they deem best." [45]

He lived these three vows with great fidelity. All of the witnesses agreed that Damien always remained faithful to his vow of chastity, although gossip was unavoidable in the microcosm of Hawaii. Despite his strong character, obedience was not an empty word for him: he faithfully obeyed his superiors even when he disagreed with them. We will return to this later. Likewise, poverty was no idle word for Damien, who had hardly any possessions. Money matters did not interest him, as his letters to his mother indicate. He kept an account book but admitted to not always being meticulous about recording the finances. He was content with what he had. His meals were utterly simple, and he never threw away food.

He imagined he was the disciple whom Jesus asked: "When I sent you out with no purse or bag or sandals, did you lack anything?" And he would answer, in full accord with the truth: "Nothing, Lord." [46]

Father Damien's rule of life

Personal Rule of August 1880 [47]

5:00	Rise without hesitation—short prayer—choose subjects for meditation—wash up and dress neatly.
5:15	Enter church—morning prayer—read about subject of meditation—avoid every distraction.
6:00	Prepare for Mass—wait for the faithful to arrive—start Mass between 6:00 and 6:30 (on Sundays continue with meditation until 7:00).
After Mass	Instruction on subject of meditation, unvest, clean up—put everything neatly in its place, never leave sacristy in disorder—afterward at least half an hour of prayer of thanks—in silence.
8:00	Light breakfast—no meat, no *poi*, only coffee, bread, and some eggs—afterward smoke pipe—discuss a little and arrange household affairs, the chickens, the children.
9:00	Divine Office—avoid interruptions—if called away for nonurgent matters, say you are busy—after breviary, study of theology and sacred Scripture until noon.
12:00	Lunch—no familiar conversation with cook—afterward visit the sick—on horseback only for long distances, otherwise by foot—before departure a short visit to the Blessed Sacrament—on the way no idle conversations—be friendly to everyone without being familiar—do not waste time talking—return home at the latest at 5:00.
5:00	Vespers and compline—if people come, catechesis.

6:00	Supper—in the winter a little earlier so that there is no service personnel in the house after dusk (be strict with any woman or girl who remains in the park after sunset).
7:00	Rosary—followed by breviary, matins and lauds and spiritual reading.
9:00	Evening prayer in the church, followed by meditation—go to sleep at the latest at 10:00.
10:00	If not sleepy, read a chapter in the New Testament.

5. Love overcomes many boundaries

It belongs to the wonderfully evangelical dynamic of Damien's life that he was a celebrity already during his lifetime. The further he removed himself from the inhabited world, the more famous he became. The more he gave himself away, the more radiantly his star shone. By giving himself completely to a small band of outcasts on a godforsaken piece of island, he became a figure emanating a universal power of attraction.

Damien was a man who knew to go far for love of the Gospel. As a young missionary, he went to the other side of the globe fully aware that he would never again see his family and homeland. In his mission field, Hawaii, his spiritual journey continued. Arriving with the prejudices of the missionary bringing civilization to "savages", gradually his appreciation and love for the Hawaiians deepened. This did not mean that he could not teach and give them much: in the first place, his faith and his love. In giving himself to the very poorest of God's creatures in the extreme conditions of the Molokai leprosy colony, his journey became a spiritual adventure. His example of self-giving yielded much fruit, even during his lifetime, and inflamed the faith, love, and generosity of those who witnessed him in action on Molokai or who heard of him through the media. The story of Damien's life is the story of a grain that died in the earth and brought forth a rich harvest.

Damien did not aspire to be the lonely hero he was all too often made out to be. He repeatedly prayed for new vocations and requested support and assistance. He tried to stay on good terms with his confreres, his superiors, and the civil authorities; but the well-being of his exiled lepers, whose voices were too little heard, was paramount. The arrival in Hawaii of the Franciscan sisters of New York under the leadership of Mother Marianne Cope raised Damien's hopes for the fulfillment of his dream, the granting of his prayers, though he had to exercise great patience before the sisters finally made the crossing from Honolulu to Molokai.

One of the many boundaries that Damien's love overcame was that between Catholic and Protestant Christians. Formed in the categories of Catholic missionaries of his time, he had been taught to see Protestants as heretics he had to bring back to the true Roman fold. But that did not impede his love: by living among many Protestants, by attempting to establish good relations with everyone in the interest of his lepers, and especially by trying to be a father to all lepers, his understanding and love grew, including for those he did not manage to bring to his faith. That did not make him into a "progressive" priest,[1] a nonsensical contemporary category to apply to a missionary formed in the ultramontane Catholicism of his day; rather, one could say that Damien found, in the Catholic tradition itself, in the cultural changes that went hand in hand with the globalization of his time, and especially in the ways of the heart, breeding ground for his new ecumenical openness.

It is significant that Damien's love was returned from the Protestant and Anglican sides. While his superiors and confreres admired his commitment but were also rather fixated on what they regarded as his lesser sides, it was often non-Catholics, in Hawaii and the wider Anglo-Saxon world, who were touched by the unique greatness of his life. Through the extraordinary admiration for the figure of Damien and the generosity that his witness awakened in the Protestant world, he certainly counts, without having sought this himself, as a forerunner of the ecumenical movement. For his life exemplified what is central in Christianity. Sincere Christians, irrespective of their tradition or confession, could not remain insensitive to that. Unconditional love always attracts. That too is the spirit of Damien.

From competition to magnanimity

The religious climate on the Hawaiian Islands in the nineteenth century, like that in many mission regions, was marked by robust competition between Protestant and Catholic missionaries. Protestants had been active on the islands since 1820, so the situation was to their advantage. Most communities had American, Congregationalist leanings, with full autonomy and without institutional presiders. However, the majority of the Hawaiian royal family belonged to the Episcopalian church, the American variety of Anglicanism. Initially the anti-Catholic spirit was strongly present: the Catholic mission was opened in 1827 but was twice closed. In 1839 it was reopened, under French pressure, and entrusted to the Congregation of the Sacred Hearts. In 1850 the Mormons also came, and in 1862 the Anglicans.

When Damien arrived in 1864, the Catholic Church had gained a firm foothold, and the faith spread among the population. As remarked already, the initial years of Damien's mission on the island of Hawaii were lived out in that atmosphere of intense competition.

The rivalry with Protestants persisted but took on a different expression in his life among the sufferers on Molokai. He aspired to be a father to them all, including those who did not convert to his religion. When distributing relief goods, he always took care to treat everyone equally, never discriminating on the basis of faith, which was not the usual way of doing things.

As a result of Damien's generosity of spirit and fatherly presence, the allure of the Catholic Church in the colony naturally rapidly increased. "I went to Honolulu and pleaded for my poor unfortunates and got enough clothes for three hundred! Everyone is beginning to see that the Catholic priest is a common father of the poor and unfortunate. Therefore, our heretics over here lose confidence", he wrote after only a couple of months.[2]

In the extreme circumstances of Molokai Damien lost his nagging side, insofar as this would have characterized him previously. What remained were service and friendliness toward each inhabitant of the colony. When a member of the royal family, Peter Kaeo, was exiled to the leprosy colony, Damien came to introduce himself, as he usually did with newcomers. Knowing that the man belonged to the Anglican communion, Damien avoided the subject of religion. "I have had a call from the Catholic priest", Peter Kaeo wrote to Emma, the dowager queen. "He is a very nice man."[3] This resulted in a long letter written by the queen to the prominent leper, filled with admonitions about the dangers of Catholicism.

Damien wanted to be a source not of division but rather of reconciliation. "I try to be everyone's friend, people of the government as well as the sick", he explained to his superior general. He was pleased to report that none of the sick seemed to hold anything against him—perhaps only the Calvinist minister, "who is more consumed by jealousy than by leprosy". The minister wrote anonymous pieces against Damien and tried to tarnish his good name. "I know where it comes from and do not need to refute it", Damien said, adding magnanimously: "I forgive him wholeheartedly." [4]

The influence Damien radiated was immense; his commitment spoke for itself. The German Picpus Father Hermann Koeckemann, who in 1882 succeeded Maigret as apostolic vicar, was pleased to note at his installation: "More than half of the population of the leprosarium is Catholic; many heretics and unbelievers have been converted by the grace of God and the gratitude for the dedication of the Catholic priest." [5]

Damien nurtured his relationship with the civil authorities. He realized that the settlement could be made more humane only by using all the available resources of people of goodwill. That required not narrow-mindedness but magnanimity. Over the years, he developed a good relationship with the settlement's superintendent, Rudolph Meyer, a native German who lived on a farm on top of the hill. Meyer was a Protestant, but that did not hinder the mutual good feelings between them. To Hermann Koeckemann Damien wrote: "Your friend Meyer spent a whole week with me. His company was very beneficial for me, and he has only to take a small step to be a good Catholic." [6] Undoubtedly that was meant as a huge compliment.

Tribute

The leprosy settlement welcomed distinguished visitors in mid-September 1881. The Hawaiian princess Liliuokalani, who later became queen, landed with her entourage, members of the Board of Health, and a number of journalists in tow. Eight hundred lepers, dressed in their Sunday best, welcomed her with the traditional aloha, the Hawaiian welcome. Meyer and Damien accompanied the princess from Kalaupapa over the dusty sand road to Kalawao, where they gave her a tour. The princess entered some of the neat, tiny white houses and visited approvingly the boys' and girls' orphanages and the Protestant and the Catholic churches. Damien and Meyer thought to spare her a visit to the hospital, but she insisted on making it. She was not prepared for the sight of the swollen and mutilated faces staring at her from their small mats on the wooden floor. She braced herself and tried to smile at a leper with an empty eye socket and swollen earlobes reaching to his shoulders. When she spoke with a severely deformed and crippled girl, her eyes filled with tears. The Hawaiian press reported in great detail and in lyrical words on the emotional royal visit.[7] Journalists reported that, just prior to her departure, the girls' choir, which had prepared for weeks, sang a couple of additional songs and serenades. When they finished, they all looked, full of expectation, toward the princess for her words of farewell. The princess rose and told the patients how proud she was of the courageous way they dealt with their illness and separation from their loved ones. Then the tears streamed down her cheeks, and she could not speak for minutes. Finally she promised that the Kingdom of Hawaii would do all it could to improve the living conditions in the colony.

The lepers had made an impression on the princess. And so had Damien. When she returned to her palace in Honolulu, she reported on her experience at Molokai. She praised the efforts of the energetic Catholic priest to improve the lot of all of the exiles regardless of their religious convictions. Also full of praise for the work of the Catholic missionary were Rudolph Meyer, the members of the Board of Health, and the resident physician, all committed Protestants. The princess proposed to honor Damien, together with the departing apostolic vicar, Louis Maigret, with the title of Commander of the Royal Order of Kalakaua, the highest honor in the kingdom.

A few days later Damien received a letter.

Reverend Sir:
It is my desire to express to you my great appreciation of your heroic and self-denying labors, among the most unfortunate of the subjects of this Realm, and in some public manner to testify to the fidelity and

patient, loving care with which you labor for the physical and spiritual good of those who are necessarily shut off from the tender ministrations of relatives and friends. I am aware that your labors and sacrifices are dictated solely by a desire to benefit your unfortunate fellow men and that you look for your reward and inspiration to the divine Father and Ruler of us all,—never the less, in furtherance of my desire I ask you, Reverend Father, to accept the Order of Knight Commander of the Royal Order of Kalakaua in testimony of my sincere appreciation of your efforts in alleviating the distresses and mitigating in many ways the sorrows of the unfortunate lepers of Kalawao, as I had occasion to observe during my recent visit to that place.

I am your Friend
Liliuokalani, Regent[8]

The royal family asked the new apostolic vicar, bishop Hermann Koeckemann, to deliver personally to Damien the letter and accompanying medal. Koeckemann had never been in the colony and was terrified of leprosy. He would have preferred that Damien come to Honolulu. But because he feared the public reaction in the press and could not refuse the princess, he made the journey. On October 3, sick from the voyage, he went ashore at Kaunakakai, on the other side of Molokai, where Damien was waiting for him in the moonlight. Together they rode to the top of the *pali*, from which they started the descent to Kalaupapa. For Koeckemann it was a true Calvary: "We began our two-thousand-foot descent on a small and steep path with courage and gaiety of heart. We made headway with hands and feet, sometimes sliding on our backs faster than we wanted, which lasted an hour and twenty minutes. After walking for fifteen minutes, I could no longer carry the suitcase. Father Damien, who is as strong as a Turk, took the case on his own and brought the heaviest objects to the foot of the mountain."[9]

The ceremony itself went smoothly. To Koeckemann's relief, the contact with the lepers turned out better than expected. The entire colony, lepers and healthy kokuas, Catholics and Protestants, had gathered for Damien's tribute. The ceremony concluded with a great feast of roast pork, fresh fruit, and, of course, *poi* for everyone.

Damien took advantage of the presence of the new apostolic vicar to communicate two concerns: because of the growing number of faithful, the tiny church in Kalaupapa had to be enlarged to a cross shape, as had been done in Kalawao. Additionally, he asked for a confrere to serve the other part of the island. For, since the departure of André Burgerman the previous year, he was alone again. Damien obtained permission for the first request, but the bishop could not fulfill the second.

The following day, after Mass, Koeckemann was greeted by a delegation of Protestants, who, together with Damien, saw him off in a festive procession to the foot of the *pali*. Damien recorded with delight that these Calvinists, separated brothers, "demonstrated that, while there is no unity of faith, at least there is a good relationship between the two parties".[10] Together with his bishop, who was relieved to head back to the safety of Honolulu, Damien made the arduous hour-and-a-half climb. It was to be the only time during his long term in office that the bishop visited Damien in the leprosy settlement.

The down-to-earth Fleming was not overly impressed with his honor of receiving the title of Knight Commander. It was not for this that he was on Molokai, as the princess had accurately suggested in her letter. While the bishop received visitors, "the knight is in the confessional", Damien wrote to his brother, not without self-mockery.[11] He never wore his medal, not even on the occasion of the rare visits to the colony of members of the royal family. Superintendent Ambrose Hutchison regarded Damien's humility "too great to take advantage of this honorable decoration".[12] For the writer Stoddard, who came to visit Damien, he dug out his decoration only after his visitor insisted a great deal. The neat morocco case in which it was kept was covered with a thick layer of dust.[13]

The missionary might not lose sleep over the decoration, but he did not underestimate the influence of the recognition that had fallen to his lot. Not only was it Hawaii's highest national distinction, but it had been awarded to him by a Protestant royal house. At the announcement of the news, the national press did not spare its praise for that magnanimous gesture. The Hawaiian Gazette, owned by Walter Murray Gibson, which already had sung Damien's praises, wrote on this occasion: "Father Damien receives a mark of

distinction for self-devoted services which few men would under-
take. We have ever regarded this gentleman's work as one of the
noblest that man can do. A man without any desire for earthly
reward, who willingly takes up his abode among the unhappy sufferers of Kalawao, devotes himself to the good of the poor lepers,
and runs the risk of taking a loathsome disease that will eat his
body piecemeal." [14]

The story of the princess' visit to the leprosy settlement and the
high honor conferred on Damien inspired the Hawaiian press and
public opinion for quite some time, the result of which was a renewed
interest in the banished lepers. A wave of solidarity was rising. Islanders of all confessions collected money and sent relief aid. Clothing
was especially welcome to the leprosy patients, who complained
about the cold, which was a consequence of both the weather conditions on the peninsula and the progression of their disease.

Interest in Damien's work on Molokai and the solidarity with him
were not limited to Hawaii. After the reception of his medal he became
more and more known throughout the Anglo-Saxon world, from Great
Britain, the leading nation at the time, to the United States of America. It was remarkable that the celebrity of the self-sacrificing Catholic missionary grew especially through the Protestant network.
Donations from all varieties of religious communities and philan-
thropic organizations started pouring in. Damien had never sought
celebrity; nor had his missionary congregation ever specially publi-
cized his work. It must have seemed strange to Damien's immediate
superiors that this should happen precisely to him, who was neither
their best-formed priest nor the easiest one to get along with. They
did not know how to react to his celebrity. It was wonderful for the
aura of the Catholic mission, but did the other missionaries not do
good work too? Would this go to Damien's head?

Reinforcement . . . but not for Molokai

Princess Liliuokalani's visit to the leprosy colony and the great
response to Damien's royal tribute had yet another immediate consequence. The question of the leprosy policy was again high on the
political agenda.

The princess had heard from sick inhabitants of the immense aversion to the brutal and swift manner in which the potentially sick on the Hawaiian Islands were detected, judged, and deported.

The heavy-handed segregation policy caused great dissatisfaction across broad layers of the population. There was hardly a family unaffected by the epidemic, and everyone knew someone who was banished to die on Molokai. Some of those infected with the disease took flight or were hidden by family and friends, often for years. Besides, it was a public secret that some lepers from affluent circles received privileged treatment and were not exiled. Instead, they received permission to seek treatment on the American mainland.

That unjust selection policy angered many, even if the principle was scarcely questioned. Moreover, the medical examinations were often conducted in a superficial way, without a thorough examination and without the possibility of a second opinion. Yet the symptoms of leprosy in the early stages were far from unambiguous. It regularly happened that men and women were exiled to Molokai and that after some time it was determined that they suffered from another disorder. While they then were allowed to leave the place of quarantine, they had been needlessly and cruelly separated for a time from their loved ones.

The dissatisfaction was smoldering. A serious incident nearly led to an outright uprising on the islands. One day in October 1881 the *Warwick*, the ship that usually transported lepers to Molokai, could not anchor in Kalaupapa due to heavy weather. The captain ordered twenty-two patients thrown overboard, forcing them to swim ashore. What possessed him is unknown, but the message conveyed by such an action was clear: exiles on Molokai would die sooner rather than later; their lives were of no value. Shocked inhabitants of the colony, including the Belgian priest, dove into the roaring surf, risking their own lives, to save the new arrivals. For the most part it turned out all right, though two unfortunate ones died on the beach, one in the arms of Damien.[15] The scene has been strikingly portrayed in Paul Cox's film *Molokai: The Story of Father Damien*.

The incident caused a wave of criticism in the Hawaiian press concerning the Board of Health's policy. The government had treated the lepers "like dogs thrown to the sea".[16] Pamphlets appeared demanding the closure of the leprosy settlement on Molokai. If those demands were not met, plantations would be set ablaze, resulting in widespread destruction. On the island of Kauai some rebels carried out the threat.

Under pressure of an incensed public and smoldering rebellion, Hawaiian officials realized that the leprosy policy had to be relaxed and made more humane. However, they did not want to rescind forced segregation, which they regarded as the only effective response to the epidemic. They decided to found a new hospital, where those suspected of having the disease could remain for a while and be given further examination and not be immediately exiled. There was space for two hundred patients. It would be, not a prison, but a place where they could receive visits and care from their families. Princess Liliuokalani donated a piece of land on a spot called Kakaako, situated between Honolulu and Waikiki.[17]

The head of the Kakaako hospital was George L. Fitch, a boastful, self-satisfied American doctor who had acquired a certain reputation in the area of fighting leprosy. He did not turn out to be a happy choice. The man was more a charlatan than a real doctor. He had no feeling for the human drama of the patients. He could be bribed, with patients paying to avoid banishment to Molokai. In no time the new structure was overcrowded.

Furthermore, Fitch advanced the theory that leprosy was the fourth stage of syphilis. The leprosy epidemic, according to him, was essentially a venereal disease and entirely rooted in moral licentiousness.

Fitch was also appointed the doctor for the leprosy colony. He occasionally visited the settlement, but it scarcely interested him. The leprosy policy remained a huge human and political drama. The Kakaako hospital, where the hygienic and human situation also left a lot to be desired, did not bring improvement under Fitch.

The prime minister at the time, Walter Murray Gibson,[18] who as a publisher-editor had often written about Damien with admiration, could not stand by and watch it any longer. The editor-politician was an eccentric figure with an eventful past, perhaps the most colorful figure in Hawaiian history. He had been a widower since age twenty-two and had once been imprisoned on suspicion of complicity in a coup attempt in the Dutch colony of Sumatra.

As an active member of the Church of Jesus Christ of Latter-day Saints, better known as the Mormons, he persuaded church president Brigham Young to allow him to establish a Mormon colony in the Pacific region. He was later excommunicated from the church community, having been accused of embezzling church funds.

Gibson was a man of many talents and boundless ambition who was convinced he had an important mission in life. He took special interest in the leprosy epidemic. It was his great dream and aspiration to turn the Hawaiian Islands into a model in the fight against leprosy. As such he was one of the harshest critics of the Board of Health.

Although Gibson had many rivals and adversaries on the islands, he managed, clever and ambitious as he was, gradually to amass political power.

Gibson published a handbook on leprosy that conflicted with the theories of Doctor Fitch. It contained an accurate description of the bacillus theory, which had become well known following the discoveries of the Norwegian Gerhard Hansen in 1873, and provided practical advice on how contagion could be avoided. He scored highly with King David Kalakaua and became his confidant. He became a member of the Board of Health and quickly managed to become its head. Similarly, in his political career, he found success through his friendship with the king, through his oratorical skills, and through his ability to play to public opinion. He was named a minister and rapidly became the most powerful man in the archipelago. Nicknamed the "Minister of Everything", he became prime minister of Hawaii in 1882; he also served as minister of foreign affairs, justice, and war.

As a politician Gibson had a great appreciation for the work of the Catholic mission. In return, the Catholic superior had a warm heart for the former Mormon leader. At a time when the political future of Hawaii was highly uncertain owing to immigration and American pressure, the Catholic Church played the Gibson card. That became an important element in the story of Damien.

Gibson was determined radically to overhaul the leprosy policy. He wanted to turn both the quarantined settlement on Molokai and the hospital of Kakaako into model places. To do so he sought to recruit new people. In the medical realm, he contacted a German doctor,

Eduard Arning.[19] He was trained in the school of scientists like G. H. Armauer Hansen, the discoverer of the leprosy bacillus, and the German Robert Koch. The latter had devised a methodology to prove scientifically that a certain microbe causes a certain disease. This methodology involved experiments on living fiber, and also on human beings. The hope was that Arning could not only determine the causes of leprosy but also discover a medical treatment for it. For this Hawaii was the ideal laboratory, where he could find not only many lepra bacils but also many human guinea pigs.

Gibson was not only interested in the scientific and medical aspects of leprosy. He was also convinced that the care given to those suffering from the disease had to be improved. Both in Kakaako and on Molokai there was need for quality nursing. As funds for professional nurses were lacking, Gibson thought to ask religious sisters to provide the care. On January 4, 1883, he wrote a letter to apostolic vicar Koeckemann requesting him to invite "eight or more Sisters of Charity".[20] The bishop put his friend Léonor Fouesnel to work. The French missionary wrote to fifty different religious orders in North America. Only one of them was willing to take on the task, the third order of Saint Francis from the city of Syracuse, New York. On November 8, 1883, seven sisters landed at Honolulu on the Mariposa, coincidentally the same ship on which the German doctor Arning was traveling. The sisters were led by Mother Marianne Cope, a nun of exceptional character and refinement.

The impulse given by Gibson, the appearance of a young and ambitious doctor, and especially the arrival of the sisters were an important turning point in the battle against leprosy and a more humane treatment of the sick in Hawaii. Damien grasped that immediately. The arrival of the sisters filled him with great hope and joy and was the topic of conversation during the entire year of 1883. The missionary assumed that a number of sisters would soon come to his aid, for which there was urgent need. No matter how colossal his efforts, the conditions in the settlement remained especially tragic.

Damien painfully miscalculated. It had been owing to his efforts that the leprosy problem was placed on the political agenda and that politics and church had sought reinforcement overseas. But the arrival of seven Franciscan sisters set in motion a different set of dynamics. The condition in the Kakaako hospital was as appalling as that on Molokai. But Kakaako was centrally located, right next to Honolulu and Waikiki, an eyesore for many traveling business-men and tourists. It was a visible stain on the Hawaiian image. Molokai, on the other hand, was hidden from view, with Damien and his lepers a day's journey away.

As is often the case, the political and church leaders gave prior-ity to what was thrust on them, to what lay close at hand. It has to be said that Mother Marianne and her sisters did wonderful work in Kakaako. They took the situation firmly in their own hands, and the conditions improved appreciably.

As a result Koeckemann turned a deaf ear to Damien's impatient pleas that the sisters come to Molokai. As long as the sisters were right next to Honolulu, Koeckemann could keep an eye on things him-self. And did Damien not always exaggerate? Did he not constantly ask for more?

Damien could not count any longer on strong man Walter Gib-son. The widower had developed a platonic love for Mother Mar-ianne since her arrival. His diaries reveal that he constantly sought out her company. "His love for Marianne had become obsessive. On Sunday mornings he would hurry to the cathedral, hoping to sight her. He phoned the convent repeatedly, wrote her note after note", John Tayman noted.[21] After one of his visits Gibson wrote with delight: "A happy hour with my little girl—so faithful to her duty—so good—so pure. What a noble character. I reverence as well as love her." [22] He did not give a single thought to letting her depart for Molokai.

Meanwhile, on Molokai, where there were five times as many leprosy patients as in Kakaako, Damien could use all the help he could get. J. H. Stallard, an English doctor who visited the colony in March 1884, wrote a highly critical report. According to him, the mortality rate was ten times that of any ordinary community of an unhealthy type. In 1883, 150 men, women, and children had died, with the number of deaths for 1884 already one-fourth higher.

Stallard denounced the government for its gross neglect. He wrote bluntly that the leprosy patients were dumped on the island and left starving and uncared for. The shortage of food, which was espe-cially evident, was a consequence of government frugality.[23] Damien could not have written something like that. Besides, he had experienced much worse conditions in the initial years.

Rudolph Meyer, the superintendent on Molokai, tried to gloss over the outsider's stinging indictment. He was of the opinion that, given the limited resources, the government was doing its best. The ailing exiles lived an average of five years, and that was not bad at all. They were "comfortable and happy",[24] and their banishment was not inhumane.

Damien for once completely disagreed with Meyer. He shared the view that there was too much suffering in the colony and that it had to be alleviated, no matter what the cost. But in Honolulu they had gotten used to the fact that Damien again banged his fist on the table. His complaint was hardly heard. His ecclesial superiors were in the first place focused on Kakaako. Nor could he expect priority treatment from politicians. Gibson would not let go of his Marianne. Again Damien had to exercise patience. Once more he had to rely on himself.

Stoddard's visit

Damien was not a man to seek his own publicity. During his initial years on Molokai, his brother Pamphile had a number of his letters published. That, however, angered the superiors of the Congregation of the Sacred Hearts in Hawaii. They feared that the portrayals of the appalling conditions in the leper colony would reflect negatively on the Hawaiian authorities. The Catholic mission, which still felt like a threatened minority on the islands, did not wish needlessly to offend the local authorities.

Nor was Damien keen to obtain the status of a hero. "The desire not to come across as important in the public press is the reason why I respond so late to your letter and to that of the superior general last year", he wrote to Pamphile. As a consequence he played down his work: "Every day my occupations are the same, and I am in a certain sense outside this world. I have nothing interesting to report to you."[25]

Damien, however, was also not stupid. He understood very well the direct link between the news coverage of the lepers of Molokai and the gifts and support that arrived.

And with a Board of Health and a Catholic mission that were continually short of money and that talked more about economizing than investing, he could make good use of the money and support to improve the living conditions in the colony. "In the first years of my work of service, I often received considerable alms through the intervention of our procurator in Paris, but because I never acted like a public beggar, the overseas caritas seems to have forgotten the poor lepers of Molokai", he noted in a bitter moment.[26]

Damien did not have to take care of his own publicity. Others would do that for him. In that regard the visit of the American writer Charles Warren Stoddard (1843–1909) and the little book he later wrote about it played a role that cannot be overestimated.

Stoddard was a homosexual and a rather eccentric writer of travel stories.[27] Critics sang the praises of his remarkable talent, which, however, was diminished by laziness. He grew up in San Francisco, where he came into contact with famous authors like Walt Whitman and Mark Twain, the latter of whom hired him for a while as his secretary. Later he met the Scot Robert Louis Stevenson, who was seven years younger and an admirer of his. They became friends and maintained an intense correspondence throughout their lives. Stevenson only visited Molokai shortly after Damien's death. Together the two eminent authors have contributed much to the propagation of Damien's name.

Stoddard had previously visited Hawaii on one of his peregrinations in 1869. He did not conceal the fact that he was searching on the Sandwich Islands for a lifestyle that could be reconciled with his sexual orientation, a lifestyle that, according to him, was not possible even in tolerant California. During this journey he also visited Molokai, spending a few days in the leper colony. The settlement had existed for only three years, and Damien had not yet arrived. It was his first encounter with leprosy, but it is unknown whether the disease made any impression on the writer. Rather, he associated Molokai with a young Hawaiian there, with whom, in his own words, he experienced the "sweetest idyl of my life".[28] After that trip, when the writer's life had gone downhill, the nostalgia for Hawaii and Molokai kept nagging him. He sang to Stevenson of "the singular loveliness of the place", with "its abrupt walls, hung with tapestries of ferns".[29]

In 1884 Stoddard visited Molokai a second time. On this occasion his attention was focused entirely on the leper colony and the figure of Damien, who fascinated him. Stoddard had earlier converted from strict moralistic Calvinism to the Roman Catholic faith, as he described it in *A Troubled Heart and How It Was Comforted at Last*. Nonetheless, he had not yet found the peace of soul and genuine happiness he was desperately seeking. His meeting with Damien, a joyful missionary living in the midst of the greatest suffering, inspired him in his search, as he described afterward in his successful little tome *The Lepers of Molokai*.

After some insistence, Stoddard had received permission to visit the colony. The members of the Board of Health preferred to keep the curious at a distance, but they speculated that the reporting of this journalist, who had visited the colony in its utterly wretched initial period, would be advantageous.

Stoddard, who traveled in the company of Doctors Fitch and Mouritz, later described his first encounter with Damien as follows: "The chapel door stood ajar; in a moment it was thrown open, and a young priest paused at the threshold to give us welcome. His cassock was worn and faded; his hair tumbled like a schoolboy's, his hands stained and hardened by toil; but the glow of health was in his face, the buoyancy of youth in his manner." The writer was immediately taken with Damien's "ringing laugh, his ready sympathy, and his inspiring magnetism".[30]

Stoddard's view was likely somewhat clouded by his enthusiasm and his presumption that God protected his servant against the disease. Doctor Mouritz, on the other hand, who traveled along with him and became from then on the colony's resident physician, later said that he had recognized in Damien from the first glance the signs of the onset of leprosy. Did Damien already suspect it as well? When at Stoddard's request Damien showed him a photo of himself, Damien added with a laugh: "Looks like a leper." Stoddard later noted guardedly in his diary: "And so it does."[31]

The American writer was impressed by the progress the colony had made since his first visit fifteen years earlier. On the material level the living conditions had improved considerably. He saw how Damien had a crucial hand in this. "The neat white cottages which have taken the place of the thatched huts of the natives were erected under his eye; and, furthermore, he personally assisted in the con-struction of most of them." [32] The energetic Damien was always busy. When the writer looked for him, he found him "now at the top of a ladder, hammer and nail in hand; or in the garden, or the hospital ward, or the kitchen, or away on a sick-call, as the case might be. It was seldom he could sit with me, for not a moment was he really free." [33]

Stoddard was even more impressed by Damien's service to the lepers, his personality, and his concrete spirituality. Sitting on the veranda of the rectory while the priest prepared him a simple eve-ning meal, he noted in his diary: "How charming he is, how beau-tiful in his devotion, how sincere, how charitable." [34] In his book, he later sang the praises of this Jack-of-all-trades: "physician of the soul and of the body, magistrate, school-teacher, carpenter, joiner, painter, gardener, house-keeper, cook, and even, in some cases, grave-digger. Great was his need of help, and long was he in need of it before it came. More than 1,600 lepers had been buried under his administration, and a death-bed was always awaiting him—sometimes two or three of them." [35]

Death remained omnipresent on Molokai in 1884, and the "busy hammer" with which coffins were constructed "seemed never idle". Stoddard reported many horrific cases, such as the time he entered the hospital and bumped up against a soiled blanket, under which appeared to be a child. Damien tried to prevent him from looking, but the writer did so nonetheless. "A corner of the blanket was raised cautiously: a breathing object lay beneath; a face, a human face, was turned slowly toward us—a face in which scarcely a trace of anything human remained." The young patient was near death. "The dark skin was puffed out and blackened; a kind of moss, or mould, gummy and glistening, covered it; the muscles of the mouth, having contracted, laid bare the grinning teeth; the thickened tongue lay like a fig between them." The child's eyes were open, "the eyelids, curled tightly back, exposed the inner surface, and the pro-truding eyeballs, now shapeless and broken, looked not unlike bursted grapes." [36]

Yet one reads in the travel narrative how the romantic writer found, amid the disease and death, an unforgettable witness of faith. He described how Damien, in his miserable modest Church of Saint

Philomena in Kalawao, presided at High Mass amid his disfigured faithful: "There was scarcely a form in that whole congregation from which one would not turn with horror, and many of these worshippers seemed actually to have risen from the corruption of the grave." But all of the worshippers "seemed to be singing, or trying to sing, simple refrains, that sounded strangely enough in the hoarse throats of the singers" while "with the greatest sweetness and gravity the celebrant proceeded." The fetid odor of the assembled community was hardly bearable, but "the solemn boom of the sea-surf was fit accompaniment to that most solemn service", and the salty sea breeze struck him as "a sigh of sympathy". Stoddard observed: "This is the Feast of the Master as celebrated at Kalawao; and to celebrate it thus is Father Damien's blessed privilege." The writer was reminded of the Gospel passage in which Jesus enters a city and ten lepers call out to him, "Have mercy on us." He concluded: "Verily their prayer is answered; for He hath mercy on them, and blesses them in the person of His servant." [37]

Stoddard was deeply moved by his visit. He himself was a rather unhappy, romantic figure struggling with his feelings, his sexual orientation, and his health problems. "I wonder if you are truly happy", he once had written to a priest friend. "I am not; I cannot remember when I was for any length of time." [38]

On Molokai, however, he understood something of the mystery of true happiness. Not long after his departure, Stoddard wrote to Damien that he envied him in his peculiar life: "You seemed to me to be happy, much happier than those who live in the world." [39]

Mother Marianne (1838–1918)

The "mantle of Damien" on Molokai was taken up by the American sister Marianne Cope. Until her death in 1918 she untiringly dedicated herself with her fellow Franciscan sisters to the lepers in the settlement, with a special interest in the orphans. The sisters' arrival on Molokai at the end of 1888, a few months before Damien's death, was an enormous consolation to him, the fulfillment of his hopes and prayers.

Marianne Cope was born as Barbara Koob on January 23, 1838, in Hessen, Germany, into a family of ten children. The year after her birth, her parents immigrated to Utica, New York, where they anglicized their last name to Cope.

Already at a young age the girl felt called to the religious life, but because of a shortage of money, "I was obliged to struggle and wait nine years", she wrote about her youth, "before it pleased God to open the convent gates to me." At age twenty-four she could finally enter the Saint Clare convent, where she took the name Sister Mary Anne. That soon became Marianne.

After teaching for nearly ten years, she began a new vocation in 1870 as chief nurse and administrator of Saint Joseph's Hospital in Syracuse, New York. There she acquired medical experience, and her leadership skills became apparent. The latest techniques for disinfecting were applied meticulously. The institution she ran excelled in cleanliness, order, and efficiency.

Although "Mother" Marianne was criticized for admitting difficult cases, such as alcoholics, into her institution, she was generally known for her friendliness, wisdom, and practical attitude.

In 1883 as provincial superior in Syracuse she received the letter of Father Léonor Fouesnel with the request to send sisters to run a medical institution in Hawaii. Fouesnel did not say a word about leprosy. His reluctance was unnecessary. The letter touched Marianne's heart, and she replied enthusiastically: "I am hungry for the work and I wish with all my heart to be one of the chosen ones. . . . I am not afraid of any disease, hence it would be my greatest delight even to minister to the abandoned 'lepers'." [40]

Together with six of her fellow sisters, she arrived in Honolulu in November 1883. After a year and a half of the sisters working in the hospital in Kakaako, near Honolulu, the conditions for the two hundred leprosy patients were greatly improved. In 1885 the sisters also opened the Kapiolani girls' home for healthy children of parents suffering from leprosy.

In 1888 Damien's constant prayer that they also come to Molokai was finally answered. Together with two fellow sisters, Mother Marianne arrived in Kalaupapa. They assisted Damien during the last weeks of his life. The assurance that they would also take over Damien's home for boys in Kalawao was a great consolation to him.

In the difficult living conditions of the peninsula of Kalaupapa, Mother Marianne was an example of persistent hopefulness, serenity, and trust in God. Unlike Damien, the sister did not contract leprosy. Although she had initially thought that her assignment in Hawaii would last only a year, she never returned to New York. She died at the age of eighty in Hawaii on August 9, 1918.

On May 15, 2005, she was beatified by Cardinal Jose Saraiva Martins, the first beatification during the pontificate of Pope Benedict XVI and the first since 1971 in which a cardinal, rather than a pope, presided over the beatification rite. On the Hawaiian Islands she is revered and mentioned in the same breath with Father Damien.

6. Stubborn obedience

Bullheaded. That is how Damien is often portrayed. He comes across not only as enterprising, a go-getter, but also as foolishly stubborn. That certainly is how he was when it came to defending the cause of his people, to organizing life in the community entrusted to him, to following his own vocation. Without that character trait, he probably would not have achieved much in the challenging setting of Molokai. Damien's perseverance, however, cannot be disconnected from a profound fidelity to his evangelical vocation: to give himself fully to the least of Jesus' brothers, the diseased outcasts with whom he shared his life and for whom he was prepared to give his life.

That fidelity to his calling did not always make for the smoothest of relationships with his confreres and superiors. These tensions form the thread in recent biographies. They satisfy the journalistic penchant for conflicts, which are more newsworthy than amicable relationships, and the widespread allergy to anything smacking of superiors and hierarchy. Damien can partly thank the rebellious nature attributed to him for his present-day popularity.

While Damien's sometimes-difficult relations with his confreres and superiors have been exaggerated, they were indeed real and explain in part why the beatification and sanctification process took so long. Some negative comments of his superiors sowed doubt: was Damien obstinate to the point of being disobedient? And was he really "holier" than his confreres, or was he merely better at self-publicity? Was he egocentric, as some of his superiors suggested? After the Second Vatican Council, when the notion of holiness and the criteria for canonization were adapted, an additional examination into the figure of Damien was requested. One of the issues examined was precisely Damien's relations with his confreres and superiors.[1]

Top: Apostolic Vicar Hermann Koeckemann (left) and Father Wendelin Moellers.

Bottom: Léonor Fouesnel, by his incomprehension and disrespect, brought on Damien the most difficult trial in his life.

Not all of Damien's relations with his superiors were troubled. Both Modeste Favens, his direct superior and provincial, and Bishop Maigret, the apostolic vicar in Honolulu until 1882, had very positive relations with Damien, despite his strong temperament. They thought that he occasionally moved too fast, but they valued the zeal of the missionary and guided him in his work. Damien realized that he often reacted strongly. "I have such an impetuous character if one pushes too much", he writes in one of his letters.[2] Relations were very different with Favens' and Maigret's successors: Régis Moncany (vice provincial from 1878 until his death in 1883); Léonor Fouesnel (vice provincial from 1883 until 1898); and Hermann Koeckemann (1828–1892), bishop of Olba, who succeeded Maigret in 1882 as apostolic vicar in Honolulu.

What were the tensions about? In the first place, there was Damien's relentless insistence that he be sent a confrere. He especially wanted a confessor, but also someone with whom to share his missionary work. In making that request, Damien in fact did nothing other than follow the constitutions of the Congregation of the Sacred Hearts. Article 420 reads: "The general rule is that no member of the community, whether a priest or a brother, will be sent out or remain on the islands alone."[3] Damien never wanted to be a lonely hero. He wanted a brother by his side. This desire expressed not only fidelity to the rule of the Picpus Fathers, in which he was schooled, but also the Gospel's vision of mission: did Jesus not send his disciples out two by two?

But when a confrere was sent, the relationship with Damien did not always go smoothly. Such was the case with Father André Burgerman, who resided on Molokai from 1874 until 1880, and to a lesser degree with Albert Montiton, who was there from September 1881 until March 1885.

Damien's superiors were sometimes critical of him for taking too much on his plate and then doing it in too much of a hurry. Especially at the beginning of his missionary work, he was quick to baptize, and he blessed marriages without checking whether the would-be spouses fulfilled the Church's conditions. As he grew in experience and wisdom, he became more careful in these matters.

The rule stipulated that Picpus missionaries keep close contact with their provincials and submit to them all questions of a material nature;

for questions of a spiritual or pastoral nature, they direct themselves to their ecclesial superior. It is true that contact and communication were not always easy, which in practice gave the missionaries on the Hawaiian Islands a certain freedom vis-à-vis their superiors. Damien's superiors thought he sometimes wanted too much freedom or presented them with a fait accompli.

Gossip was unavoidable in the microcosm of Hawaii and Molokai. A popular theme in Hawaii was alleged affairs of celibate priests with women, or sometimes children. In a few cases something was going on. Damien too had to defend himself several times against persistent rumors about alleged infidelity to his vow of chastity. It did not help that he was succeeded in his first post in the district of Kohala by a priest who left the congregation in 1880 following an illicit sexual relationship with a woman. Nor did it help that this missionary's name was Fabien (Schauten), which could be confused with Father Damien.[4]

Finally, there was a lot of petty jealousy, since Damien received a great deal of attention, far beyond Hawaii, as well as substantial financial gifts. It is painful to see how many conflicts revolve around money. Unfortunately, in this regard the Church sometimes does not differ much from the world.

Lack of reason and good judgment

Régis Moncany (1827–1883), the French vice provincial, thought that Damien lacked good judgment and *savoir vivre*. In a letter from the end of 1879, Moncany wrote to the superior general in Paris about Damien: "To tell the truth, he is almost *sine concilio et sine iudicio* [without consultation and without judgment]."[5] Half a year later he wrote: "Without questioning his virtue and his zeal, the formation in Louvain once again has delivered a failed priest. On top of it, he has no brains and he lacks *savoir vivre*."[6] That was a harsh judgment from a direct superior. How did Moncany come to this view?

It had everything to do with the disagreements between Damien and Burgerman, his confrere on Molokai from 1874 until 1880. Unfortunately, the six letters that Damien wrote to Moncany were lost. But from the totality of the correspondence, one can deduce that the vice provincial attributed the origin of that conflict at least as much to Damien as to Burgerman. He could have known better, however, because as he himself remarked, "Father Damien was always on terms with the civil authorities of the leprosy settlement", while Burgerman was "almost always at war with them." [7]

Who was Burgerman? The Dutchman from The Hague (1829–1907) was ten years older than Damien. He was not easy to get along with. "I am a proud man, and I'm proud of it", [8] he used to say. He was a restless soul who first worked a couple of years in different Picpus colleges in France and subsequently was sent on mission to Tahiti (1863–1870). After difficulties there and stays in Chile and France, he arrived in 1873 in Hawaii. Maigret sent him to Molokai, where he stayed six and a half years. Father André had a great fancy for medicine. Already in Tahiti he had a reputation as a healer, and also during his mission in Hawaii he cared for the sick and wounded. For the first four years, Burgerman was assigned to topside of Molokai, but his attention naturally turned to the situation in the leprosy colony below. In him the vocation of doctor often was stronger than that of missionary. From the beginning Damien saw a danger in that: for Damien, the primary reason for their presence among the lepers was pastoral and missionary in nature. Of course, the lepers had to be cared for—and he did not spare himself in that regard—but care for the body was a way to practice care for the soul. He noticed that for André the priorities were different.

Already on March 14, 1876, Damien wrote confidentially in his annual letter to the superior general in Paris that Father André was "out of place" on Molokai, and even in Hawaii. "His way of acting and speaking has convinced me that he is not particularly attached to this place, nor to the mission, nor to the congregation." [9] This was, in fact, an astute judgment.

The relationship between the two might have been difficult, but it was not especially bad. Every two months, Burgerman came down the *pali* to hear Damien's confession. All in all, Damien was fond of his only companion and did everything possible to get along with him: "He does not interfere with my work, and out of prudence I do not interfere with his." [10]

Several times Damien and André switched places, so that Damien could build chapels and little churches on topside. For André did not know the first thing about carpentry. And that way he could take Damien's place with the lepers. In 1874, for instance, Damien worked for a few months on the Church of Our Lady of Seven Sorrows, of which a later replica can still be admired on Molokai.

In his good moments Burgerman was rather positive about his confrere. In 1875 he wrote to his provincial: "After two years the mission is well installed on the island of Molokai. The tireless Father Damien has built or is building six chapels on the island. He serves three of them; I serve the other three. Since my arrival I have baptized 140 people. Damien did 300 or 400, so we should not complain." [11]

Yet in the course of the years, it became more and more evident that Burgerman aspired to the position of medical doctor. He showed great interest in succeeding William Ragsdale, who died in 1877, as *luna* or chief supervisor of the leprosy colony, a government-paid position. According to Damien, his confrere was even ready to leave the priesthood for this. Damien was absolutely opposed to Burgerman's getting the appointment. As a consequence he himself was appointed superintendent for a few months. However, he refused any payment for this. "If my mother would hear that [i.e., that he would receive payments], she would not recognize her child any longer." [12] Self-giving, free service, in which the care for the soul was, if possible, more important than that for the body, was evident for the missionary Damien. Not so for Burgerman.

The latter was appointed at a certain moment to Kalaupapa, the landing place on the volcanic tongue of land, while Damien remained active on the other side, on Kalawao. At the end of 1878 Damien wrote to his provincial: "My great concern is that I witness my only companion drift away more and more from the congregation and the mission, from his superiors and companion." [13] Damien was concerned about his confrere, seeing him slowly distance himself from the congregation. When Burgerman as much as admitted that in an angry letter, Damien promptly went to visit him. After an "animated nocturnal conversation", Burgerman decided not to leave the Picpus Fathers after all. It is clear that Damien had the interest of the congregation in mind, as well as that of his confrere. He updated his superior by letter and sought his advice. [14]

"That does not look like the behavior of a man without good judgment"[15] was the conclusion of those who in the 1970s conducted the Vatican's investigation into Damien's relations with his confreres.

Their paths parted ways in 1880, the result of a bizarre incident. It seems that in the summer of that year, Burgerman had threatened to kill Damien. "Je vous brûle la cervelle!" (I'm going to blow your brains out!) he shouted following an argument at his home, after which he went inside to look for his pistol. Whether things actually went that far remains uncertain, but it prompted Damien to write a letter the following day to Doctor Nathaniel B. Emerson, chief supervisor of the leprosy colony at the time, to ask for Burgerman's permanent removal from Kalaupapa.[16] Church authorities had in the meantime already decided to transfer Burgerman. Doctor Emerson, who also came to blows with Burgerman, reported that the priest was together with a woman.[17]

Burgerman was a missionary for nine more years on the island of Maui before going to Honolulu in 1889. He survived Damien by nearly twenty years. That he did not leave the priesthood was probably, to a great extent, due to Damien. He died on September 3, 1907, in Honolulu as a missionary whose piety was no longer called into question—and who himself, after Damien's death in 1889, had probably come to the realization that he had lived in close proximity to, if not a saint, then an exceptional confrere.

No wonder those in Rome who examined Moncany's judgment of Damien ended up doubting the good judgment of the superior himself. Granted, as a Breton and a Frenchman, he seemed to prefer the formation in Paris above that in Louvain ("encore un prêtre manqué dans le moule de Louvain" [yet another failed priest in the mold of Louvain]). Nevertheless, Louvain in those years brought forth a number of solid missionaries. Likewise, many superiors, including Koeckemann himself, were formed in Louvain. Worse was Moncany's inability to judge the exceptional character of Damien's life among the lepers, seeing only a lack of insight and *savoir vivre*. Still, in a moment of rare introspection, the superior wrote of himself: "I do nothing of value, mess up the work of others. . . . I don't have a head for leadership."[18] That was probably the most lucid judgment he made about himself.

Yet another difficult confrere

After Burgerman's departure in the summer of 1880, Damien was once again alone. He was the only priest on Molokai, and he suffered from his isolation. Owing to an epidemic of chicken pox on the Hawaiian Islands at that time, it was forbidden for months to travel between the islands. It weighed heavily on Damien not to have a confrere and be able to make his confession. He sought and found consolation near the altar and the Blessed Sacrament. In a letter to Pamphile, he wrote: "As I was temporarily the only priest on the island of Molokai, I had to take as a confessor our Lord, who remains in the tabernacle. Alas, my dear brother, it is at the foot of the altar that we find the necessary strength in our isolation. There I meet you every day and all the dear fathers of our beloved congregation. Without the Blessed Sacrament, a situation like mine would be untenable. But with our Lord at my side, I'm always joyful and content." [19]

After a year without a brother and companion, a new confrere, Father Albert Montiton, arrived in the summer of 1881. That was a great joy for Damien, but it also meant new heartache. Montiton had heard rumors in Honolulu about Damien's alleged relations with women in his previous mission on the island of Kohala. Apparently Montiton attached credence to the rumors, because immediately after his arrival on Kalaupapa he spoke about this for three consecutive days, which caused Damien a great deal of pain. [20]

Montiton was fifteen years older than Damien, had studied more, and had considerable experience with missionary work, including in French Polynesia. But he had contracted a persistent skin disease—which for a long time was thought to be leprosy—and had anything but an affable character. His superiors were aware of this, describing him alternately as "a man who always boils over", "a madman", "a confused spirit", and "someone who was never satisfied" and "with whom it was difficult to live in peace". "In five years he returns to Chile. *Optime* [Good!]" Father Régis Moncany wrote. [21]

Missionaries were often hardened men, individualists who lived their calling in the most difficult circumstances. To get them to cooperate was not easy. But in the case of Damien, as Steven Debroey remarked in his biography of him, it certainly looked "as if he got only helpers who were not desired anywhere else".[22]

Hermann Koeckemann, as apostolic vicar the highest-ranking churchman on the Hawaiian Islands, foresaw difficult relations between the two. So he suggested that Damien minister in Kalawao while Father Albert serve in Kalaupapa. Damien disagreed with this, complaining in a long postscript in a letter to Koeckemann:

> As to the impossibility of a cordial agreement, that will not be my fault, because I do not insist on anything and I am willing to give in on everything. That's why I'm only half behind the proposal to form two separate parishes. That was already a plan of Father André that has caused many difficulties, criticisms, jealousies, and ultimately the catastrophe [André's affair that led to his departure]. That would not have happened if we had stayed together. Besides, for my honor and my reputation, which are now being called into question by Father Régis and Father Albert, I would prefer that the good Father Albert see me busy every day and not remain a witness at a distance.[23]

Damien, who himself remained firmly faithful to his priestly vow of chastity but did not shy away from interaction with women, would rather have his confrere close by than far away. The company of a confrere, as prescribed in the rule, was not only a remedy against the acute loneliness that pushed a number of religious into the arms of a woman but also, Damien thought, a sound means of defense against the false accusations leveled against him. It is notable that Damien, in his continual plea for a confrere, followed more closely than his superiors the spirituality of the founders and the rule of the congregation.

Relations between Damien and his French confrere gradually improved. But they were two strong characters, which unavoidably led to friction. For instance, Damien reacted forcefully against nonmarital cohabitation, which was rapidly increasing in the leprosy settlement under the influence of Mormonism. Albert thought Damien exaggerated. Further, Damien had taken a number of orphans under his care. With great persuasiveness he had obtained permission from the Board of Health. Albert did not regard this as a task for a missionary. Sometimes the friction became too much for Damien, who had been slaving away for nine years to improve the situation in the settlement. "If my attitude, which is not shared by Father Albert, does not please you either," he wrote to Koeckemann, "then I will gladly leave the island of Molokai."[24] It is the only time that Damien made such a threat. He was tired of being continuously opposed by confreres of his own congregation. He had more pleasant and cooperative relations with people from the outside, such as the Protestant Doctor Fitch, who visited the settlement once a month. Damien considered him a friend, and together they often made plans to invite hospital sisters to Kalawao.[25] At the bottom of the letter, he added: "If you do not try to temper the intolerance of Father Albert, you will soon see me appear before you without an assignment. I do not wish to live any longer at war with confreres being sent by my congregation to Molokai."[26]

Koeckemann tried to appease Damien. He did not want to question his goodwill, nor that of his confrere. Still, he knew Montiton's difficult character enough to say that "you need a good dose of patience to live near him."[27] He told Damien to be careful and if necessary forsake good deeds if those give rise to jealousy or other problems. Yet Koeckemann was not displeased with the general course of affairs. At the end of the year, he wrote to Superior General Bousquet: "You will be pleased to learn that a good spirit is reigning among our fathers. With the exception of some small clouds between Father Albert and Damien, which dissipate rather quickly, the unity and charity are perfect."[28]

The Christmas celebration of 1882, of which Damien left behind an extensive description,[29] shows how, despite everything, the missionaries kept doing beautiful work in the leprosy colony.

Koeckemann had invited Damien to Honolulu for Christmas, but Damien chose to go only after the holiday. He had several catechumens who were to be baptized, including three Kanaks and four Chinese. It had not been easy for the latter, but thanks to the help of two older Chinese Christians, Damien had been able to teach them the most important doctrines of the Catholic faith—enough, in any case, for him to be able to baptize them. Damien was extremely pleased with the way the midnight Mass went. Albert delivered a beautiful homily, which impressed its listeners, and Damien was pleased to note that, despite his age, Albert had managed to master the local language.

Having celebrated Christmas and having heard confessions in his parishes on topside, Damien set sail for Honolulu. The visit was good for him. "Our house in Honolulu is for the missionaries like the motherhouse",[30] he wrote with gratitude. Damien also praised the apostolic vicar, Bishop Koeckemann, a good administrator who was also appreciated by non-Catholics. The bishop took Damien along on New Year's Day for a visit to Prime Minister Gibson in the royal palace. There followed a pleasant meeting with Queen Kapiolani. She was happy to learn that the sisters would soon come to take care of the sick. Damien kept hoping that some would come to the leprosarium of Molokai.

On January 6, the Feast of the Epiphany, Damien took part in the Solemn High Mass in Honolulu's cathedral. Bishop Koeckemann presided; Father Clément was the assisting priest. Damien was given the role of deacon, which was no longer so familiar to him. "Kamiano is more used to being among lepers than at the side of a bishop",[31] he reported about himself. But with the assistance of Father Sylvester, who as subdeacon gave occasional directions to Damien, it went reasonably well. Damien was asked to deliver the homily. He developed the themes of the vocation of the three wise men and the glorification of the Child, and he gave a moral explanation of the gifts of the wise men. He did not manage to keep to his half-hour limit, for which he was teased afterward. Damien knew that he often preached too long, and so he often asked for forgiveness for this at confession. In Honolulu he received a letter from Father Albert in Kalaupapa: that writing showed his character. Even his New Year's wishes for Damien contained a certain criticism of him. The rest concerned mostly practical matters, demonstrating that the two confreres had built a normal work relationship. Albert reproached Damien for not finding the time during the past half year to come and repair the lock on his tabernacle. During Mass in Kalaupapa the previous Sunday, Albert had not been able to open the tabernacle, which caused confusion.[32]

Damien was impressed by the many people at Mass in Honolulu on Sunday, January 7. It reminded him of parish Masses in Belgium. The singers and the sister at the organ would not have been out of place in the Church of Saint Peter in Louvain, he thought to himself. Damien also paid a visit to a new Catholic school and paid several visits to the leprosy hospital in Kakaako. On January 8 he returned to Molokai. The inhabitants of Kalawao gave him a heartwarming welcome. Ordinary life and the daily bickering with Albert could start anew.

With time it became clear that the recurrent troubles between Damien and Albert were due to the latter, who was not an easy man to live with. When in 1884 Albert received treatment for his skin disease while in Honolulu, everyone was happier to see him going than coming. "In spite of his talent, his zeal, and quite some virtues, he never was at peace with his superiors, his confreres, the faithful, and outsiders. He sticks to his own point of view, and if he wants something, he cannot be stopped", Koeckemann remarked.[33]

In the spring of 1885 Montiton left Hawaii and returned to Tahiti. "I am going, with or without your permission",[34] he let Koeckemann know.

Fouesnel becomes vice provincial

In August 1883 vice provincial Régis Moncany died of consumption. The French father Léonor Fouesnel was appointed his successor. The appointment had enormous consequences for Damien during the final years of his life. If his relations with Moncany were difficult, those with Fouesnel were absolutely awful. With him Damien experienced the most painful ordeals of his life, as he himself later wrote. It turned out to be a great exercise in patience and obedience.

The Breton missionary with the impressive beard was a logical choice. He was without doubt a man with many positive qualities. He and Apostolic Vicar Koeckemann had arrived together in Hawaii in 1854, and they complemented each other well. Whereas Koeckemann had been a pastor only in Honolulu, Fouesnel had experience of life on various isolated mission posts. In addition, he was skilled and artistically gifted. As pastor in Wailuku, he had overseen the building of a beautiful church. Fouesnel was active, handy, and good at managing material matters.

But as a religious, and certainly as a superior, he failed in his duties. This we know from a highly critical report on him that was dealt with at the congregation's general chapter of 1893, ten years after his appointment.[35] Superior General Bousquet had the report drafted after he had received complaints from different corners about the provincial. This report shows that Fouesnel could be as hard on his subordinates as he could be soft on himself. He enjoyed eating and drinking, which he forbade to others. He was known as "a tyrant, harsh and without compassion, everything but an exemplary person". In another document, Father Corneille Limburg, a valued missionary, asked the superior general of the congregation to "send a father, but then a father who was ready to sacrifice himself in the interest of his children and not one who is seeking only his own comfort." [36]

Fouesnel and Damien knew one another, though not very well. They first met on May 4, 1873, at the consecration of Fouesnel's church in Wailuku, the occasion when Damien offered to go to Molokai. When Fouesnel was not yet a provincial, he visited Molokai on August 15, 1874, to consecrate the Church of Our Lady of Seven Sorrows, which Damien had built in Kaluaaha. On that occasion he paid a brief visit to the leprosarium of Kalaupapa, leaving that same day. The sight of the leprosy victims was too much for him. He had a strong physical aversion to the disease and was deadly afraid of contagion. In the first seven years as vice provincial, which corresponded to the last seven years of Damien's life, he did not visit Damien once, not even when he already was gravely ill. That is an especially remarkable fact. Nonetheless, he was convinced that pastoral visits were necessary, reproaching Koeckemann that he had only life in Honolulu in mind. "Some of our fathers need to be encouraged, others need direction, some need to be admonished softly. That's not possible by letter. It is by going to the place itself that you can bring forth some solid fruit", he once wrote to the superior general.[37] Only once did Koeckemann set sail for Molokai, the island closest to Honolulu, but owing to bad weather he could not go ashore. He left it at that one attempt. During the same period, he traveled at least seventeen times to the island of Maui, eight times to the big island of Hawaii, and at least five times to Kauai.[38]

When he took over as vice provincial in 1883, Fouesnel described Damien as "a good religious, a good priest, a very industrious missionary, exaggerated in his devotion to the lepers".[39] Fouesnel indeed thought Damien exaggerated. According to Fousnel, Damien did not understand the art of *sapere ad sobrietatem* (sober self-judgment),[40] and he was blinded in his zeal. Not once did Fouesnel give the impression that he understood that the exceptional situation of the place of banishment for the victims of leprosy demanded an exceptional love and "exaggerated" zeal. On the contrary, he regularly indicated to Damien that he had to know his place, that he should not be different from the others. In his letters, Fouesnel often used a rude style, for which he excused himself in subsequent letters. This reinforces the impression of an unbalanced man with limited self-control.

Damien knew from the beginning that Fouesnel did not have a high opinion of him. "Again I read in your letter how little you trust me.... Really, I did not know that my superiors had such a low opinion of me", Damien wrote in November 1883.[41] What was that first argument about? Damien had long hoped that the sisters who had answered the call to care for the leprosy sufferers of Hawaii would also soon come to the leprosarium of Molokai. That seemed self-evident to him, for there the need was surely greatest. His superiors and the politicians saw it differently: their attention was given in the first place to Honolulu. Molokai could wait. Besides, they had many worries about how the sisters would be able to live in such an unwholesome place. Fouesnel pressed Damien several times not to talk about this matter in public. Damien replied that he had never done so but that he could not refrain from insisting in private on an exploratory visit by the sisters. "In case of a visit of the superior and another sister, even in your company, I would only have to sweep my house a bit, and all three of you would be housed well, amid an entirely Catholic village." [42] Damien was not insisting for himself: so great was his desire that the sisters come to Kalawao that he was willing completely to efface himself, to the point of humiliation: if his presence was not desired, he would go away for a while.

If Fouesnel was at all impressed by the letter, one would not know from the tone of his reply. "If I have offended you, then I ask your forgiveness. By God's grace I well hope that I never hesitate to humiliate myself before a subordinate whom I might have insulted or hurt by words that were not measured enough." [43] At the end of the letter, Fouesnel was even more personal, remarking on his own unsuitability for his function: "Because I have given you a proof that I am not the man who is needed on the spot where our superiors have placed me (against my wishes), I would be grateful if you could obtain my removal from those same superiors." He suggested that Damien cooperate to this end with others who were not pleased about his appointment. "More and more I see that the task surpasses my powers. And that I am not at all capable of giving good direction."

Fouesnel would swing from one extreme to the other. Often he complained in his letters about his unworthiness and ineptness as a superior; however, this did not prevent him from writing harsh words again the next day. What stands out is the fact that it is always about Fouesnel himself. In his letters, one rarely, if ever, reads genuine concern for Damien and his spiritual or physical well-being.

Did Fouesnel really regard himself as unsuitable? Koeckemann did not seem certain about this when the generalate asked him whether it would not be better to replace Fouesnel with another. "Father Léonor certainly suffers from the burdens of his task; he sincerely asked to be discharged from it; still, without realizing it himself, he likes to exercise authority." [44]

Damien, in any case, did not consider pursuing the removal of his superior. He had promised obedience to his superiors, whoever they were, and was ready to go to great lengths in this. His priorities lay elsewhere. In obedience too he could be stubborn, more than Fouesnel ever realized.

A leper among the lepers

Several times prior to contracting leprosy, Damien thought he had detected the signs of the disease, but it always turned out to be a false alarm. In the course of 1884, however, the signs became undeniable. Yellow spots appeared on his back and arms, while his left foot became increasingly numb. He was expert enough to recognize the symptoms: he tried to keep track of whether the numbness in his left foot, which was evident for a long time, was spreading.

"Father Damien has leprosy", Fouesnel reported to the superior general in Paris on September 23, 1884.[45] Damien himself was still hesitant about the diagnosis. In a letter to the German physician Arning, he apologized for not having kept him informed of his condition. "I thought it is better to wait a little and see the progress of the disease, and if new indices appear to corroborate the verdict of true genuine leprosy."[46] He expressed confidence that medicine would slow the progress of the incurable disease and that he would be able to devote himself to many more years of service: for a while he took arsenic pills and underwent a treatment involving electric shock.

At the beginning of 1885, however, doubt was no longer possible. He decided to inform his brother. In a reply to Pamphile, who had complained about his own physical ailments, Damien wrote:

> I can no longer conceal from you that I too am being threatened by a disease that is worse yet than consumption. I have lived almost twelve years among the lepers. Leprosy is a contagious disease. I think I cannot complain about the visible protection that God has given me. The Holy Virgin and Saint Joseph also have something to do with it, because I am really still as strong and robust as when you saw me depart in 1863, with the exception of my left foot, which has lost all feeling for the past three years. It is deceptive venom that threatens to poison my entire body.[47]

In a letter written that same day to his mother and other brothers and sisters, he did not mention the news. He wanted to spare them that grief. But between the lines you could read the verdict: he mentioned the burning of his foot in boiling water and also that some doctors had proposed that he go home for some rest. He wondered whether there would still be a room for him at home in Ninde. But returning was not at all Damien's intention. "I am happy here and content and still capable of doing some good. But don't hope to see me again in this world."[48]

The rumor went around that Damien's infection was the consequence of venereal disease. The theory that syphilis and leprosy were linked was widespread at that time. Damien too subscribed to the hypothesis, but he was at peace about his own behavior, having always kept his vow of chastity. He had to undergo a humiliating examination by Doctor Arning. Doctor Mouritz, who was present, felt embarrassed for the ill missionary and was amazed that he did not display the least resentment.

Damien accepted his disease and invested it with a religious meaning. It helped him to die to self. To Bishop Koeckemann he wrote: "The memory of the fact that twenty-five years ago I lay under a funeral pall on the day of my ordination has allowed me to run the risk, in fulfilling my duty, of being infected with that horrible disease and to die to self more and more. As my disease develops, I feel content and happy in Kalawao." [49]

He saw leprosy as a sign and pondered its meaning. He waited a long time before informing his superior general about his condition, but eventually wrote: "So don't be too surprised or distressed to learn that one of your spiritual children has been decorated not only with the cross of the Order of Kalakaua but also with the heavier and less honorable cross of leprosy, with which I, with the approval of our Divine Savior, was marked." [50]

Although Damien never stopped hoping for a cure or treatment, he gradually accepted the disease as a "providential agent" to help him detach his heart from all earthly affection and prompt the desire of his soul "to be united—the sooner the better—with Him Who is her only life". [51]

The hardest ordeal

Becoming sick and being less and less able to get around was a terrible test for the energetic Damien. But the loneliness was even harder on him. He had lived the greatest part of his missionary life alone, but now he felt even more the need of a confrere's company. From 1885 on, Damien was alone on his peninsula. For a brief time the leper priest Father Grégoire Archambaux had joined him, but he was ill at ease at the colony and had one asthma attack after another. [52] After a few months he obtained exceptional permission to leave the place of quarantine. The obstinate Montiton left too, despite Damien's insistence that he stay. Over the years, Damien had come to appreciate the company of Montiton, who had been a good confessor. Damien would have liked to keep him with him until his death.

For a while it appeared that his former companion André Burg-erman would be banished to the colony because he too might have contracted leprosy. But the superiors realized that such a transfer would not be a good idea. Damien informed them that under no circumstance did he want to live with the priest again.

Damien lodged his complaint with Koeckemann. He dragged his leg and would be lame the rest of his life. Never again would he be able to climb the *pali*. Even going to the hospital, five min-utes away, required great effort. "If I'm really attacked by this hor-rible disease, then one has to recognize that death is approaching with little steps. Without being too preoccupied with my body, I mostly have to be concerned about my soul. And that requires a good confessor." [53]

Koeckemann and Fouesnel acknowledged the problem but had no solution. The mission suffered from a chronic shortage of priests, and there was more than enough work everywhere. Father Colomban Beis-sel was asked to go regularly to Molokai to hear Damien's confes-sion. Because he had to come from the island of Maui, that happened only every two to three months. Besides, Colomban got seasick eas-ily. To Damien's repeated pleas Fouesnel replied curtly that he deplored not being able to send a permanent confessor. "Your position is excep-tional. Let us pray that the difficulties are solved." [54]

Damien then adopted the plan to go to Honolulu. He could get some medical care there and make his confession. But his superior flatly forbade it. Damien was a leper, and Prime Minister Gibson was already under fire for his lax segregation policies. An excep-tion had been made for the sick Father Grégoire; Damien had bet-ter stay where he was.

Damien screamed out his need to Pamphile. He had not felt so lonely since the departure of Albert. "Since that time I am, con-trary to an article of our holy rule, always alone." He tried, despite all, to be resigned in his suffering. "I surrender to Divine Provi-dence and find my consolation in my only companion who does not leave me, i.e., our Divine Savior in the Holy Eucharist. I often confess at the foot of the altar, and there I seek alleviation of inte-rior pains", he wrote.[55]

For the rest it was not a sad letter. Damien was still active and had his hands full with his two parishes. It was a pleasure to care for his orphans. Pamphile should hear them sing at High Mass once. Or hear them play the organ with their leprous hands.

There was no end in sight to Damien's isolation. He almost never saw a confrere anymore, and he himself was no longer allowed to leave the settlement. He felt locked up and let Bishop Koecke-mann know it at the end of the year. "I murmur a little against the somewhat tyrannical manner in which this good father [Fouesnel] thinks to be able to incarcerate me here", he wrote, tempering his own feelings. "As long as my health allows it and the government does not oppose it, why then should my superiors not grant me freedom of movement if there would be need for it?" Koeckemann could have detected that Damien's complaint was also directed against him. Damien knew they would regard his repeated request as a sign of his bad character and stubbornness. "*Poo paakiki no o Kamiano*", he added playfully. "A bullhead, that Damien." [56]

And indeed Fouesnal did not show the slightest concern for the leper Damien. He could have visited Damien, as his predecessor, Modeste Favens, had done in 1873. But Fouesnel was occupied by life in the capital, Honolulu, and the idea of a visit never seemed to enter his mind. Fatherly and pastoral sensitivity were lost on him.

When Fouesnel heard that Damien kept insisting that he be allowed to come to Honolulu, he dipped his pen once more in vinegar. "There is again a rumor that you want to come here. It is *my duty*, my very dear Father, to remind you again of the decision taken *by the provincial council*, and not by me." But that was not true: there is no evidence of the provincial council prohibiting infected religious from leaving the place of exile. Further, there was never a question of such a prohibition in the case of Father Grégoire Archambaux, who had been allowed to leave the leprosy settlement. But if Damien dared to show up in the mission, Fouesnal warned, he would be confined to the leper quarters. Nor was he welcome in the hospital of Kakaako. He would not be allowed to say Mass, because no priest would dare to use the chalice and vestments that a leper priest had used. And he concluded: "Your pretensions, my dear Father, prove to us that you have neither tact nor charity toward your neighbor and that you think only of yourself. That is too much selfishness." [57]

For those[58] who later conducted the investigation into Damien's alleged disobedience, Fouesnal's remarks went way too far. "Rarely will a subordinate have heard such harsh words", they concluded.[59] It was hard for Damien to bear the attitude of his vice provincial and direct superior. To Koeckemann, the apostolic vicar, he lodged his complaint: "The absolute refusal, expressed more in the tone of a gendarme than of a religious superior, and that in the name of the bishop and the minister, as if the mission was placed under quarantine, gave me, I frankly confess, more pain than I have ever suffered since my childhood." But Damien would not have been Damien had he not resigned himself to that fate. "I responded with an act of absolute submission because of my vow of obedience. We continue to love one another."[60] Also in his obedience Damien was stubborn and persistent.

Finally, after insisting for almost a year, Damien was allowed to make the trip to Honolulu. That occurred in July 1886. Doctor Mouritz, the physician at Molokai, and Chief Superintendent Meyer had insisted on this with the civil and religious authorities. They understood that even a brief treatment with the sisters in Kakaako would have a positive effect. Damien nevertheless had the feeling that he was escaping to Honolulu "almost against the obedience that I owed my superior". Still, he was very relieved to be able to make his confession to Bishop Koeckemann, not having seen a confessor for three months.[61] In the end, he stayed only six days in Honolulu, from July 10 to July 16. It was the last time he left the leprosy settlement and the last time he saw his superiors.

Those few days in Honolulu were indeed good for Damien. The strict quarantine rules were not enforced. His stay was also inspiring for the Franciscan sisters who took care of the leprosy patients in the hospital and whom he would have liked so much to come to Molokai. "His presence fanned our zeal, because we knew how much he had done. All those days he talked about his lepers, never about himself",[62] they later testified. Only Gibson was not pleased with the visit: he feared that Damien might sway Mother Marianne and take her away from him.

The day before Damien's departure, the king, the prime minister, and the bishop visited him. Probably they all realized that his end was near. It was no different for Damien. "I don't ask anything more than to stay and die in Kalawao. Whether a leper or not, let me *perficere cursum meum usque in finem* [finish the path of my life until the end]. I am content and happy for the rest—and don't complain about anyone." [63]

Ultimate fidelity

On reflection it appears that what his direct superiors took for stubbornness and unreasonableness was in reality a form of ultimate fidelity: to the rule of the congregation, but equally to the vocation he knew to be his. Damien undoubtedly felt that not all of his superiors and confreres shared his enthusiasm. His zeal did not diminish because of this; nor did he rebel against his superiors, though some of them took an outright hostile attitude toward him during painful moments. When he felt that insisting did more harm than good, he preferred to remain silent.

With time, Damien learned not to be dominated by his character. He tried to control impulsive reactions and to act as a priest should in those circumstances. If he was stubborn in anything, it was in his obedience to his vocation, to his order, and to his superiors, even if they took an unreasonable and unsympathetic attitude toward him. In this his exceptional humility manifested itself: he never placed himself on center stage, not even if he had good reasons for feeling unfairly treated.

Damien kept living a "great" life, also in the bitterest difficulties. He did not fall into the self-pity to which he was fully entitled, nor did he let himself be paralyzed by the difficult relation with his superiors. Rather, during moments of anguish, he feared that he himself was unworthy of heaven. He reflected a lot about honor and shame, about pride and the true imitation of Christ. "Pray to achieve the spirit of humility, so as to desire scorn", he wrote in his little notebook with personal comments. The crown of thorns and the scorn that Christ suffered before Pilate were kept concretely before his eyes. "If one is scorned, may one rejoice in it. Let us not be touched by the praises of men; let us not be self-satisfied; let us be grateful to those who cause us pain or treat us with scorn, and pray to God for them." [64]

A beautiful day in Kalawao

Along with the trials and the sickness, Damien knew many happy moments. This comes out in a letter he sent to his superior general describing the Feast of Corpus Christi on June 27, 1886.[65]

Last Easter Sunday it was determined that on Corpus Christi Day we would celebrate at Kalawao with a procession. My two choirs of singers, at a meeting held at Kalaupapa, decided that they would prepare themselves by learning appropriate music for the High Mass and benediction. With a surprising perseverence for natives—and sick natives—they practiced each intervening day in their respective school houses, meeting together on certain of these days at either Kalawao or Kalaupapa.

The celebration was fixed for the Sunday in the Octave. On this beautiful day, the majority of my people of both parishes assisted at the first Mass, having prepared themselves by a good confession. (From Wednesday until Saturday the curé had been occupied to the limit of his strength in the confessional.) At ten o'clock we had the High Mass.

The church being too small to accommodate all the faithful, the seats were given up to those who came from the other portions of the settlement and the residents of the immediate vicinity of the church remained outside, about the door and windows. The singers, not wishing to use the harmonium [reed organ], placed it outside to make room for the whole choir. In all, they numbered about forty—all but three or four being lepers—well exercised under the direction of a blind leper having considerable musical talent, who struck the measure. Their singing would compare favorably with that heard in many cathedrals.

It was my sermon only that fell short of the general standard. Was too fatigued to enter fully into the deep subject of the feast, and, besides, I wished to avoid my habitual fault of preaching too long sermons. Immediately after Mass, without leaving the curé time for breakfast, the procession was formed, the cross and the great banner being in advance, then came the drum and the musical instruments of tin. (May some charitable soul supply us with some brass instruments.) Then two associations bearing their Hawaiian flag, followed by two lines of Christian women. Then came the men, and after them the singers, always directed by my good blind

Petro under a parasol and guided by another native. Then came the incense bearers before the canopy. At each corner of the canopy walked a lantern bearer. Each lantern being carried upon a staff and beautifully ornamented with flowers. The portable repository, well decorated, augmented this display.

Arriving at the residence of the superintendent, the repository was placed under the veranda. And then I exposed the Blessed Sacrament. Favored by the prolongation of the chant, we had the opportunity to rest ourselves upon the grass after our march. The benediction given, the procession returned to the church by the route it came.

After the religious exercises, the Christians were all refreshed by the agape [meal of fellowship], consisting of *poi* (the native dish) and a pig weighing 300 pounds. By this, you will see that our Blessed Lord granted us at times consolation with our afflictions.

7. We lepers

After it was determined with certainty that Damien had contracted leprosy, he lived nearly five years with what he called the "terrible disease".[1] The malady was worst during the first year and a half, from 1885 to mid-1886. Not only did he suffer great physical pain, but, even more trying, his spiritual distress was enormous: it was the period when he went without a fellow priest on Molokai and could only rarely make his confession. For him the prospect of dying without receiving spiritual consolation was much worse than death itself. His loneliness was compounded by his superiors' lack of sympathy for his situation: not only did they not visit him or consider it a priority to send a fellow priest, but they prevented him for many months from coming to Honolulu even once for bodily and spiritual care.

Following his brief visit to Honolulu in the summer of 1886, things improved significantly. His last years were actually the most beautiful of his life. Although the disease disfigured his face and limbs more and more, physically he remained remarkably strong and active. He served two parishes on his own, built new orphanages, and enlarged the church. At the same time, he broke out of his sense of desolation. The news that he had become a leper among lepers traveled around the world and multiplied support and expressions of sympathy. Above all, he was graced with new companions and co-workers: Joseph Dutton, Lambert Louis Conrardy, James Sinnett, and, eventually, Mother Marianne and her fellow sisters, as well as Father Wendelin Moellers. Under Damien's cross, a new family gradually formed. In his last years, a great tranquillity and gentleness came over him, which nothing could disrupt. His letters increasingly exhibited an unprecedented spiritual depth. Identification with the suffering servant became complete. The full meaning of his prophetic phrase, "We lepers", became palpable. The school of suffering wrought a divine grace from the human drama of the "terrible disease".

A companion at his side

The visit to Honolulu in the summer of 1886 had been good for Damien. The hot baths and the therapy of Doctor Masaano Goto helped him physically. The prospect of continuing the therapy back on Molokai filled him with new hope and strength. He had been able to step out of his isolation, talk with the sisters—again encouraging them to come to Molokai—and make his confession to apostolic vicar Hermann Koeckemann. And as an unexpected bonus, on the last day of his stay, he received the honor of a visit from King David Kalakaua and Prime Minister Gibson.

On his return, even better news was awaiting him. Unexpectedly he received a companion who would prove invaluable. On July 29, 1886, Joseph Dutton set foot in Kalaupapa. Dutton was a colorful figure, whom Doctor Arthur Mouritz described as follows: "He wore a blue denim suit, which fitted his tall, well-knit, slim, muscular figure. He stood about five feet seven inches tall; had dark brown hair and grayish blue eyes; a low voice, placid features, and a pleasant smile. He was reserved and thoughtful, had nothing to say about his past life or the reason for his seeking seclusion and work at Molokai, and turning his back forever on the world."[2] Dutton was forty-three, three years younger than Damien. The former Civil War soldier and alcoholic had converted to Catholicism following an adventurous and agonizing past and was searching for a different life. After reading about Damien's life and meeting with the writer Stoddard, his decision was made. On July 20, 1886, he showed up unannounced at the Board of Health in Honolulu and offered to volunteer at the leprosy colony. Gibson described him as "a religious enthusiast".[3] When it became clear that he was not after any salary, he received permission to go to Molokai. For Koeckemann too, this was not a bad solution to the problem of finding a companion for Damien.[4]

The Liege missionary Lambert Louis Conrardy followed in Damien's footsteps.

Bottom left: The American penitent "Brother" Joseph Dutton remained on Molokai serving the leprosy patients until his death in 1931. Bottom right: Mother Marianne Cope, American Sister of Saint Francis, arrived on Molokai several months before Damien's death and remained for thirty years until her own death in 1918.

Brother Joseph Dutton (1843–1931)

Ira Barnes Dutton was born in Stowe, Vermont, on April 27, 1843; in 1847 his family moved to Janesville, Wisconsin, where he grew up. During the Civil War (1861–1865), he fought on the side of the northern states. Afterward he worked for the army, locating the hastily buried dead scattered on the battle-fields and reburying them with a solemn funeral. According to Dutton, he and his men collected more than six thousand corpses. His disastrous marriage failed within a year, leading him to become addicted to alcohol. He estimated that he drank about 32 gallons of whisky per year over ten years. "Conditions that were repugnant I submitted to without resistance. Even going of my own will into them", he later wrote in his memoirs of that decadent decade.[5] One day he was shocked into the real-ization that he was wasting his life and underwent a radical con-version. On his fortieth birthday he became a Catholic, taking the baptismal name Joseph, and resolved to spend the rest of his life atoning for his transgressions. Initially, the strict life of a Trappist monastery seemed the best place for this, but after two years in a Kentucky abbey he decided it was not his vocation. By chance he read in a Catholic publication a brief account of Father Damien on Molokai. The seeker in Dutton was imme-diately sold. "There is the work that I have been looking for!"[6]

In his search to learn how to get to Molokai, he went to see Charles Warren Stoddard, who had visited Damien in 1884 and was then teaching the history of literature at the University of Notre Dame in Indiana. When Stoddard confirmed to Dutton that he definitely could be of service to the leper priest, he went with some letters of introduction in his pocket to San Francisco and from there on to Hawaii. On July 29, 1886, less than two months after he had first heard of the place, he landed at Kalaupapa. There he would spend the second half of his long life. Even though they had an occasional conflict, Dutton was a real companion and friend of Damien, and a humble disciple too. After Damien's death, Dutton carried forward his work in the leprosy settlement. His thousands of letters provide a good portrait of the man. In the United States this fascinating native penitent was almost as renowned as Damien himself. In 1907 President Theodore Roosevelt ordered the U.S. Pacific Fleet to pass by Molokai and dip its colors in honorary salute to Dutton.

"Brother" Joseph Dutton never contracted leprosy and lived to be nearly eighty-eight years old. He died on March 26, 1931. Shortly before his death, he wrote: "I guess that I have come to the end of the trail; that my work is finished. I hope that God approves." And he expressed his last wish: "Though unworthy, I wish to be buried at the feet of Damien." [7] There his body still rests, near the Church of Saint Philomena and Damien's grave, where now only Damien's hand is buried. President Herbert Hoover wrote on the occasion of Dutton's death: "I am deeply interested in the romantic story of Brother Joseph Dutton, whose life as a pioneer, soldier, and great humanitarian is so characteristic of our people in its variety, picturesqueness and idealism. His service to the lepers of Molokai crowned his life with saintly glory." [8] Plans exist to ask for Dutton's beatification. Along with Saint Damien and Blessed Mother Marianne, he would be the third blessed springing from the leprosy colony. The holiness of one person undeniably inspires and attracts the greatness of others.

At that time, Damien had been pinning his hopes on the arrival of his brother Pamphile. In several letters, he had urged him to come to Molokai to help him. Finally Pamphile agreed and requested that the congregation permit him to go to his sick younger brother and assist him at the end of his life. But the congregation was not as convinced. Was Pamphile not needed in highbrow Louvain? Did Superior General Bousquet suspect that the priest-professor, who had spent his life mostly among books, was not suited to a hard life among the lepers? In retrospect he was right: Pamphile's stay on Molokai, a few years after Damien's death, was not a success. Besides, Pamphile should not think that Damien was so unhappy or lonely, Bishop Koeckemann wrote soothingly from Honolulu: "Father Colomban went to visit him every two months. And every week he could communicate with Honolulu and the other islands." [9] Thus the bishop painted a misleadingly rosy picture. With characteristic

obedience Damien entrusted himself to the judgment of his superiors. To Pamphile he wrote: "The best for you, as for me, is to let
the ecclesiastic and religious authorities decide whether I will have
that consolation, to see and to work with a brother, to whom I am
indebted, after the good God, for having been chosen for the
missions." [10]

Dutton's arrival was for Damien a true gift from God. Damien
called him "Brother Joseph". The man turned out to be industrious, dedicated, and exceptionally calm in all circumstances. Damien
built a house for Dutton, close to his own house, the Church of
Saint Philomena, and the cemetery. That spot, with its unique view
of the blue ocean, pleased the American very much. "The prin-
cipal graveyard back of my cabin", he wrote in 1887, "has about
two thousand graves and nearly one thousand are buried elsewhere.... Take it all in all, this is a fine locality for meditation,
surrounded by the best symbol of eternity, the boundless ocean." [11]
Dutton, who obediently placed himself at Damien's service, was
immediately put to work. Dutton served at Mass, took the orphan
boys under his care, and did not mind finishing the many building
projects that Damien had begun, whenever Damien felt called to
do another work before the previous one was finished. And there
was an immense amount of work. As the only priest on the peninsula, the missionary had to serve both the parish of Kalawao and
that of Kalaupapa. "Instead of serving one village of lepers and one
church, I now have two. That means double service every morning and evening, and all Sundays and holy days", he informed the
superior general.[12] In addition, he wanted to use his temporarily
regained strength to complete a number of building projects. Most
of all, he wanted to build the warm-water baths required for the Goto
method. While waiting for the necessary deliveries, he started to build
a bathroom for himself and a number of orphan boys. Damien was
convinced that the Goto method was beneficial: he himself felt better during that period, and he attributed it to the therapy. But the
Board of Health began to have its doubts. In the end, the promised
therapy was never introduced on a large scale on Molokai.

Damien was pleased with Dutton, "a middle-aged, well-
educated man". The convert, who had decided to devote himself to a penitential life, wanted to sacrifice himself completely.

"He resides here with me and as a true brother helps me, caring for the sick. He too, though not a priest, finds his comfort in the Blessed Sacrament. You will admire, with me, the almighty power of grace in favor of my new companion", Damien wrote enthusiastically.[13]

After a long day's work, Damien and Brother Joseph often spent the evening together. Damien taught him Hawaiian expressions, and after only a few months Dutton mastered the language fairly well. But Dutton was most useful in his work with the lepers. He was not at all afraid to contract the disease and showed no disgust, not even with the most disfigured cases. He wanted to learn how to take care of the lepers' wounds in order to lighten Damien's work load. Doctor Mouritz taught him the basic principles of wound care and bandaging and was delighted with his pupil. Dutton was methodical and accurate and before long acquired such expertise that the pupil surpassed his teacher. "Whatever Brother Dutton undertook to do he did it well", extolled Mouritz.[14]

Unexpected solidarity with an ecumenical touch

In 1886, three years before his death, Damien's fame spread even further. *The Lepers of Molokai*, the account published by Charles Warren Stoddard after his trip to Molokai, was well received throughout the whole Anglo-Saxon world.[15] In his travel report, the author glorified the great contrast between the terminally ill community of Molokai and the unblemished, heroic priest. But just before the story went to press, Stoddard received news that Damien too was infected. In an epilogue, he published one of Damien's recent letters in which he mentioned his disease: "Those microbes have finally settled themselves in my left leg and my ear, and an eyebrow begins to fall. I expect to have my face soon disfigured. Having no doubt myself of the true character of my disease, I feel calm, resigned, and happier among my people. Almighty God knows what is best for my own sanctification, and with that conviction I say daily a good *fiat voluntas tua*—your will be done." [16]

When Damien saw Stoddard's work, he was embarrassed. "Stoddard speaks too much about me", he wrote wearily to Bishop Koeckemann when sending him some leaflets.[17] He left it to his bishop to decide about the circulation of these brochures. Yet Damien also realized what were the opportunities presented by this publication, with the intention to make the history, present situation, and needs of the leprosy settlement known. He was in contact with an Irish sister of the Paridaens Institute in Louvain who was willing to provide a French translation. The French version did not appear immediately, but the generalate in Paris was in favor of the idea.[18]

The news that the "Apostle of the Lepers" or the "Leper Priest" was now himself a leper went around the world. The notice in the missionary magazine *Les missions catholiques* in April 1886 shocked the French-speaking and European world. Damien's mother, who had been ill, died on August 6, 1886, which was, according to some, shortly after she had learned the news of her missionary son's mortal illness. In October of that year, *Le courrier de Bruxelles* even wrongly announced that Damien had died.

The news had an impact on his work. In the Anglo-Saxon world "Father Damien" became a well-known name, even though notoriety was the last thing he sought. Expressions of sympathy and gifts started pouring in from all over the world. Damien's correspondence from that period includes quite a few letters exchanged with admirers. His replies express his concern for the well-being of the lepers, especially the orphans, but contain not a trace of vanity. Personal fame did not interest him; rather, he preferred to remain in the shadows. But there was no antidote against the status of hero that he attained overseas, which he neither asked for nor wanted. So Damien decided to make the best of it: at least his fellow lepers could benefit from it.

One of Damien's special friendships was that with the Anglican priest Hugh B. Chapman, pastor of the Church of Saint Luke in Camberwell, London. Chapman was a great admirer of the Catholic missionary and carried on an intense correspondence with him. Chapman was personally touched by Damien's testimony of faith. "You have taught me more by the story of your life than all the commentaries I have ever read; and the Blessed Sacrament is more to me since I have read of a voluntary leper than it ever was before", he wrote to Damien.[19]

As soon as he heard that Damien had become ill, he organized a large fund drive. The energetic Chapman[20] was infused with an authentic ecumenical spirit. It is remarkable that the Anglican clergyman was convinced from the start that his supportive action had to overcome the three-centuries-old split between Anglicans and Catholics. He asked for and received the support of Henry Edward Cardinal Manning, archbishop of Westminster and the most important Catholic prelate of England. Critics from his own communion publicly denounced him for endeavoring to "create sympathy for an idolatrous priest of that abominable religion".[21] Did the priest's work not make his proselytes "twofold more children of hell than he is himself"?[22] Chapman had a ready answer for his critics: "Such a life makes one's own appear very easy and selfish, and I consider it an honor to lay the slightest offering at the feet of the man who is brave enough to lead it." [23] The leading London newspaper, the *Times*, gave full coverage to the collection for Damien and made space available for the discussion it set off. The international admiration—not least in London, then the world's capital—the public aspect of the fundraising, the interchurch cooperation, and the unavoidable polemic were all elements of modernity that the contemporary reader undoubtedly recognizes. They took place far away from Damien, and mostly without his awareness. But it was his radical work of service that set into motion their dynamics.

The London fund drive exceeded expectations. Substantial sums of money were donated to Damien. In 1886 Chapman sent 975 pounds sterling, and during the following years a total of 2,625 pounds sterling. That amount was more than mere alms; it equaled the amount that the Board of Health allocated to the leprosy settlement over several months.

Hero of Molokai or incorrigible troublemaker?

"Almost every week, I receive letters from America and England", Damien wrote to Apostolic Vicar Koeckemann, a bit too enthusiastically, at the end of 1886.[24] The expressions of sympathy clearly lifted his spirits after a year in which his illness and isolation had weighed heavily on him. "Please pray that I will not get a big head because of the praise of sympathizers." Damien mentioned several donations in his name but from which the entire mission benefited. And he added, in a somewhat defiant manner, in Hawaiian: "*Maikai nale no ia, mai ohumu nui olua i ko Kamiano no pepine.*" This translates roughly as: "That is a good cause: your two friends don't have to fret about Damien." He was likely alluding to Prime Minister Gibson and vice provincial Léonor Fouesnel.

The universal praise Damien received from outside the Catholic mission did not sit well with his immediate superiors in Honolulu. The jealousy only deepened once money entered the picture. There was a political component as well. Prime Minister Gibson was annoyed by the worldwide praise the Belgian missionary was receiving, which, whether explicitly or implicitly, amounted to a criticism of his policy. Every hymn of praise sung to the hero of Molokai and every gift donated for his labors was a stain on the reputation of the Board of Health or the authorities; at least that was how Gibson saw it. But that was not at all the intention of Damien— nor of Stoddard, who had written that the royal family and the Hawaiian government probably had done everything possible to alleviate the suffering in the leprosy settlement. Nor was Stoddard at all critical of the mission of the Sacred Hearts Fathers.[25] Besides, it was clear that the existence of the missionary post of Molokai had always been due to the charity and the gifts of benefactors. Hawaiian Queen Kapiolani herself was among those who occasionally donated warm clothing to the lepers.

None of this mattered. Gibson was fighting for his political survival. The opposition, which denounced, among other things, his lax leprosy policy, had momentum. Fouesnel and Koeckemann, fearing that the Catholic mission would lose Gibson's support and that Protestant forces would take over power, sided against their missionary. Apparently they shared the view that Damien exaggerated the conditions in the leprosy settlement in order to place himself in the spotlight and attract gifts. But that unwanted publicity damaged Hawaii's image. This led to bitter words in the bishop's correspondence with Damien. But a visit to the leper missionary to ascertain the situation on the ground was out of the question. Once again Damien had to endure the lack of understanding and the reproaches of his superiors. But that seemed to bother him less and less as time went on. His conscience was clear.

At the beginning of 1887 Damien mentioned to his bishop certain gifts he had received, including the 975-pound donation from London. How should he handle these funds? Should he turn them over to the Church? Or did he have permission to keep the money and use it for the good of the lepers, for whom it was meant after all? Further, several religious sisters had offered to come and help him. Damien did not dare to hope any longer that they would receive permission. "Given the enormous *hoohoka* [disappointment] we have had on Molokai regarding the Franciscan sisters, I have barely any hope that they might receive a favorable response, despite our great need of good nurses."[26]

Vice Provincial Fouesnel and Apostolic Vicar Koeckemann reached the same conclusion: the praise had gone to Damien's head and was becoming a problem for the mission. Koeckemann's answer was especially harsh. There was no question of another congregation besides the Franciscan sisters establishing itself on Molokai. And if women volunteered to come as religious, they first had to go to Syracuse in the United States and complete the novitiate with the Franciscan sisters. Mother Marianne concurred. Koeckemann did not want to touch Damien's money, though he could not refrain from saying that "the mission in general could use it more than the leprosarium." He warned Damien: "It's up to you to arrange with your religious authority how to safeguard your vow of poverty." Lastly, he reproached Damien for his self-importance: "I don't want to diminish at all the glory of your heroism, which rightly earned you the sympathy of the entire world. I myself have often contributed to that. But the affair also has its prosaic side, since a great deal of money is involved. From what I understand from the newspapers, the world is under the impression that you are head of *your* lepers, their provider, their doctor, their nurse, their gravedigger, and so on, as if the government had done nothing." Koeckemann thought that the king and Gibson were justified in feeling offended. He also felt unjustly treated: "The Catholic mission too, with its ecclesiastic and religious authorities, feels that it has been pushed to the background. It is indirectly, and sometimes directly, criticized, so that the hero can shine even more brightly."[27]

The reproach must have sounded particularly unfair to Damien's ears. He himself had never sought fame. But now that he had acquired it, he felt he must put it to the best use. He had never wanted to put himself in the limelight, let alone accuse the government or the mission of negligence, even though he had many reasons to do so. Damien felt misunderstood by his superiors, who seemed unable to imagine what life was like in the leprosarium, to grasp how great the needs still were. They did not seem to comprehend that his offering of his life was not for the sake of his own honor and glory but rather was the result of his steadfast love for his Lord and for the outcasts entrusted to him. Could he help it that others saw that? In a letter to his bishop, he wrote resentfully: "After having received incense and gold from all over, I did not count on receiving myrrh from my superior."[28] In his reply, which displayed traces of both magnanimity and severity, Koeckemann wrote: "After gold and incense, myrrh was not to your taste. You have spat that into my face together with an old supply of bile in your heart. Let us hope that now there is none left. From my side, I have never stopped admiring your heroism and publicizing it on every possible occasion. If I have counted too much on your humility, I am angry about that.... I forgive you all the more readily because you do not perceive wrongdoing on your side."[29]

The bitter verbal dispute could not stay restricted to the Hawaiian Islands. Koeckemann reported his version of the facts to the generalate in Paris.[30] According to him, Damien had received so many accolades that he now seemed in danger of losing the equilibrium in his head, "which nonetheless had always been hard enough".[31] In a long enumeration, he commended the government's efforts to provide the exiles with the best possible care in their place of banishment. According to him, most were better off on Molokai than at home. Moreover, the Catholic mission had made all the necessary efforts for Molokai. "Following my ordination, my first visit was to them."[32] He neglected to add that he had gone to the colony only because he had been asked to deliver Damien's royal decoration personally. He also, wisely, did not mention that he never again visited Damien and that the religious superior, Vice Provincial Fouesnel, had never visited. The letter reveals the bishop's blindness to the exceptional situation of the leprosy settlement. He did not deny Damien's praiseworthy achievements, but he thought Damien exaggerated them. "The Reverend Father

Damien, who devoted himself in such a generous manner, exclusively to the lepers, seems to think that the government, the mission, and the sisters should, like him, concentrate their efforts on behalf of the lepers, and take orders from him." [33] What is more, in his impatience Damien had sent letters to the four corners of the world filled with exaggerations about the lepers' material plight. Unconsciously, or perhaps consciously, he put a stain on the efforts of the government and the Church. Because of the flood of gifts, Damien now had more money at his disposal than was good for him—more than six thousand dollars, the bishop specified. Damien informed him about the funds in a "triumphant manner", even though in reality no trace of triumphalism can be detected in Damien's letter. The bishop even saw the devil at work in Damien's attitude. When the bishop had made a few remarks, Damien reacted in an unworthy manner. "His response does not bear the mark of the humility suited to a great saint whose glory has been published in the two worlds", he wrote sarcastically. "I fear that the devil has a hand in this, jealous of the good that might come of it for the Catholic religion." [34]

The bishop was painfully mistaken, especially in the light of Damien's later canonization. He probably meant well, being convinced he was taking the pastoral approach. But he had not understood that Damien's "exaggerations" and the international praise he received were not the fruit of misplaced human arrogance but rather an expression of God's "exaggerated" preference for the poorest. He showed no empathy for the difficult situation of Damien, who was destined to die of the disease. Examination of Damien's relationship with his superiors brought yet another interesting fact to light: in the letters and reports Koeckemann sent during that period to the Propaganda fide in Rome, he did not once mention the name Damien. Likewise, nowhere was the leprosarium on Molokai mentioned, unlike the one in Honolulu. Given the importance of what was happening on Molokai and the renown of the Leper Priest, that could not have been an innocent oversight. [35]

As often happens, exceptional love and faith painfully highlight the pettiness and lack of understanding of one's associates. Damien's superiors today look like tragic figures. It is the irony of history that Koeckemann's insensitivity and blindness to the exceptional in

Damien's life added yet more color and luster to the saint's life. As usual, the short-tempered Vice Provincial Fouesnel, who had taken a personal aversion to Damien, added insult to injury: "This brave priest passes himself off as the lepers' consoler, provider, nurse, shrouder, burier, and so forth, but he is no such thing." Damien deserved all the praise he got for his willingness to sacrifice his life and freedom, but unfortunately it went to his head. "He has swallowed it and become drunk and now is becoming dangerous."[36] Damien had suggested that Fouesnel put in his own name the money destined for Damien, but Fousnel judged that inappropriate and left it with Damien: "He should deal with it himself; it is too delicate with a man who has become so bossy, unpredictable, and arrogant from all the praise he has received."[37]

Immediately Fouesnel ordered Damien to forward to him all of his correspondence, except that with the superior general, so he could read it first. He wanted to prevent more of Damien's exaggerations from appearing in the press. Such an order was especially unusual, "and was never given by another provincial besides Father Léonor, who was especially strict toward others and not toward himself", as Idesbald Verhaeghe, provincial of the Hawaiian mission from 1937 to 1947, remarked about his predecessor.[38] Damien followed this humiliating order in an exemplary way. Léonor kept insisting with Damien that he had the best intentions. As had happened on other occasions, he doubted his own pastoral capacities. "If you want to shake off the yoke and think and say that I am neither worthy nor capable of directing you, then it will be a thorn that you will pull out of my foot", he complained again.[39]

To make matters worse, the rumor was spreading that the leprosy settlement had caused such a sensation in London Protestant circles that Episcopalian sisters were preparing to go to Molokai to devote their lives to the lepers. If that news proved true—afterward it turned out to have been nonsense—it would have meant direct competition with "heretics". That had to be avoided at all costs. Koeckemann realized that it had to do with the fact that the Franciscan sisters were not yet on Molokai, against Damien's insistent pleas.[40]

Koeckemann, who had never lifted a finger in this regard, now for the first time was willing to consider the option. He gave as an excuse for the delay the fact that, in addition to the needs of the lepers of Molokai, there were many other needs demanding the sisters' attention. Perhaps Damien was only looking out for his lepers, but he had to keep the entire mission's well-being in mind. Still, this time he dropped his passive attitude and discussed with Mother Marianne the possibility of sending some sisters to Molokai. The superior seemed very interested. Gibson too supported the plan. But Koeckemann worried about a lot of practical matters. How would it work with communion? The sisters could not be expected to receive it from the hands of a leper priest. So he would also have to send a healthy priest to Damien, but there were no obvious candidates. And owing to the moral depravity on Molokai—about which, according to him, Damien never talked—there had to be greater separation of men and women to be able to send the sisters in good conscience.

Fouesnel described the situation in his usual blunt manner. According to him, the Franciscan sisters would go quickly to Molokai. "Their sacrifice is greater than that of Father Damien", he added spitefully, "because they go there first of all to treat the lepers, and what is even more horrible and terrifying, they will have to receive holy communion from the hand of a leper." Fouesnel could hardly conceal his disgust for Damien and his disease. He still could not manage a word of sympathy for his suffering subordinate. Quite the contrary: "It is he who with his imprudent and even deceitful writings forces those poor girls to make that sacrifice." [41]

The critical reactions and nervousness of Damien's superiors cannot be separated from the political context. They did not want to fall out of favor with the king and prime minister. In the spring of 1887 the government was plagued by all kinds of scandals. It was in the center of a political storm. Pressure from the opposition kept mounting all the time. The political opposition, united in the Hawaiian League, was Protestant. Its leaders, such as Lorrin A. Thurston, were descendants of Protestant missionaries. The Catholic mission, which had always maintained good relations with King Kalakaua and Prime Minister Gibson, was afraid of a change of power. It was becoming more probable every day that the cabinet, or even the entire regime, might fall. Catholics would lose their only friends at the highest political levels.

At the same time, the government had to be careful not to be seen to be too friendly toward the Catholics. After reports appeared in the *Honolulu Advertiser* about the gifts Damien had received, the opposition demanded and obtained an investigation into the considerable sums of money that the government had spent on the lepers on Molokai (ten thousand U.S. dollars in two years) as well as the destination of the funds and gifts that Damien had received. The investigation found no irregularities. The money and gifts had been used as intended.

Nothing could save the government. On June 30, 1887, the revolution broke out. Prime Minister Gibson was deposed and imprisoned for a while, but he was released shortly afterward. King Kalakaua was obliged to sign a new constitution, the so-called Bayonet Constitution, which took away practically all his powers. However, it soon became evident that the new political situation was not so disastrous for the Catholic Church in Hawaii. Only then did Koeckemann and Fouesnel take a more pastoral tone in their relationship with Damien. But it never became genuinely cordial.

Besides, Damien felt appreciated because of the warm letter he received from Superior General Bousquet in Paris, who was pleased with Damien's exceptional service and the publicity it received. They were working on a French translation of Stoddard's publication. The superior general's secretary, Janvier Weiler, regularly wrote encouraging words in Bousquet's name, even though Bousquet could not intervene directly from Paris in the problem of Damien's isolation and lack of opportunity to confess and receive the sacrament of penance. With an eye to publishing something in *Les missions catholiques*, he requested more information about Damien's work and photos of the leprosy settlement. The Paris motherhouse thought that the Sacred Hearts Fathers talked too little about their missions and about Molokai in particular: "If the Jesuits had a Molokai, the news would never dry up, and alms would keep pace." [42]

Constant isolation

In the middle of 1887 the problem of Damien's isolation was still unresolved. He was already two years without a confrere. His superiors were working on it, but it clearly was not a priority. "So

Koeckemann at any point could have redeemed himself, his mission, and his Congregation from the criticism to which he was so sensitive by arranging to send Damien a colleague, some solid, reliable, and willing member of the Sacred Hearts. But Koeckemann did not", Gavan Daws remarked. "Over the years, Damien was alone at Kalawao more than half the time." [43]

The coming of two new Sacred Hearts Fathers, Sylvester and Xavier, filled Damien with new hope. Could one of them join him? However, it quickly became clear that their arrival in Hawaii would not mean a solution to his problem. Both Koeckemann and Fouesnel were of the view that they could not send a new missionary to the leprosy settlement. Their solution was to entrust Father Sylvester with confreres Gulstan Ropert and Colomban Beissel in Wailuku on the island of Maui, which should allow Father Colomban to travel more to Molokai to hear Damien's confession. Koeckemann wrote in justification: "It is not possible, at least for a year, to send him [Colomban] permanently to Molokai. . . . We feel very badly for Reverend Father Damien and Molokai. But if we were to send the new missionary there, he [the new missionary] would be disgusted from the time of his arrival. Nonetheless, Damien is too isolated." [44]

Damien was disappointed. He insisted, sounding out the bishop once again on the possibility of sending the sisters and asking about the other newcomer. Sending Father Xavier was likewise not an option, Koeckemann decided. He did not have the right to ask something like that of the new missionary, who spoke neither the indigenous languages nor English. Besides, he did not seem like someone who was up to sharing the heroic life that Damien lived on Molokai. "If you can persuade him to join you in the leprosarium, I will not put any obstacle in the way. But to be honest, I will tell you confidentially that we're not counting much on his heroic dedication." [45] Damien once again had to practice more patience. As far as the sisters were concerned, in those times of great political uncertainty, their coming was out of the question.

Meanwhile, there developed some discord in the relationship between Damien and Dutton. Dutton wanted to become, with Meyer's support, head of the hospital in Kalawao. Damien did not like this; he wanted to keep Dutton at his disposal. There was a

lot of work in the leprosarium, and Damien was ill. Dutton complained about Damien to Koeckemann, the ecclesial superior with
whom he could communicate directly. He considered Damien often
too demanding, and at the same time too impudent, too familiar.
Further, he, who was not a leper, had to receive communion on
his tongue from a leper's hand.[46] Koeckemann tried to soothe the
disturbance from a distance. He kept Dutton where he was but
recommended to Damien that he give Dutton some more freedom
and take into account human weakness. "Give him the orders that
you deem necessary, but leave him a bit of freedom in the sphere
you assign to him." [47]

The change of political regimes in Honolulu had considerable
consequences for life in the leprosy colony. The new leadership
thought Gibson had been too lax in implementing the exile policy. Henceforth anyone showing signs of leprosy would be banished without exception. Damien experienced the increase firsthand.
"Now the government is sending dozens of new lepers each week,
and it is expected that shortly our number will double or even
triple", he wrote to his brother.[48] He was responsible for over
fifty orphans, a number that increased quickly. Fortunately, the
pains in his feet had subsided, and despite his illness, he was still
strong. "Although the leprosy has a firm hold on my body and
has disfigured me somewhat, I continue to be strong and robust,
and the terrible pains in my feet have disappeared. Until now the
disease has not yet deformed my hands, and I continue to say
Holy Mass every day. This privilege is my greatest consolation,
for me as well as for my numerous companions in misery, who
every Sunday fill my two churches, in which I continuously reserve
the Blessed Sacrament." [49]

The stricter exile policy meant that the leprosy patient Father
Grégoire Archambaux was required to return to the settlement.
The erratic and physically weak priest had already spent some time
in the colony, four years before, which had not been a success.
Still, Damien was pleased he would no longer be alone.[50]

The superiors postponed Grégoire's transfer as long as possible,
suspecting that he and Damien would not get along. Besides, Grégoire would be incapable of adjusting to the colony. "Grégoire would
soon die of sadness", Fouesnel thought.[51] When Grégoire's exile

became unavoidable, the bishop named him pastor of Kalaupapa. That solved Damien's confession problem; at the same time, Grégoire was far enough away to be able to live with Damien's "hard and intransigent character".[52] Vice provincial Léonor Fouesnel asked Damien to look after his confrere: "We count on your great charity to take good care of him, and on your courage to encourage him."[53] Sometime later, Léonor asked Damien to make sure Grégoire did not drink too much wine, as alcohol was harmful for leprosy sufferers. "How is his health? Can he reasonably maintain himself?" he asked. "He is very sensitive to the cold. Can he cover himself sufficiently at night and during the day? Maybe a good heavy coat would do him well and please him?"[54] The tone is notable. Léonor, who himself regularly remarked in his letters that he did not regard himself as a good provincial, was clearly capable of warm, pastoral concern for the confreres under his charge. How then is it possible that he so rarely adopted that tone toward Damien? That he never once inquired into Damien's health, even though he communicated almost daily with him about all kinds of practical matters? That he showed so little understanding for Damien's spiritual need in being deprived of a confrere? Many of Damien's biographers have been struck by Fouesnel's obvious bias against the Belgian missionary. He had constructed for himself an image of Damien as an unreasonable, stubborn, and exaggerating man. Even Damien's physical and spiritual needs did not alter the vice provincial's view. It is noteworthy that Damien no longer complained about this treatment. He accepted everything with full obedience and without any resentment against his congregation. In his letters to Pamphile, where he usually unveiled his heart the most, he kept repeating how happy he was as a missionary. "Having a lot of work, time seems quite short to me. The joy and contentment of heart that the Sacred Hearts provide me makes me the happiest missionary in the world."[55]

Once again Father Grégoire's stay in the leprosy settlement was not a success. His egocentricity was in sharp contrast to Damien's attitude. He complained constantly about everything, including about Damien, who paid him too little attention. He suffered from one asthma attack after another and showed signs of hysteria. To help him escape his lonely existence in Kalaupapa, Damien even brought him to Kalawao. But there too Grégoire was difficult to handle. Nothing seemed to be able to calm him down. Koeckemann and Fouesnel officially petitioned the Board of Health to make an exception and allow Grégoire to leave the place of exile. Amazingly, with the help of Doctor Nathaniël B. Emerson, the new president of the Board of Health, their petition was granted. On March 15, 1888, the priest departed Molokai for Honolulu, happy to leave the condemned island. In the tranquillity of the Kakaako hospital, and probably thanks to the good care provided by the sisters, Grégoire's health improved. He no longer suffered from asthma, was satisfied with his neat room, and resigned himself to his illness in a happier mood. "I cannot forget the trouble I caused you; accept my sincere gratitude", he wrote to Damien when he had regained his calm.[56] Grégoire died some months later, on November 12, 1888.

Conrardy's arrival

The presence of the long-hoped-for confrere, in the person of Father Grégoire, had been a burden rather than a help to Damien. But perhaps salvation was at hand. At the beginning of November 1887, Damien received a warm letter from Lambert Louis Conrardy. This missionary priest from Liège, who was active among the Native Americans in the Rocky Mountains of the United States, was long intrigued by the story of his Flemish compatriot among the leprosy victims of Molokai. Conrardy, already in the first letters of his decade-long correspondence with Damien, had volunteered to go help him in his apostolate. Though that did not happen at that time, the two kept up their correspondence, about one letter per year.

Conrardy had a profound admiration for his fellow Belgian that only deepened once he learned that Damien had contracted leprosy himself. He did not hesitate to call him a saint. In his eyes, Damien, who like Job was struck by God with many trials and maladies, was a great example for the world. "The good God is marvelous in his saints."[57]

Conrardy, aware that Damien was still alone, again offered to go help him. He wished to go immediately, if Damien thought he could be of use. If necessary, he was willing to enter the Congregation of the Sacred Hearts. The arrival of the Jesuits in his mission region in the Rocky Mountains meant that there was less need for him there. Conrardy recommended himself to Damien: he had worked for thirteen years with Native Americans and was used to the rugged existence of a missionary. He was healthy and hoped to be able to work at least another twenty years.

Damien was more than delighted with this offer of help from a fellow countryman, a Walloon, whom he had never met and who did not even belong to his own congregation. He pleaded with Conrardy from the bottom of his heart to come as quickly as possible, to help him, and to succeed him.[58]

To Damien's great relief Fouesnel and Koeckemann did not respond negatively to the prospect of Conrardy's joining him. But they did indeed see a problem. Conrardy was a diocesan priest. If he wanted to enter the Congregation of the Sacred Hearts, he would have to follow the usual procedure of at least one year of novitiate. The best place to do this would be in Paris or Valparaiso, Chile. Conrardy made a counterproposal. He would assist Damien as a diocesan priest on Molokai. Living for a time at Damien's side would help him become a suitable candidate for the congregation. Later he would do his novitiate. A close listener understood the unstated: after Damien would have died.

Koeckemann hesitated. He could accept Conrardy's paying a visit to Molokai on his way to the novitiate. "But if he wants to settle with you straightaway, it would be embarrassing for me to accept him, an outsider to the congregation, despite his undoubtedly good qualities", the bishop wrote.[59]

Damien exploded. There was an ever-growing amount of work. Due to the new policy, the number of exiles was rising rapidly. He felt his powers diminishing. He looked forward to welcoming a priest who could help him in his pastoral duties and assist him in his debilitating disease and inevitable death. Besides, Conrardy had a great deal of experience and showed that he was capable of handling the strenuous life of a missionary. He seemed to be made of the right stuff. And still the bishop and vice provincial would send him to do the first year of his novitiate! Conrardy would never accept that; he would choose other missionary work. In a letter to the bishop dated February 2, 1888, Damien wisely softened his tone. He made a counterproposal. Why not let Conrardy come immediately to Molokai? He could bind himself by temporary vows to the bishop's authority, as Brother Dutton had done. If that worked out satisfactorily, he could eventually be admitted to the congregation. "The circumstances in which I find myself are exceptional— why not come to my aid in ways that are a little exceptional too?" he asked boldly. It was a logic that pastorally minded superiors could have worked out for themselves. At the end of his letter, Damien requested the fatherly blessing of the bishop, adding: "Have mercy on us" [60]—something he had never done before.

Koeckemann could not resist Damien's passionate pleading. On top of that, a severe storm had recently caused terrible destruction on Molokai. One night, the tower Damien had built for the Church of Saint Philomena was blown over, and a substantial portion of the building was in rubble. That had to be rebuilt. Koeckemann acceded to Damien's "ardent desire". Conrardy would be permitted to go straight to Molokai without first completing a novitiate. "It is because of your health that I have consented to deprive him of the benefits of religious profession." [61] Rarely had Damien received a message from his bishop that filled him with as much joy as this brief letter.

Koeckemann, however, was not entirely convinced, as can be ascertained in the version of the facts he presented to the superior general in Paris. "We expect here in a few weeks a Belgian priest, Father Conrardy, who for a dozen years was a missionary to the Indians in Oregon. Father Damien does not want to give him time to do his novitiate in Valparaiso or Europe." Not a word about the real reasons that had convinced the bishop to give his permission. In the epilogue, it emerged that two things still bothered him. First, it now appeared as though the fathers of the Hawaiian mission were not charitable enough to go to Damien's assistance on Molokai. Second, the newcomer was another Belgian. Now they would receive all the praise linked to the fame of Molokai. "We must not be jealous that Belgium reaps all the glory of the mission", he wrote, thereby illustrating the contrary.[62]

Even more salt was poured on the bishop's wounds when a Protestant newspaper in Honolulu, the *Hawaiian Gazette*, announced in especially flattering terms the arrival of the Belgian missionary. "Every Christian, Catholic or Protestant, must respect and admire the zeal and self-denial of this minister of Jesus Christ, who voluntarily sacrifices himself for love of poor suffering humanity, just as Father Damien had previously done." [63]

Koeckemann vented his gall on Superior General Bousquet. Damien had ordered Conrardy to come to Molokai immediately, without doing a novitiate. "He sees only the leprosarium and himself; all the rest has to fit his ideas." But the bishop could not have opposed Damien, who would have denounced him to the four winds as the enemy of the lepers. Damien liked to twist the truth: the government, the mission, and the congregation were all, directly or indirectly, unjustly blamed for casting shadows on the hero. The newspaper article about Conrardy reinforced the impression that not a single missionary of Damien's own order had been willing to go to Damien's assistance, "whereas several of our fathers are ready to go at the first signal." [64] But Damien was not easy to get along with, the bishop went on. Even Damien's relationship with Dutton had soured. It remained to be seen how long Conrardy would stick it out with Damien.

The news of Conrardy's arrival, with all the publicity it garnered, created a lot of ill feeling on the part of the missionaries of the Sacred Hearts. Many of them were enthusiastically prepared to assist Damien, but no one had ever asked them to go! Koeckemann saw it differently: if he had never sent anyone to Damien's side, that was because of the lack of missionaries. He simply did not have enough men. But was that really true? The German Picpus Father Corneille Limburg, a young missionary who often had sound judgments about the state of affairs in the mission, slammed his fist on the table: it was an outright scandal for the mission that not a single one of their own confreres was sent to Damien. It would have been sufficient for the bishop to send a circular letter to the missionaries asking for a candidate. Once that priest was chosen, others should see about replacing him. Monsignor Koeckemann followed Limburg's advice. Within two weeks nearly all of the missionaries volunteered—many full of enthusiasm, most with the obedience that the rule required of them.[65] Léonor mentioned an "avalanche" of letters.[66] It was decided that Father Wendelin Moellers would be sent to Molokai.

Conrardy arrived in Hawaii on May 12, 1888. Koeckemann kept him a few days in Honolulu to assess him. The impression was negative: he was dim-witted and eccentric. He drank too much. "By himself he drank a whole bottle of wine—without water", he specified. And he was full of himself. "In the three days he was in Honolulu, he saw more people than I visit in a whole year", he complained, though that said more about himself than about Conrardy. His decision was made: the Liège priest must first do his novitiate, which could only do him good.[67]

When Damien learned of the decision, he reacted angrily. "Conrardy is my man", he said. Now that a fellow priest was finally coming, he did not intend to give him up just like that.[68] Koeckemann defended his decision to Damien but refused to explain his motives. Would a year-and-a-half delay in Conrardy's coming to Molokai really matter? The bishop had still not understood how pressing time was, nor the extent to which Damien was in spiritual need.[69] And Vice Provincial Fouesnel continued to be against the appointment. He indeed had resolved to have nothing more to do with Damien because of the damage that he and his fellow countryman had inflicted upon the missionaries. But financial matters eventually led him to take a different decision. As usual, he complained about his own health without asking about Damien's. And he lashed out at Damien: "Be prudent, my dear Father, and before you write to your superiors, meditate on humility. Remember that a haughty manner can bring myrrh from those who before were so lavish with their gold and incense." After all, why was Damien so anxious to have a confrere join him as soon as possible? From the moment he could no longer administer the sacraments himself, a confrere would be sent to his side.[70]

Fouesnel expressed himself even more sharply to the superior general, describing the problems with young missionaries. He criticized Koeckemann for not daring to say anything about that for fear it would anger them. "But the worst of all", so Fouesnel judged, "is the Reverend Father Damien, who has been raised so high on a pedestal by his heroism that now no one can bring him back down. As for myself, I stick to keeping his accounts and filling his orders for supplies in silence."[71] That last assertion was definitely not true—just like the rest; it was to be feared, according to Fouesnel, that after all of Damien's work and sacrifices, "the flattery and honors are going to divest him of any merit." As far as Conrardy was concerned, Koeckemann would do everything he could to get rid of him, but that probably would not work. "He is too eager for the glory that has brought Father Damien the title of 'hero', a title for which he is ambitious himself." [72] Damien had no luck with his immediate superior, who seemingly was incapable of seeing the self-giving service taking place before his eyes in categories other than those of glory and ambition.

On May 17, 1888, less than a year before Damien's death, Conrardy landed at Molokai. The seasoned missionary was prepared for everything, even to die a martyr. Yet the impact of the brutal reality of Molokai was enormous. The newcomer's eyes provided a fresh view of life in the settlement and on Damien's condition. Damien's physical appearance was even more pitiable than Conrardy had anticipated. His ears were terribly swollen, his face, neck, and hands covered with tumors and swellings of all kinds. Above all, Conrardy, who shared living quarters with Damien, had a hard time with the repugnant odor. The first weeks, he could hardly bring himself to eat. Avoiding direct contact with the germs was impossible for a priest, he quickly realized. The germs were everywhere: the leper boys sought out his company; leper butchers handled the meat; lepers touched the food; Damien's chickens were picking on rotting flesh, so that not even the eggs were safe any longer. In order to discuss confidential matters, Damien often came close by.

Conrardy was convinced, in line with the prevailing view of the time, that leprosy was highly contagious. Even for a man like him, who was prepared to make the ultimate sacrifice, the prospect of contracting the disease was difficult to stomach. [73]

The new missionary was overwhelmed by omnipresent death. Due to a deadly flu epidemic, the mortality rate reached its peak during the first weeks of his stay, with no fewer than ninety deaths out of a total number of inhabitants of at most seven hundred. Eleven died in one day in June.

Conrardy was impressed by the extraordinary work rhythm Damien maintained: besides administering the sacraments and visiting the sick, he provided care for more and more boy orphans, already numbering eighty. With the support of the Board of Health, he started the construction of two new dormitories for the boys. He was also busy with the reconstruction of the tower destroyed at the Church of Saint Philomena. He was looking for money for that also: he did not want to appeal to his superiors, as Fouesnel was already being difficult about everything, even about one hundred dollars in import duties for a beautiful altar piece he had received as a gift from the United States. Damien did not want to use gifts destined for the lepers to pay for the construction work. He asked his Anglican friend Chapman to seek support from Cardinal Manning.[74]

In a letter destined for a meeting of the general chapter of the Picpus Fathers, Damien sang Conrardy's praises. Because his ailing hand would not cooperate any longer, Damien had to dictate the letter to Conrardy. "He has lived here with me for over two months as a very good confrere and companion, leper though I am. He performs many services in our large leprosarium."[75] As Damien put it, he behaves like "one of us"—meaning a Picpus Father—and followed in an exemplary way the vows of poverty, chastity, and obedience. He asked the superior general and the chapter to find a different way from the usual novitiate for Conrardy to enter the congregation. For he already had substantial missionary experience, and if he is not given a different option he will pursue his vocation elsewhere. Then Damien would have lost once again his sorely needed assistance. In a postscript, Conrardy confirmed in his own name: "If I'm forced to leave the leprosarium, I will prefer to return to my old mission post rather than to go spend a year and a half and more in Europe."[76]

Around the same time, Koeckemann, for whom the newcomer was a "fifth wheel on the wagon", offered opposing advice. Priests from outside the congregation were nothing but trouble: "They begin with a perfect submission, next they want to do it their way, and bit by bit they want to rule everything." A conversation of a quarter of an hour in Honolulu had convinced him that things would not be different with Conrardy. Besides, in his eyes Damien was the worst possible mentor for instilling the spirituality of the Sacred Hearts into Conrardy. For Damien seemed to "have entered a separate order beyond all religious and ecclesial authorities". Scornfully, he added: "If those two heroes stay together a long time, it is to be feared that they will end up by putting the mission to shame, either by their direct complaints, or by their self-praise, as if they are the only ones dedicated to the work, or by false reports, which sooner or later will provoke opposition." Bishop Koeckemann did not see a serious reason why Conrardy could not first go to the novitiate. Did he perhaps feel too inadequate to go through a novitiate? Or, perhaps more accurately, already too perfect? Koeckemann did not say a word about the urgent situation facing Damien.[77] Two days later Léonor Fouesnel added his judgment: "The incensing he received because of his heroism has made him drunk, and the gold he received and still receives has made him blind. . . . He is excessively difficult, not to say impossible, to direct."[78]

In Paris, Bousquet weighed his response. He knew his people in Hawaii well and did not want to turn a deaf ear to Damien, whom he admired. He temporarily put off his decision, but he did argue, to Koeckemann's displeasure, that Conrardy was better off on Molokai than in any possible novitiate formation.[79] Koeckemann sensed which way the wind was blowing and expressed regret to Janvier Weiler, the general's assistant, for his harsh words about Damien. Damien might indeed be utterly stubborn and have poor judgment, but ultimately he meant well and undeniably had a good heart. But deep down the superior stuck to his judgment: Damien did not live in the true familial spirit of the Sacred Hearts. He saw only the needs of the leprosy victims and not those of the entire mission; he was imprudent; all too often he had created publicity for his work without rectifying the mistakes in the reporting. Koeckemann offered as advice: "After his death, we can grandly and publicly sing his praises; but during his life, I recommend to you a certain reserve."[80]

In the meantime, Koeckemann had changed his mind about Conrardy. He saw that he devoted himself unconditionally to the lepers and was well liked by them. If he dared to take him away, the leper faithful would likely turn against him. Besides, it started to get through to him that Damien's health was rapidly deteriorating. On October 15, 1888, Damien fell at the altar during High Mass. He was no longer capable of finishing the Mass.[81] Under those conditions an extra priest in the settlement was not a luxury.[82]

Koeckemann now even called Conrardy a sign of Providence.[83] Damien's helper also made a very good impression on Father

Corneille, who stayed on Molokai for a few days at the end of that year and wrote a detailed report.

Father Corneille thought Conrardy did his work very well: he was active, was industrious, lived poorly, and fortunately had a cheerful character, which was absolutely necessary. Conrardy had admitted to having been somewhat incautious in not sufficiently specifying in a number of newspaper articles that many Sacred Hearts Fathers had also been prepared to go to Molokai. "He behaved in a very correct way toward me as a confrere. He respected me and listened to me as if I were his superior. And yet he is forty-seven, and I am only forty", he added.[84]

Lambert Louis Conrardy (1841–1914)

Lambert Louis Conrardy,[85] born in Liège, Belgium, on July 12, 1841, was of the same generation as Damien and in many respects was an equally remarkable man. If there is an unsung hero in Damien's story, it is Conrardy. No challenge was too great or too difficult for this Walloon priest, convinced as he was that a Christian is called in this short life to perform great deeds. "Since I was twelve years old, I prayed that I would die one day as a martyr of the faith. But I did not know how I could sacrifice myself for Christ, and so I prayed every day that I could do this in the most awful places in the world", he later wrote.

Conrardy was ordained a priest in 1867. As assistant pastor in Stavelot, near Malmedy in the Diocese of Liège, he distinguished himself during the cholera epidemic of 1869 by caring for the sick day and night, even offering his own bed to them. But the great challenge and wide horizon beckoned: the vocation to the missions, and even to martyrdom, was unstoppable when in 1870 he learned of the martyrdom of Marie-Josèphe Adam, who together with nine sisters of the Daughters of Charity was killed in the Chinese Tianjin Massacre. Three hundred Daughters of Charity went to replace their fallen sisters, which speaks volumes about religious ardor in nineteenth-century Europe. Conrardy could not remain behind. He became a kind of *fidei donum*-priest *avant la lettre*, a secular priest who did missionary work.[86] He spent a year in the seminary of the Société des missions étrangères in Paris, in the hope of going to China. Instead, his superiors sent him, in 1872, to the French mission in the southeast of India (Pondichéry). He could not tolerate the humid climate, and in 1874 he was back in Belgium. After studying at the American College of Louvain, he was sent to the Archdiocese of Oregon City, in the mountains of the northwest United States. He followed in the footsteps of the "Great Blackrobe", the Belgian Jesuit Pieter-Jan De Smet, who had died the previous year. Archbishop Gross of Oregon entrusted him with the mission on the Umatilla Indian Reservation. Conrardy traveled tirelessly through his vast mission field by horse; he built churches and taught. He was remembered in the area for generations.

Archbishop Gross, who kept in close contact with Damien, told Conrardy of the work of "the Apostle of the Lepers" on Molokai. Beginning in 1877, Conrardy and Damien kept up a correspondence. In an 1881 letter to the bishop of Honolulu, Conrardy asked to be allowed to go help Damien on Molokai. The Catholic mission in Hawaii was reluctant, however, because he did not belong to the Congregation of the Sacred Hearts, and they had had no good experiences cooperating with priests outside the congregation.

When Conrardy learned that Damien had contracted leprosy and had no successor or fellow priest on Molokai, he again offered to go. With Damien's help he convinced the mission to allow him to come. He landed at the leprosy colony on May 17, 1888. He became Damien's fellow priest and intimate friend during the last eleven months of his life, attending him on his deathbed and administering the last sacraments.

Conrardy remained in the leprosy settlement for six years after Damien's death. Damien's brother Father Pamphile De Veuster went to Molokai in 1895, and the congregation sent five brother-nurses. The Liège missionary decided that the time had finally come for him to realize his China dream. Conrardy launched a plan to found a settlement, along the lines of Molokai, in Chinese

Canton to deal with its numerous leprosy patients. However, both the ecclesiastical and civil authorities required that such a project be run by a medical doctor rather than a missionary. Even that did not impede the extremely driven Conrardy, who entered the University of Oregon Medical School in Portland at age fifty-five. Thanks to his enormous zest for work, his iron self-discipline, and his unwavering confidence in God, he graduated in April 1900.

However, he was not yet able to realize his project: he still had to study Chinese and raise the needed funds, a work that consumed him between 1900 and 1908. He worked as a mendicant preacher in various European countries, including Belgium, as well as in the United States and Canada. No difficulties or setbacks were too burdensome for him. Referring to the bloody Boxer Rebellion in China, he wrote in 1905 from England: "Riots or not, I won't be deterred. If I had enough money to start my work, I would go immediately." [87] By 1908 he had raised thirty thousand dollars, enough to start his project. That was not the sole fruit of his labors: roughly two hundred missionary vocations are attributed to his passionate preaching.

Robbed of part of his collection in San Francisco, Conrardy continued on to China. In May 1908 he arrived in Canton. On the islands of Shek Lung, not far from Hong Kong, he bought land and established his leprosy settlement in the face of many difficulties. When on August 24, 1914, he died of pneumonia at age seventy-three, Shek Lung was home to seven hundred leprosy patients. He was buried wrapped in a braided mat between two lepers. Owing to the outbreak of the First World War in Belgium, his death as well as his remarkable and fruitful life remained unremarked and unknown.

8. A new family under the cross

In the fall of 1888 Damien felt his physical strength quickly fading. Being an expert in leprosy through experience, he saw how the disease was increasingly undermining his body. His eyes were infected. Letter writing became more and more difficult, as did reading from his breviary. Conrardy provided a heartrending description of Damien in a letter to a friend, later published in Belgium: "He is completely deformed, his voice almost extinguished. If you could see him in his room, lying on his mattress on the floor, tears would fill your eyes."[1] But fortunately he still managed quite well with his hands and feet. Conrardy hoped that Damien would live for at least another year. There was much work to be done. Conrardy was in charge of one hundred orphan boys, and every day more were added. Besides, he realized, amid the desolate leprosy of the diseased peninsula: "It is better to be here with two than alone."[2]

Damien, on the other hand, felt his end coming. He had long lived in the presence of finality, but now he felt the hour of death quickly approaching. In his letters, he regularly gave a hint: "I feel my disease has gone down to my lungs, and very soon I hope all will be right—when the body is under the green coverlet."[3] Likewise: "Our Divine Savior knows ... what is best for my poor soul.—I leave to Him the prolongation or shortening of my days. Since I wrote you last I have made many steps toward our graveyard."[4]

It is part of the miracle of Damien's story that in the last months of his ailing existence he was able to experience the consolation he had so desired. Among others, the Franciscan sisters finally settled in Kalaupapa. For years Damien had hoped for their arrival, prayed for it, and strongly insisted on it, until he nearly became fatalistic. That he might receive this consolation so close to his death was an incredible mercy. For years Damien had struggled alone, but in the end, together with Dutton and Conrardy, a small family formed under his cross. Likewise, the arrival of the Irish American nurse James Sinnett, in whose arms Damien would die, was welcomed. But Damien's greatest joy was the visit of the painter Clifford, a friend of the Anglican priest Chapman. Until the very end Damien was capable of engaging in new friendships.

Arrival of the sisters and a refreshing visit

The sisters' arrival was preceded by a great deal of difficulties. "Very strange", Father Damien says in the film by Paul Cox. "The voyage from New York to Honolulu took just a few weeks, but that from Honolulu to Molokai more than four years." The real Damien must have harbored similar thoughts. In the course of 1888 the plans to settle some sisters in Kalaupapa finally became a reality. A motivating factor certainly was the fear that, after Gibson, the Board of Health would again be completely in Protestant hands and might recruit Anglican sisters or nurses for Molokai. Damien's fame and the enormous sympathy he aroused in Anglican and Episcopalian circles in England and the United States fed that fear. As it turned out, the Protestant power holders recognized and appreciated the qualities of the Catholic Church. After a meeting with the Board of Health in Honolulu, Conrardy noted how much credit Catholics had gained with the civil authorities through their care for the sick. "Where shall we find men and women willing to sacrifice themselves for the lepers except in the Catholic Church?" a prominent member of the Board of Health had said to him. Conrardy correctly remarked: "There was a time when the Catholic religion was barely tolerated in the kingdom, but things have changed." [5]

Mother Marianne decided to lead the Molokai mission herself; two other sisters would join her. But first a series of practical problems had to be solved. More so even than the sisters themselves, the ecclesiastical authorities, Koeckemann and Fouesnel, were worried about the conditions in which they would live. "I do not think that Father Léonor is against their coming, but his tender heart is sensitive to the isolation in which they would find themselves if they came", Rudolph Meyer, the Board of Health's representative

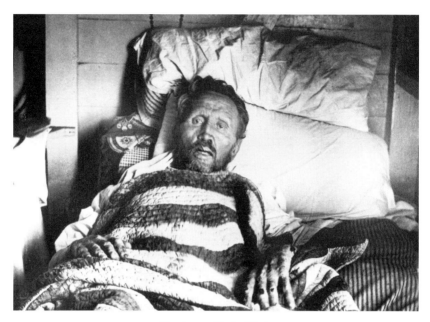

Damien on his deathbed.

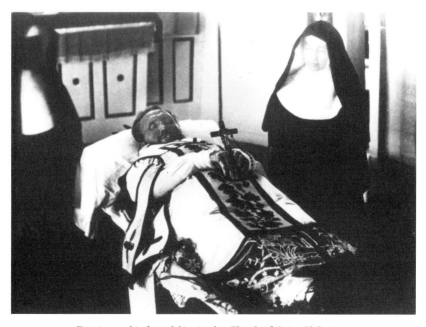

Damien on his funeral bier in the Church of Saint Philomena.

on Molokai, wrote to Damien.[6] Certainly that was a side of Fouesnel unknown to Damien.

In the summer, thanks to a donation from the wealthy Protestant banker and Hawaiian benefactor Charles Reed Bishop, two houses were built in Kalaupapa: the Bishop Home for girls, who were cared for by the sisters, and a house for the sisters themselves. At the same time, the much-needed water system for the second leprosy village, which had been put off for such a long time, was finally built. All that remained was the problem of a chaplain for the sisters. Receiving communion from the hands of a leper like Damien was unthinkable. The idea alone filled the fathers in charge with disgust. Conrardy, then? Mother Marianne opposed this. Why is not fully clear, but she was resolute in her rejection.[7] Ultimately the choice was made for the German father Wendelin Moellers.

On a Wednesday morning, November 14, 1888, Mother Marianne and two fellow sisters disembarked at Kalaupapa. Their boat also transported forty lepers. The sisters went at once to the modest cloister that was built for them. Damien came to welcome them. A dream had been fulfilled.

Father Corneille was also there, waiting for Father Wendelin, his replacement as pastor of Kalaupapa. He remained twelve days on Molokai and delivered an interesting report about it to Apostolic Vicar Koeckemann and to Superior General Bousquet. He could not say much yet about the sisters: he had consecrated their cloister and dedicated it to Saint Elizabeth. He had encouraged them in taking on their new, heavy responsibility. The English painter Edward Clifford, who visited the colony at the end of the year, was impressed by Mother Marianne. He described her as a very friendly woman and a remarkable organizer with an appreciation for art and beauty. He regretted that she had so little opportunity to develop her talents in such a desolate place.

Father Corneille, a keen observer, was very impressed by his confrere Damien. Although Damien exhibited all the signs of leprosy and struggled with various ailments, he remained robust and active. His pleasant mood was especially enduring. "He is happy, working, taking care of the sick as if he is not sick."[8] Once when Corneille visited him in Kalawao, Corneille was surprised to find the ill missionary on the roof of the Church of Saint

Philomena, coordinating the reconstruction work on the building, giving good-humored orders to the bricklayers and carpenters. His orphans, now counting more than one hundred, were well fed and lodged. One morning he found Damien with severely infected eyes. He had gone out the previous night to administer the last sacraments to the dying. Corneille proposed that he pray the rosary instead of reciting his breviary. This, however, was out of the question for Damien, who was reading with difficulty: since his first ordination he had never skipped his breviary. For Father Corneille Limburg, there was no doubt: Father De Veuster would quit only when he literally collapsed.

November 20, 1888, was an unexpected feast day in the life of Damien. That day Wendelin Moellers finally arrived, the missionary who would administer the sacraments to the community of sisters. Moellers, Conrardy, and Corneille traveled together to Kalawao to visit Damien, who was beside himself with joy. Four priests in Kalawao—that was unheard of. How long had he hoped for such a moment of fraternity? On top of it, Colomban Beissel, who had accompanied Moellers, stayed on topside to paint his three chapels. That made five missionaries on Molokai. In his great joy, Damien wanted to call out to the *pali* to invite Beissel to come and join him.

What most impressed Corneille was a funeral ceremony he happened to witness in Damien's parish. "If you haven't seen that, you haven't seen anything",[9] Damien told him. The funeral procession was accompanied by drum, flute, guitar, and other instruments. To Corneille's surprise, the lepers sang a German song he recognized, *Muss ich denn, muss ich denn.* The missionary had to smile: the soldier's song was about a young man who was called up and had to leave behind his village and his beloved. It sounded odd in that remote leprosy settlement, but when one considers it more closely, it was not so incongruous. Following the service, a long row of women and girls accompanied the coffin to the cemetery, to the playing of music. They were dressed in black, one group with red scarves, the other with white ones. Damien explained proudly that he had established different funeral organizations. The men too were dressed agreeably in black. A funeral worthy of the capital, Honolulu, Corneille concluded. Here he approached the genius of Damien, who had turned a group of outcasts condemned to death into a close-knit community. Even though death was omnipresent and newcomers had a life expectancy of five years in the colony, beauty, joy, and dignity were not far away.

Corneille also had his criticisms of Damien. Likely inspired by the gossip about Damien that he too had heard, he found him to be rather childish and careless in his statements. Did he not complain everywhere about the dreadful conditions on the leper island? Had he not received many gifts because of this while at the same time offending the Board of Health and the authorities? Yet Father Corneille saw with his own eyes that the Board of Health had indeed invested in the settlement and that the peninsula had turned into a decent place. He probably underestimated the impact of Damien's obstinacy and selflessness on the undeniably positive evolution. Or did he after all? In a postscript to the superior general, he praised the quality of the mission work in Hawaii. He acknowledged that there had been a time when the lepers were not well cared for and that it was necessary to come to Damien's aid. He suggested that the story of the leper colony be put in writing in an orderly way and published. That would interest many, he thought, and would do honor to the mission. Perhaps it was a little late, but better late than never, he thought.

"I was sick and you visited me"

The small steamer *Mokolii* reached the turbulent coast of Molokai on Tuesday, December 18, 1888. Landing at Kalaupapa was impossible because of the heavy surf, so sails were set for Kalawao on the other side of the peninsula. On board, along with thirteen leprosy patients who had parted forever with their loved ones in Honolulu, was the English painter Edward Clifford. To Clifford's surprise, he recognized Damien from far off. The missionary, wearing his characteristic straw hat, was standing at the shore amid his fellow lepers.

Clifford's visit to Molokai during the last two weeks of 1888 undoubtedly belongs to the most beautiful experiences in the final months of Damien's life. Clifford left a moving account of his visit.[10]

The Anglican visitor and the Catholic missionary had never before met, though they had exchanged a number of cordial letters. They had a common friend, the London Anglican priest Hugh Chapman, who was so generous to Damien and had set in motion in London and far beyond a seldom-seen wave of ecumenical solidarity. At the start of December, Chapman sent another letter to Damien, in which he included a check in the amount of one thousand pounds sterling. Damien could do with it as he desired. The money, given mostly by Protestants, was destined for the reconstruction of the Catholic Church of Saint Philomena, a remarkably ecumenical and magnanimous gesture.[11] Chapman's letter contrasted painfully with a letter Damien received at the same time from his immediate superior, Léonor, which contained the usual fault-finding about Damien's expenses. As far as the ambitious construction of a larger church was concerned, Damien should realize that the poor mission could not afford such a project and that he could do something at less cost. Damien could have gotten permission for that construction work, but it would have required him to take care of financing himself.[12]

Chapman deeply regretted that he himself was not able to visit Damien—he had neither the time nor the money—but he was happy that his friend Clifford, who was making a voyage around the world, planned to stop in Molokai during his passage through the Pacific Ocean.

Clifford was impressed by Damien. Damien's calling him "Edward" without hesitation took some getting used to for the Englishman, who was accustomed to more formalities, but he felt immediately at ease. He described the Belgian missionary as a figure who must have been very impressive but who was now debilitated by leprosy. His forehead was swollen and wrinkled, his eyebrows had fallen out, his nose had collapsed somewhat, and his ears were considerably enlarged. Yet Clifford found it pleasing to look at that disfigured face in which he detected much intelligence and benevolence. That is also how he portrayed Damien in the famous paintings he made of him. The two men hit it off immediately: during their walk from the landing place to Kalawao, Clifford discovered that Damien was an even more charming man than he had imagined from their correspondence. Damien talked without interruption, in rather fluent English, and shared with him various bits of information about the surroundings. When Clifford wanted to pause for a while to freshen up in the sea, Damien sat down to read his breviary. Afterward they happily continued the conversation.

Clifford did not come empty-handed. He brought along a large crate filled with gifts, which could not be brought ashore because of the weight and the rough surf. So the crate was unpacked on the boat and the presents brought ashore one by one, under the astonished and excited gaze of curious onlookers who had gathered. For Damien he brought gurjun oil, a treatment for leprosy produced in British India that seemed to be effective. Damien was skeptical but willing to try it. There were also engravings and paintings from several of Damien's admirers, including a watercolor painting of the vision of Saint Francis of Assisi. Clifford helped Damien select places to hang them in his simple house and in the church. Damien himself seemed most delighted with a bunch of grapes from America, a welcome delicacy and variation from his monotonous Hawaiian diet.

To the great delight of the orphan boys, the English visitor also brought a "magic lantern", a sort of box with illuminated images from the Gospel, which Damien used to give a catechism lesson to the boys. Clifford was impressed with Damien's fatherliness and great willingness to listen to his boys. There was also, to the pleasure of all of Kalawao, an Ariston, or small barrel organ, with many hymn tunes. "Before we had been at the settlement half an hour Father Damien was showing his boys how to use it, and I rarely went through Kalawao afterwards without hearing the ariston [sic] active." [13]

Clifford lodged in Damien's guesthouse, near the Church of Saint Philomena. The first evening, they dined together, with Conrardy, Dutton, and Sinnett, the lay nurse who was staying in the settlement at that time. Damien ate separately to avoid passing on the infection. "But he was close to us, and we were happy together." [14] Conrardy lived downstairs, from where steps led up to the balcony. There two doors opened out, one to Damien's austere bedroom, the other to a simple workroom containing some books and a world map. Some of Clifford's "happiest times at Molokai", [15] he later wrote, were spent on Damien's little balcony. There he produced the famous portraits of the missionary, which today can be viewed in Damien's childhood home in Tremelo. But principally, he listened for hours on end to the stories of a man whom he began to regard as a saint. Not that Damien gave himself airs of being a martyr, a saint, or a hero. On the contrary, "a humbler man I never saw." [16] While Clifford painted and drew, lepers continually came to look at the work's progress. The painter was struck by their happiness and obvious ease with the Belgian priest. The ground floor too was often alive with conversation and joyful laughter. Of course, there were occasional frights, as when Clifford saw a severely disfigured ten-year-old boy with the face of an old man. But in general, to his own surprise, the lepers filled him with less disgust than he had feared. He had prepared himself for a stay in a wretched place of disease and devastation, but now he was moved by the cheerfulness and joy of living he experienced on Molokai. The settlement had more than a thousand inhabitants, and Clifford experienced a pleasant busyness. He described how the lepers often walked up and down from Kalawao to Kalaupapa, or traveled the two and a half miles by pony, while greeting one another and him in a friendly way. He was surprised by "the cheerful people, the lovely landscape, the comparatively painless life". [17]

For his part Damien was struck by Clifford's portrait of him. Did he really look like that? Then it would be better not to give the portrait as a present to Pamphile, as Damien originally had thought to do. His brother would be too pained by his disfigured face. Only then did Clifford realize that mirrors were a scarce item on Molokai.

The Anglican regularly attended the Mass. Though he did not understand the liturgy, he was inspired by Damien's animated sermons and by the dignified attention of the faithful, who invariably filled the modest church. The Christmas celebration was an especially unforgettable experience. Clifford's description allows one to appreciate how moving *Adeste fideles* sounded out of the raw leper throats. He was even more touched by the "Leper's Song", composed by a native poet, about the lot of the colony's inhabitants.

> When, oh when shall it be given to me
> To behold my God?
> When,
> Oh when shall the captivity of my wretched soul

Cease in this strange land where night and day
Weeping,
Weeping alone is my portion;
When oh when shall I leave this valley of sorrow,
Where the only bread I eat is my continual tears?
When, oh when shall I see my well-beloved Lord?
Prince of the heavens is he,
Guardian of my soul, my Hope, my Savior,
My All.[18]

Better than previous visitors, such as Father Corneille, who was on the island a month earlier, Clifford understood the extent to which Damien's beneficent presence and kindhearted sternness had transformed the once-wretched place into a human place, where now there was music and joy. He asked Damien endless questions about his years on Molokai, and Damien, who could otherwise come across as somewhat stiff and focused on practical matters, took pleasure in talking for hours. Damien recalled how from the beginning he had addressed the lepers as "we lepers". Now it was a reality. "People pity me and think me unfortunate, but I think myself the happiest of missionaries."[19] Clifford started to understand something of that mystery in the brotherly and amicable closeness of Damien.

The friendship that developed between the two men demonstrated that Damien, from his place of exile, was capable until the end of opening himself up for others and looking beyond frontiers. The same was true of the English visitor, who was moved by Damien's reputation while he was still on the other side of the world. Their conversations, in the company of Conrardy and the convert Dutton, often dealt with theological or church-related themes. Damien was astonished by the amount of sympathy that had grown for him in the Anglican world. "He was, of course, desirous that the English friends whose sympathy and affection have helped him should belong to his Church," Clifford remarked, "but I was glad to find in conversation with him that it was no part of his belief that Protestants must be eternally lost."[20] It says a great deal about the evolution that the once-militant Damien had gone through. Conrardy and Damien, from their side, tried to convince

The English painter Edward Clifford visited Damien five months before the priest's death.

their Anglican guest of the benefits emanating from the Roman Catholic Church, with her infallible magisterium, as laid down in the First Vatican Council of 1871. Damien remarked how happy it made him to know that what he told the faithful was proclaimed everywhere by the Catholic Church. Clifford admitted that there was a certain attraction in that, but he preferred a church without a pope, being of the opinion that all too often, ecclesial authorities in their unlimited power had caused misery in the history of the Church. He preferred the Anglican system, where the power of the hierarchy could be tempered by good-willed and sensible lay people and where there was, besides orthodoxy, also some freedom that allowed for the development of church doctrine.

The friendship between the men transcended their theological or ecclesiological differences. Clifford brought along for Damien the blessing of the Anglican archbishop of Petersborough, who himself had surmised that perhaps Damien "won't accept the blessing of a heretic bishop" but added: "Tell him that he has my prayers, and ask him to give me his." Damien asked, "Does he call himself a heretic bishop?" to which Clifford replied that the bishop had probably used the word playfully.[21]

Their differences did not at all get in the way of their mutual understanding. Damien showed Clifford how, when relief goods were distributed, he never distinguished between Protestants and Catholics. And not once did Clifford sense any barrier between them, not even when he was expressing unorthodox opinions: "No sincere man could feel a real barrier in intercourse with one so good as Father Damien, and on his side he always showed a true and wholesome charity while he dealt with views which he considered erroneous."[22]

At the end of his life, Damien received from the Anglican the kind of tender appreciation and brotherly friendliness that he, in his raw and lonely existence, had been deprived of for all too long. Clifford recorded: "We must all be happy that the Roman Catholic Church produces such saints, and not hesitate to accord them the fellowship, the sympathy, and the hearty honest praise which they deserve. To Damien we render more than praise. He has our love."[23]

Damien reciprocated that love wholeheartedly. On a simple little card with a drawing of flowers from the Holy Land, Damien wrote:

"To Edward Clifford, from his leper friend, Damien." It greatly pleased the painter, all the more so because he knew that Damien was not a sentimental man. What to think, then, of what Damien wrote with his leper hand in Clifford's Bible? "I was sick and ye visited me." [24] It was the most beautiful gift Clifford could take along from Molokai when he departed on December 31, 1888.

Nunc dimittis

Damien let Chapman know how much happiness the visit of their common friend, Clifford, had given him. He had brought enjoyment with his magic lantern, his music box organ, and "his own sweet voice". [25] For a time Damien thought that the gurjun oil Clifford had given him revitalized his body. But he quickly felt his strength undeniably diminishing.

In the meantime the Franciscan sisters and Father Wendelin had adopted a plan to move the church of Kalaupapa. It took the sisters a few minutes to walk to the church's present location from their convent, so the plan was to move the church closer to the convent. Their plan entailed Damien doing the work. The apostolic vicar and vice provincial urged him from Honolulu to start the work immediately. Damien did not like the plan at all. Probably he felt his powers diminishing and saw other priorities, such as finishing the Church of Saint Philomena in Kalawao. [26] Fouesnel spurred Damien on to obligingness: "It is appropriate that the decision be taken by him [Wendelin] rather than by you, or that the outcome is to his satisfaction rather than yours. Don't be so obstinate in your ideas." [27] Meyer let Damien know from topside that he too did not see any reason to move the Kalaupapa church. However, as an agent of the Board of Health, he could not interfere in Church matters. [28] Still, Damien won the battle: the church remained where it was. It had only to be enlarged somewhat. [29]

Koeckemann felt he was still in a position to complain about Damien and Conrardy. New publications in American and European newspapers offended him, as had the publication in *Annales catholiques* of one of Conrardy's letters. In it he saw only vanity and ambition. At the same time, he worried a lot about Wendelin, who was sick and apparently could not handle life in the leprosy settlement.[30]

Damien did not mention any of those problems to Pamphile. While the leprosarium now counted more than a thousand patients and his orphanage more than a hundred boys, at least he was no longer alone. With satisfaction he went over the list again: there were the priests, Conrardy and Wendelin; the brothers, Dutton and Sinnett; and the three Franciscan sisters. And from England he received a great many expressions of sympathy, from both Catholics and Protestants. "Still I am happy and content, and, though seriously ill, I desire nothing else than the fulfillment of the holy will of the good God." He did not conceal anything about the state of his health: "I am being gently dragged toward the grave. May the good God strengthen me and grant me the grace of perseverance and a good death." These were his last words to his brother.[31]

To Clifford, who was still on the Hawaiian Islands, Sinnett mentioned Damien's deteriorating condition: he could no longer tolerate daylight, and at night he slept at most an hour or two. Inability to close the eyes any longer is characteristic of the final phase of the disease. Damien added a salutation in his own hand: "I try to make slowly my way of the Cross and hope to be soon on top of my Golgotha."[32]

A week later, on February 28, Damien wrote one last time to Clifford: "Please do not forget to take that narrow road—we both have to walk carefully so as to meet together at the home of our common and eternal Father."[33] In the meantime the seriousness of Damien's condition had finally gotten through to the motherhouse of the mission in Honolulu. Bishop Koeckemann hurriedly put Damien's will in order. Though Damien had barely any personal possessions, he managed a large sum of money for the lepers, with $3,700 in the bank. The will he had drafted back in November of 1887, in which he left all of his possessions to the bishop and his successors, was not satisfactory. Damien had appointed his confrere Clément as an executor of his will; in February he added Wendelin. It would be too much trouble for the two of them to go to Honolulu each time for the execution of the will. It would be better for the bishop himself to appoint the priest who would manage the will's execution. He sent two copies of the new will. Damien simply had to sign them, which he did submissively.[34] The missionary was happy to have given everything away: "Now I die poor, having nothing left of my own."[35]

Fouesnel clashed one last time with his subordinate. Again he was angered by Conrardy's recently published letters, which, to his mind, contained unjust criticism of the government and the mission. And he was irritated with Damien's impatience in asking that his order of supplies—mostly the usual items needed for Mass, but also his own burial pall—be sent with urgency. Did Damien not understand that as vice provincial he did his best but could not speed up matters? "Calm yourself, then, and *do as the others do.*"[36]

From March 28 on, Damien became definitely bedridden. He no longer left his room. His confrere Wendelin left an account of those final days, which makes a lasting impression:

> Saturday, the thirtieth, he prepared for death. It was truly edifying to see him. He seemed so happy. After I had heard his general confession, I made my confession to him. Then we renewed the vows that bind us to the congregation. The following day, he received the holy viaticum. During the day, he was bright and cheerful, as usual. "Look at my hands", he said. "All the wounds are closing, and the crust is turning black. That is the sign of imminent death. I am not mistaken, for I have seen many lepers die."[37]

On April 2 he received the last sacraments from Conrardy's hand. "How good God is to have allowed me to live long enough to have two priests by my side to assist me in my final moments, and then to know that the good sisters of charity are at the leprosarium. That was my *Nunc dimittis*, 'Now, Lord, let your servant go in peace.' The work for the lepers is in good hands; I am no longer needed."[38] Wendelin asked him to leave his mantle to him, as the prophet Elijah had done to Elisha, so that he would inherit Damien's great heart for the lepers. "Oh, what would you do with it?" Damien asked. "It's full of leprosy."[39] Then, teary eyed, Damien blessed his confrere and the sisters.

The following days, Damien rallied a bit, as often happens with the dying. Wendelin was impressed by this testimony to faith. "What I most admired in him was his admirable patience. He who was so ardent, so vigorous, so robust was now nailed to his poor bed, fortunately, however, without suffering much. Like the simplest and poorest leper, he was laid on the ground on a mattress, and we had difficulty in making him accept a bed. And what poverty! He who had spent so much money to relieve the lepers had forgotten himself so far as to not even have a change of linen or sheets for his bed." [40]

On April 10, Koeckemann informed Superior General Bousquet that Damien was dying. Koeckemann had planned to travel to Molokai after Easter, but he would not make it. "As soon as we receive the death announcement, we can praise him without reservation." [41]

Wendelin underscored Damien's attachment to the congregation. Together they said the prayers of the congregation. Damien often repeated: "How happy I am to die a child of the Sacred Hearts!" [42]

Sinnett was also impressed by Damien's last days. "I shall never forget the midnight scene which every night took place from his first being confined to his bed till his death. A little after he heard the clock strike eleven, he would remind me it was time to commence the prayers preparatory for Holy Communion which he followed with the fervor of a saint that he was." Sinnett then accompanied Conrardy to get the Blessed Sacrament in the church and to bring it to the dying priest, "who received his God with the fervor of a Seraph. This solemn and impressive scene was witnessed nightly by two mortals and by myriads of angels until that last midnight. . . . It was truly affecting to witness how attached the people and children were towards him. They besieged his house night and day, and could with difficulty be kept from the sick room." [43]

Damien's last brief letter was addressed to Doctor Swift, the settlement's resident physician: "Jobo Puonua has been spitting blood from yesterday morning. Please spare a moment to go and see him—at the second house after that of Jack Lewis—and oblige your friend, J. Damien. In the same house you will find the dying woman I have spoken to you about last night." [44] Until the end, Damien's thoughts went out to his beloved lepers. His death was a real *ars moriendi*, in the school of his Lord and exemplar, Jesus, who on the Cross also thought of his disciples and his Mother.

Doctor Swift thought to take a photograph of the dying missionary. The shot of Damien, wide-eyed, with his leprous hands prominent on top of his well-worn quilt, went around the world shortly afterward.

Sunday, April 14, was Palm Sunday. The story of Jesus' passion was being read in church. Damien had first landed at Hawaii on Palm Sunday, and he would have liked to die on Palm Sunday too. But death did not come that day. "Even saints and martyrs have to exercise sometimes a little patience",[45] Meyer commented.

Monday, April 15, was the first day of Holy Week. Damien knew his hour had come. "The Lord is calling me to celebrate Easter with him." Early in the morning, Conrardy sent word to Wendelin that Damien was in his death agony. Wendelin hurried to Kalawao but on the way met a messenger who gave him the news that Damien was dead. He had died in the arms of Father Conrardy and Brother Sinnett. "I have never seen a happier death", Sinnett wrote. "He constantly was one with God through his prayer and suffering."[46]

When Wendelin arrived, Damien was already dressed in his cassock. All the marks of leprosy had disappeared from his face. At eleven o'clock, he was placed on a bier in the Church of Saint Philomena next door. Many lepers came to pray by his body.

The funeral took place the next day. After the Eucharist the simple cortege processed to the cemetery. Damien had taught his people how to see someone off. The crossbearer went first, followed by the musicians and the members of a confraternity, then the sisters, the women, and the girls. The coffin followed, carried by eight lepers clad in white. Behind the coffin, Wendelin, Conrardy, the acolytes, the brothers with their orphan boys, and all the men followed. Damien was buried, according to his long-expressed wish, near his church, on the spot where he had spent his first nights on Molokai, under the shade of his beloved pandanus tree.

9. Damien after Damien

Already during his lifetime, Damien De Veuster enjoyed in large parts of the world renown for holiness. But those who had known him up close were less sure. Without doubt he was heroic—but holy? Certain character traits of this hero did not fit the idea of holiness of those who knew him. Yet the name "Damien" has lost none of its luster as the decades have passed. On the contrary, his story has been retold again and again. It has inspired the hearts of men and women of every generation and has ultimately brought forth a hundredfold fruit. One hundred and twenty years after Damien's death, the Roman Catholic Church formally recognized that in this son God's love had been visible and at work in a special way.

Commendations and a false note

The news of Damien's death spread like wildfire. In Hawaii commendations to the Belgian priest who had sacrificed his life for their outcasts resounded everywhere. Plans were promptly made to erect a memorial both in Honolulu and in Kalawao for "the hero of Molokai". Various groups, and by no means just Catholics, started raising funds.

In America and Europe too the news got a lot of ink. The story was particularly well covered by the press in England, the superpower of the day and the country where the name of Damien was so well known. This quotation from the *Daily Telegraph* is a good example: "Fearless, serene, contented, and victorious among the direst scenes and the most dreadful visitations which can light upon humanity, this sublime priest appears to our sight one of the greatest conquerors and instructors of the age. Not only has he given solace and resignation to hundreds of his dark brothers and sisters

Left: Audrey Toguchi, inexplicably cured of cancer after praying to Damien. Right: Molokai has not forgotten its Kamiano.

Pope Benedict XVI blesses a new icon of Saint Damien days before the canonization Mass. The icon, written by Father Paul G. Czerwonka, hangs in the chapel of the American College of Louvain.

in pain and dissolution, but to his generation he has bequeathed a splendid example of the truth that 'perfect love casteth out fear.' " [1] The *Universe* already looked ahead to the future, surmising that the visitors who might go to Molokai in "generations yet to dawn" will go "with love and veneration as to a shrine, where the visitor becomes a pilgrim, and involuntarily kneels and murmurs a prayer." [2]

Pamphile De Veuster had always been acutely aware of the exceptional nature of his youngest brother's life and work. He had plans to establish a "Damien fund" to carry on Damien's work for victims of leprosy. Thus it was important that Damien's name not be covered with the cloak of oblivion. He put to paper the most important facts of his brother's life and bundled the letters he had exchanged with him in the course of the years. He no longer felt bound by the promise he had made to him not to make their correspondence public. He gave them to an English confrere who was preparing a publication about Damien's life. Before the year 1889 was over, his *Life and Letters of Father Damien, the Apostle of the Lepers* appeared in London.

Less than three weeks after Damien's death, Bishop Hermann Koeckemann presided at an official memorial Mass in Honolulu's small cathedral. Although he remained convinced that Damien had too many faults to be a real saint, he did not spare his praise: "We are assembled here to honor the memory of a man whose fame has spread over the whole globe. There is perhaps not a city, small or large, in the civilized world, where the name of Father Damien is not known. . . . He has two more glorious titles which raise him above the rest of good men—he is a hero and a martyr of Christian charity." [3]

Afterward the bishop wrote to the superior general: "In my funeral oration, I believed that I should be brief and a bit reserved, so not to discuss his private life, which I believe was holy, but not without considerable faults. His humility, his obedience, and his amicability left much to be desired. I would be insincere were I not to tell you this confidentially." [4]

Damien's name was best known in England, mainly as a result of the publication of Stoddard's and Clifford's accounts and the several fundraising campaigns that had been organized there for the leprosy patients of Molokai. Owing to Damien, greater concern was generated for those suffering with leprosy in their own British empire, namely in India. In June the Prince of Wales, the future King Edward VII, proposed the following to honor Damien:

> The heroic life and death of Father Damien has not only roused the sympathy of the United Kingdom, but it has gone deeper. It has brought home to us that the circumstances of our vast Indian and Colonial Empire oblige us, in a measure at least, to follow his example. And this not for foreigners and strangers, but for our own fellow subjects. India and our colonies with their unnumbered but increasing victims to a loathsome disease that has hitherto baffled medical skill, have a far stronger claim on our aid than the poor natives of the Hawaiian Islands could ever have had on the young Belgian priest, who has given his life for them.[5]

The future king of England then made a threefold proposal: to erect a monument to Damien on Molokai, to establish a Father Damien Ward in a London medical institution where leprosy in particular would be studied, and to fund a thorough study of leprosy in India.

The Hyde-Stevenson controversy

But Damien would not have been Damien had there not been a false note in the loudly resounding choir of commendations. It came from Charles Hyde, a prominent pastor of the Presbyterian church in Honolulu. It was Hyde who first spread the rumor that Damien was not at all as heroic as Catholics would like him to have been, that all of the significant progress in the leprosy colony of Kalaupapa was due to the Board of Health, which, if anyone needed reminding, consisted entirely of Protestants.

On top of that, Damien's illness was not the result of his heroic devotion to the sick, as Catholics pretended, but of his unchaste actions. Hyde, a firm believer in the theory that leprosy was the fourth and final stage of syphilis, thought it certain that Damien had slept with women infected with the disease.

The accusations against Damien circulated beyond Hawaii. In California the Presbyterian pastor H. B. Gage wanted to know what was true of the favorable accounts of Damien appearing in the Anglo-Saxon press. Hyde's answer, dated August 2, 1889, was not long in coming:

Dear Brother,

In answer to your inquiries about Father Damien, I can only reply that we who knew the man are surprised at the extravagant newspaper laudations, as if he was a most saintly philanthropist. The simple truth is, he was a coarse, dirty man, head-strong and bigoted. He was not sent to Molokai, but went there without orders; did not stay at the leper settlement (before he became one himself), but circulated freely over the whole island (less than half the island is devoted to the lepers), and he came often to Honolulu. He had no hand in the reforms and improvements inaugurated, which were the work of our Board of Health, as occasion required and means were provided. He was not a pure man in his relations with women, and the leprosy of which he died should be attributed to his vices and carelessness. Others have done much for the lepers, our own ministers, the government physicians, and so forth, but never with the Catholic idea of meriting eternal life.[6]

Gage had Hyde's letter published in a Protestant periodical in San Francisco. The ignominious charge was promptly repeated in Protestant publications around the world. The attack hit its mark. Damien's image was tainted and doubt sown. The plans to erect a monument to the Belgian missionary were halted.

Damien's friends and admirers were deeply shocked. A reply was called for. It came from another member of the Presbyterian church, the renowned Scottish writer Robert Louis Stevenson, author of the successful novel *The Strange Case of Dr. Jekyll and Mr. Hyde*. The famous story, which first appeared in 1886 and which would be adapted numerous times for the stage, reveals the writer's fascination with split personalities and the dual nature of human beings. That Stevenson defended Father Damien as a man of a piece against an accuser whose name, of all names, was Hyde, is a marvelous facet of Damien's story.

Stevenson, during his trips in the Pacific Ocean, was fascinated by the stories about Father Damien, and he had planned to visit the missionary. His own precarious health—he was sickly his entire life—kept him from realizing his plans in time. He was in Waikiki,

Honolulu, when news of Damien's death reached him. Motivated by the gossip that Hyde had been spreading about Damien within his church, he decided to go to Kalaupapa to question eyewitnesses. A month and a half after Damien's death, he stayed in the leper colony from May 22 to May 29, 1889 to officially make a report for his book about Hawaii, *The Eight Islands.*

Stevenson spent his stay interviewing the most important direct eyewitnesses of Damien's life: Brother Joseph Dutton; Ambrose Hutchison, superintendent of the settlement; Mother Marianne, the superior of the Franciscan sisters; and Rudolph W. Meyer, the superintendent of Molokai. They all testified to the great selflessness and love with which Damien had assisted the lepers of Kalawao-Kalaupapa, day and night, never sparing himself. According to Mother Marianne, Damien had performed "a small miracle" in the leprosy settlement. Not only had he served the lepers spiritually, full of love and compassion, but he also had contributed as "doctor and carpenter" to the material improvement of the living conditions in the colony. In her eyes his greatest gift had been the love with which he had surrounded the children in particular. Protestants too, like Hutchison and Meyer, were full of praise and esteem for Damien's lifework. Because Stevenson had won their confidence and also asked them about Damien's worse sides, they were open with him, as revealed in notes Stevenson took during his seven-day stay on Molokai. According to Hutchison, Damien was sometimes too authoritarian, as when he wanted to impose his Catholic morals on all of the colony's inhabitants. Mother Marianne thought that Damien's great weakness had been his disregard for all preventive hygienic measures, measures that were keeping the sisters free of infection. He had eaten food prepared by lepers and had shared his pipe with them. Further, he could sometimes become enraged, as when he smashed an alcohol distillery to pieces.

All of the witnesses agreed, however, that Damien had scrupulously kept his vow of chastity. Even those in the leper colony who were not favorable toward him did not call his chastity into question. Stevenson obtained the most confidential information from Dutton, to whom Damien had confided that during his early years in Hawaii he sometimes had struggled with his feelings for women but that he always had asked for forgiveness for his fantasies, in confession and at the foot of the altar. Never, however, did he—and he was adamant about it—succumb to the temptation.

The old writer left Molokai entirely reassured, and even more impressed by Damien's merits. In *The Eight Islands* he did not mention the accusations against Damien. But when he landed on the island of Samoa on December 7, 1889, in search of a better climate for his health, he realized with deep regret the damage that Hyde's letter to Gage had caused in large parts of the Protestant world.

Stevenson immediately came to the aid of Damien's memory. The result was an open letter to Reverend Hyde, a philippic of thirty-two pages in which the author did not shy away from using ad hominem arguments against his fellow Presbyterian.[7] If their own church had been lacking in love and aid for those suffering from leprosy, that was no reason to stain the Catholic missionaries who did offer love and support. "If that world at all remember you, on the day when Damien of Molokai shall be named a Saint, it will be in virtue of one work: your letter to the Reverend H. B. Gage", he sneered.

In the open letter, he refuted Hyde's accusations one by one. Damien was coarse? "It is very possible. You make us sorry for the lepers, who had only a coarse old peasant for their friend and father. But you, who were so refined, why were you not there, to cheer them with the lights of culture? . . . And in the case of Peter, on whose career you doubtless dwell approvingly in the pulpit, no doubt at all he was a 'coarse, headstrong' fisherman! Yet even in our Protestant Bibles Peter is called Saint."

Was Damien dirty? "He was. Think of the poor lepers annoyed with this dirty comrade! But the clean Dr. Hyde was at his food in a fine house." Was Damien headstrong? "I believe you are right again; and I thank God for his strong head and heart."

And so it went at some length. Stevenson's open letter also found its way to the publishers, and it spread on a large scale in the first months of 1890. The publication achieved its goal. The doubt that had arisen was skillfully refuted. One year after Damien's death, all of the projects dedicated to his memory were restarted. The Hawaiians worked on a statue in Honolulu. A large granite cross designed by Edward Clifford, to be placed on Molokai, was donated from

Great Britain. The inscription read: "No one has greater love than this, to lay down one's life for one's friends." [8]

Meanwhile, the Hyde-Stevenson controversy within Protestant circles led many in Hawaii to wonder why Damien's superiors, the provincial and the bishop, remained so quiet. Finally Bishop Koeckemann felt obliged to speak. Responding to a new attack from Hyde, published in the *Liverpool Courier* and taken over in the *Hawaiian Advertiser* in June 1890, he wrote: "As head of the Catholic mission here, a longer silence on my part would seem to credit this attack. I ask you to insert the following statement: 'I declare in the most peremptory and formal manner that there is absolutely no truth in the statements of Rev. Hyde against the moral purity of the late Father Damien.' " [9] A few months later Koeckemann elaborated on his defense of Damien, in response to the archbishop of Boston, who had pressed him to comment after Hyde had repeated his old charges once again. "The extract from the *Boston Congregationalist* is an infamous falsehood, and what is more, an atrocious calumny. It is the more injurious in that it is partly founded upon facts, which, through malicious misinterpretation and sectarian jealousy, are presented under a prejudicial light. The good works done by others do not, in the least, diminish the real merit of Father Damien." [10]

Molokai after Damien

Damien's death left a great void on Molokai. The always-present father figure, strict but loving, sick but strong, had vanished. Father Conrardy could not fill the emptiness. He was distrusted by the superiors of the mission and, what is more, was ill. Shortly after Damien's death he went to Honolulu for treatment.

The other priest in the leper colony, Father Wendelin, wrote a beautiful account of Damien's final days, but he did not follow in his footsteps. He saw it as his particular task to assist the Franciscan sisters in his role as a priest. He wanted to remain clean and avoided all physical contact with the leprosy patients.

The Board of Health took advantage of Damien's death to propose that priests and religious workers no longer be allowed to perform medical tasks. Their service would be limited to the spiritual.

Mother Teresa at Father Damien's beatification Mass in Brussels, June 4, 1995.

Bottom left: French lawyer Raoul Follereau started the "World Day for Lepers". Bottom right: Sœur Emmanuelle was inspired as a child by the story of Father Damien.

An exception was made for Mother Marianne and her sisters, who, having already been given supervision over the Bishop's Home for Girls, were put in charge of the Baldwin Home for Boys in Kalawao.

There are testimonies that after Damien's death the leper colony reverted to lawlessness. Already in July the nurse Sinnett wrote to Clifford: "Following the decease of our dear leper-priest there has been a complete change in the order of things here. It is no longer an institution where children learn virtue. They have no longer the salutary fear of Father Damien. Drunkards have recommenced drinking; the distillers, to distill; and, disorders have reappeared among the young people." [11]

A year later Provincial Fouesnel made mention of an uprising in the leper colony: "There have been, some three weeks ago, serious troubles on Molokai. At the instigation of some bad elements, Father Conrardy was threatened with being tied up, as they had tied up the administrator of the government.... The revolt has now ended, but the Reverend Father Wendelin claims that the fire still smolders under the ashes." [12]

In October 1890 Father Wendelin wrote to a confrere: "How I admire Father Damien.... He has lived alone amid a people that were more than ungrateful and more than libertine." [13]

Damien's brother Pamphile, whom Damien more than once had asked to join him, also experienced firsthand the hard life on Molokai. A few years after Damien's death, he finally made the voyage. He was already fifty-eight years old and living a devout life as a Louvain professor when Gulstan Ropert, Koeckemann's successor as apostolic vicar, asked him to go to Hawaii. Pamphile departed from Boulogne-sur-Mer on October 16, 1895, the voyage taking only six weeks. He arrived on Molokai on November 30. One can imagine his emotion upon visiting his brother's grave, near the little Church of Saint Philomena in Kalawao. But life in the remote leprosy colony was a test he could not pass. "Just as you don't become a seaman at age fifty, you don't become a missionary at age sixty", his biographer wrote. "The good father, who was used to occupying himself with intellectual matters, studies, classes, sermons, confessions, did not at all feel at home in the small chapel of Kalawao." [14] He tried to love the lepers as Damien had, but the arduous, lonely existence of a missionary was not for him. He missed

Louvain and the comfort of his familiar surroundings. "You have to be young to depart for the missions, and, no matter what, you have to be formed before age forty." [15] The oldest of the De Veusters persevered on Molokai for twenty-one months before asking to be transferred. He resumed his old life in Louvain, where he died on July 29, 1909.

As described elsewhere, Marianne Cope continued her work among the lepers. Along with her fellow sisters, she cared for the children. She continued to hold a negative opinion of Conrardy, who left in 1896, having no place among the congregation and ultimately losing his residency permit. Mother Marianne died in 1918.

An example that inspires

As materially poor as Damien was in death, so rich has been the legacy he has left behind. For generations, even until today, Damien's love for the lepers, lived to the extreme, has yielded an improbable torrent of love for those suffering from various illnesses and pushed to the edge of society, not least for leprosy patients. Whether holding Catholic, Protestant, or other convictions, many who have dedicated themselves to serving those suffering with leprosy during the past decades have acknowledged that Father Damien determined their vocation.

At the time of Damien's death, there were, outside of Latin America, but a handful of leprosaria where Catholic priests and sisters cared for leprosy patients. But the impulse given by Damien effected a true multiplication of such care. During the first two decades after Damien's death, numerous leprosaria were opened: in just about every mission post where there were lepers, it became a point of honor to set one up.

The Congregation of the Sacred Hearts felt the effect of Damien's charism in an increase in vocations. Following its foundation at the start of the nineteenth century, the congregation had known growth, but that had halted. In 1870 the congregation counted 451 fathers and brothers; in 1890 only 350. But in the ten years after Damien's death, 251 new members entered: an unprecedented increase of more than 70 percent. Wendelin Moellers correctly remarked that the congregation's growth had its roots in Damien's grave.

After the First World War Damien's appeal endured. Dozens of large leprosaria were established in Africa and Asia, where Catholic missionaries, especially sisters, gave the best of themselves. The story of Damien's life, which was intensely circulated by the missionary congregations, generated many new vocations, both in Belgium and beyond, among both men and women. Among the many so inspired was the French Belgian sister Emmanuelle Cinquin, who as a child was intrigued by the story of Father Damien. She realized her dream to follow in his footsteps only at the age of sixty-one, when she went to Cairo to work among the city's trash collectors.

It is impossible to estimate how many men and women were inspired by Damien to give their lives to the sick, the outcasts, and the poor, in whatever form they might exist.

Edward Clifford had understood it well when he wrote in his typical style: "When Father Damien consecrated his life to Christ and buried himself in the leper settlement of Kalawao, he little thought that the echoes of his self-sacrifice would not only be the bugle call to quicken the divine life in thousands of souls ... but that they would rouse an Empire. . . . No one can measure the results of the simplest act performed with a single eye from love to God and man." [16]

Damien's name remained especially linked to the fight against leprosy. Everywhere in the world, organizations came into existence that fought against the disease and gratefully used his name, like the Damien-Dutton Society in the United States, the Fondation Père Damien (Foperda) in Belgium, the Friends of Father Damien in the Belgian Congo, and the Damien Foundation in Korea.

In 1936, the year Damien's body was brought back to Belgium, the Belgian doctor and friar minor Georges Mensaert tried to coordinate the entire world's efforts on behalf of leprosy patients: such an organism present in the entire world was the real monument worthy of Damien.

The Belgian physician Frans Hemerijckx (1902–1969), a lay variation of the followers of Damien, was a key figure in the fight against leprosy. As a specialist in tropical medicine, he worked for a quarter of a century in Tshumbe, Belgian Congo (1929–1954), where he founded a leprosarium in which leprosy sufferers could live with their families. He was strongly opposed to the policy of segregation, which only deepens the stigma of the disease. He set up "clinics under the trees", a system of prevention and healing in which health care workers travel to those in need rather than segregating them. Thanks to the sulphone treatment, developed during the Second World War, he was able to give form to his dream of ambulant care.

From 1954 to 1960 Hemerijckx stayed in India, where he founded numerous "clinics under the trees". Not only the Indian government, but governments in countries like Thailand and South Korea, also followed his advice. During the final years of his life he became an advisor to the foundation Damien Action [Damiaanactie], which fights against leprosy, tuberculosis, and malaria around the world.

Mahatma Gandhi was another great admirer of Damien and his legacy. He wrote: "The political and journalistic world can boast of very few heroes who compare with Father Damien of Molokai. The Catholic Church, on the contrary, counts by the thousands those who after the example of Fr. Damien have devoted themselves to the victims of leprosy. It is worthwhile to look for the sources of such heroism." [17]

Also worthy of mention is the Frenchman Raoul Follereau (1903–1977). [18] This fervent Catholic dedicated his life to the battle against poverty; economic and social injustice; and the egoism and heartlessness of the rich. He wrote numerous novels, pamphlets, poems, and plays. He was an admirer of Father Damien and from 1933 onward joined the fight against leprosy and for the social rehabilitation of leprosy patients. In 1954 he founded the World Leprosy Day, which is still commemorated every last Sunday of January. At that time the number of leprosy patients was estimated to be around ten million worldwide. "Give me one aeroplane, each of you, one aeroplane, one of your bombers. . . . With the price of two of these death-dealing machines *all the lepers in the world* could be treated", [19] he wrote on September 1, 1954, in an open letter to the most powerful world leaders of the day: the president of the United States, Dwight D. Eisenhower, and the chairman of the council of ministers of the Soviet Union, Georgy Malenkov. "One plane less on either side would not change the balance of power. . . . You could both go on sleeping peacefully. I would sleep considerably better. And millions of poor people would sleep for the first time." [20] In the 1960s Follereau repeated variations on that proposal in his struggle against war and discrimination. In 1967 he established the Raoul Follereau Foundation, which fought against leprosy, especially in Africa. He emphasized the fact that leprosy was a perfectly treatable disease.

In that same year, Follereau organized a petition of leprosy sufferers around the world calling for the beatification of Father Damien. In April 1967 he handed to Pope Paul VI the signatures of 32,864 lepers. [21] He did this in interreligious company, together with the Indian professor T. N. Jagadisan, a Brahman who was filled with admiration for Father Damien; the Anglican clergyman D. J. N. Wanstall; and Father Henri Systermans, the superior general of the Sacred Hearts. Nearly half of the signatures were those of Hindus. The other signatories were Christians (Catholics, Protestants, and Orthodox), Muslims, and Buddhists. The petition demonstrated the great affection for Father Damien throughout the entire world. The petition was also supported by 302 Catholic bishops who were dealing with leprosy in their dioceses. Their letters from the five continents arrived at the generalate of the Picpus Fathers. [22]

In his answer, Paul VI expressed his gratitude for the petition. "I was touched by the thought that two-thirds of these testimonials come from hearts that do not share our Catholic faith but who belong to the great fraternity of men of goodwill. Believers and nonbelievers are united in the same tribute. Assure them that I share their fervent wish that Father Damien soon be raised to the honor of the altars." [23]

And yet the beatification was more than a quarter of a century away. How did that come about?

Sœur Emmanuelle (1908–2008)

Sœur Emmanuelle Cinquin, who died on October 20, 2008, less than a month before her hundredth birthday, is known mainly for her work with the trash collectors of Cairo, which began in 1971. In an interview, she described how much her reading the book *Le père Damien chez les lépreux* [*The Heart of*

Father Damien] by Vital Jourdan had influenced the course of her life.[24]

As a young girl in the period 1920–1925, I was captivated by the life story of Father Damien. It seemed to me the summit of love: to give hope to the lepers by sharing their fate. The face of Father Damien, who had become a leper out of love, fascinated me, because he had succeeded in giving himself until the very end.

I thought about walking in his footsteps to bring consolation and joy to those who suffer. While I saw how my sister found her happiness as a mother, I knew that my destiny lay elsewhere. I felt called to go take care of children suffering from leprosy. But because I did not find a single congregation that had as its mission the care of lepers, I entered the Congregation of the Sisters of Sion. In my heart, however, I preserved the memory of Father Damien and prayed that, like him, I could give myself to the most destitute of people, to bring them the joy of heaven. . . . In 1971 the vocation to help leprosy victims rose to the surface again. Our congregation's college in Alexandria was transferred to an Egyptian congregation. That gave me, at the age of sixty-one, quite a bit of free time. I was still healthy and hoped that I finally could realize my dream of following Father Damien in caring for lepers.

I received permission from my superior and the Ministry of Public Health to visit the leprosy hospital in Cairo. The sight of all those people locked away without hope reinforced in me the desire to be near them, just like Damien, in life and death. Because love is stronger than death.

However, it was not possible at that moment to obtain official permission from the authorities to stay in the leprosarium. Would Father Damien let me down?

I don't believe that Father Damien denied me his help at that moment, but he placed me on the path to a different adventure. While my girlhood dream fell through, the papal nuncio proposed that I work with the rubbish collectors, the disregarded pariahs who lived in the slums without any assistance. While driving to the slums with the nuncio, I was, just like Damien when he first came face-to-face with his lepers, staggered: by the collected trash piled high in the small streets, by the ramshackle huts, by the absence of water, electricity, school, church, dispensary. You saw only ragged children with flies in their eyes.

Then I understood that God was asking me to go live among them to serve them, following Father Damien, and with the same fire that he had. I could do that only by living from the same inspiration: the burning love of Christ. . . .

So it is thanks to Father Damien that I ended up among the trash collectors, where for the past twenty-two years I have led the most interesting life on earth, just like him. Because everyone who gives himself, like Christ, to his brothers and sisters shares the same fantastic experience: that the "bluebird" of happiness does not leave his house anymore, not even in the darkest hours, because in the depth of his soul a wondrous joy reigns. The joy of God, reflection of the perfect joy of Saint Francis of Assisi.

Veneration and canonization

Since her origin the Catholic Church has had the custom of venerating as saints those believers who have lived the Gospel with exceptional piety and love of neighbor. Over the centuries and after a complex evolution, the right to declare someone a saint became that of the pope, and the procedure for canonization became more and more formalized. In the sixteenth century the process was entrusted to the Congregation for Rites; in 1969 the Congregation for the Causes of Saints was established.

A cause for canonization has to be introduced by either a religious order or a diocese, generally the one in which the candidate saint died. On the basis of eyewitness reports and other documents, it has to be verified that the candidate saint lived the Christian virtues—more precisely, the three theological or divine virtues of faith, hope, and love, and the four cardinal virtues of prudence, justice, temperance, and fortitude—in an exceptional way. Once a commission of Vatican cardinals and bishops reaches this conclusion, the declaration of heroic virtues can solemnly be proclaimed. For beatification, which makes local veneration of the beatified possible, a posthumous miracle that can be attributed to the mediation only of the blessed is required. In order for the blessed to be venerated as a saint in the universal Church, another miracle, occurring after the beatification, is required. Normally, such a procedure takes a few decades. That time gap is also required in order to be able to verify whether the charism and veneration of the candidate saint can stand the test of time. In Damien's case, no fewer than 120 years passed. How did that all come about?

Already during his lifetime, Damien enjoyed fame as a saint. At his death an article in the *Times* of London called on the Catholic Church not to wait decades officially to bestow on him that honorary title. The first biographies of Damien clearly have hagiographic traits.

Shortly after Damien's death the then superior general of the Congregation of the Sacred Hearts, Marcellin Bousquet, assessed whether Damien might be canonized a saint. By 1898 the congregation was no longer so young, but the canonization process had not yet been set in motion for any member of the congregation. Bousquet felt that Damien could very well be the first.

It was Bousquet who started the first formal procedure for the canonization. He had everyone who had known Damien interviewed. The local superiors in the mission of Hawaii were less enthusiastic. Apostolic vicar Hermann Koeckemann and provincial Léonor Fouesnel thought that Damien had been a special man but not so different from the many other missionaries who devoted themselves with heart and soul. Besides, Damien's character, in their eyes, showed such clear shortcomings that they did not think a formal canonization to be realistic.

When the motherhouse kept insisting on a formal record of the eyewitness reports, Koeckemann charged Wendelin Moellers and Corneille with the delicate mission. They did not perform their task wholeheartedly.

What were the conclusions of their examination? Father Corneille summarized them briefly: "Father Damian sacrificed his life for the poor lepers. Everyone knows that; everyone rightly admires that. If, however, one looks into the details of his everyday life, the details of the various virtues, then you find nothing extraordinary. Just as with others, you find many shortcomings. As regards special favors or miracles obtained due to his intercession, there are none." [25]

When on April 10, 1890, Hermann Koeckemann sent the requested report to the motherhouse in Paris, he added with relief: "You will see that the result has nothing brilliant. But we can trust entirely in the reporter's judgment and truthfulness." [26]

The beatification process came to a halt. Within the Picpus congregation, Damien's confreres and immediate superiors were convinced that he had led an exceptional life, but they were anything but convinced of his holiness. The image just did not fit with the Damien they had known, who sometimes could be rough and stubborn. "From afar he might seem holy; we who knew him closely know better" was the tenor of their reasoning.

In the following generations yet other motives played a role within the congregation that kept it from hastening the canonization process. Would it not be better if the congregation's founders, Pierre Coudrin and Henriette Aymer de la Chevalerie, were beatified first? And what about other confreres, such as those who had died as martyrs in the revolutionary violence of the Paris Commune uprising in 1871?

In spite of these considerations Damien's fame continued to spread, and his story continued to be told and retold. In many Catholic families and schools—but not only there—children grew up with that story from a young age. It seemed that, as the period of his life and death receded more and more into the past, the radiance of his life increased more and more. Joseph Dutton was right when he said: "All of the complaints that one can make about Father Damien will soon disappear; what will remain will be the figure of a saint—his qualities will only grow." [27] How many vocations, how many life choices were inspired by him? It is impossible to calculate, but surely it was many thousands.

The Church in Belgium certainly benefited from Damien's example. The missionary enthusiasm knew unknown heights. In 1927 Belgium, after France, was the country that supplied the most missionaries in absolute numbers—thus, more than the Netherlands, England, Germany, Italy, or Spain. [28] It was believed that, if the influential Archdiocese of Mechelen pushed the cause of Damien's canonization, it would move forward.

When it became clear at the beginning of the 1930s that the village of Kalawao would be vacated to the benefit of Kalaupapa, the Church in Belgium, which thought it unacceptable that the grave of her saint would end up in a state of neglect, seized the opportunity. Plans to transfer Damien's body to Belgium took shape. That this flouted the will of Damien himself, who already long before his death had chosen his burial spot next to his Church of Saint Philomena, apparently was not an issue. King Leopold III requested and obtained the consent of U.S. president Franklin D. Roosevelt for the transfer of Damien's body, Hawaii being at the time a territory of the United States. At the exhumation on January 27, 1936, and at the departure of the body from Honolulu, the population stood by like orphans: their Kamiano was leaving them after all. Following a tearful farewell Mass in the cathedral, a battalion of artillerymen and their marching band escorted Damien's remains in a procession to the harbor in a heavy downpour. The U.S. Army troop ship the S.S. *Republic* transported the koa-wood[29] casket to Panama via San Francisco, where it lay in state for five days in Saint Mary's Cathedral. A steady stream of visitors paid their respects, with guards often having to restrain them from taking as relics pieces of the Belgian flag draping the casket. The most elaborate of several liturgies was the solemn requiem Mass celebrated by Archbishop John Mitty in a cathedral filled with political and ecclesial dignitaries.[30] On arrival in Panama, Damien's casket was entrusted to the legendary Belgian training ship *Mercator* for the last leg of its journey.

Almost half a century after his death, Damien was given a jubilant reception in his native land. On the quay in Antwerp hundreds of thousands of people streamed together on May 2, 1936. Among them were King Leopold III, Joseph Ernest Cardinal Van Roey, and many prominent figures of church and state. It became a truly posthumous triumphal procession, a mass display with probably no equal in Belgian history. The casket lay in state in Our Lady's Cathedral. The next day it was brought first to Tremelo and then to Louvain: there, too, people lined the way many rows deep. Finally the body reposed in the Church of Saint Anthony, the Picpus Fathers' church in Louvain. The procession also served a political aim. In times when the fascist and communist ideals touched many hearts, the Church showed through Damien what she understood to be true Christian heroism.

The Archdiocese of Mechelen lost no time over the canonization. The formal procedure was begun in 1938. The eyewitnesses—fifty years after Damien's death, there were few still alive—were formally heard and questioned about the manner in which Damien had lived the virtues.

Before the Second World War, four interrogation missions (*processi rogatoriali*) took place: in Paris; in Hainan, China; on the Sandwich Islands; and in Northampton. After the Second World War, another interrogation session was organized in Mechelen in 1947–1949. In total, forty-three witnesses were heard, among whom were ten eyewitnesses who had known Damien personally.

Every witness was formally heard and questioned about the manner in which Damien had lived the virtues. The witnesses were classified in a *Summarium*, which contains a lot of valuable information about Damien's life and especially about how he heroically lived the Christian virtues: *fides*, *spes*, and *caritas* (*in Deum* and *in proximum*); the cardinal virtues *prudentia*, *iustitia*, *temperantia*, and *fortitudo*; and the religious vows *paupertas*, *castitas*, *oboediantia*, and *humilitas*.

It is a very beautiful, sometimes moving, collection of texts, with a lot of details about Damien's life and work among the lepers as a real Catholic missionary, and especially about his strong faith and prayer life.

In April 1955 the *Summarium* was introduced in the Vatican. The case of Father Damien, who was still universally known at this time, was welcomed by the consultants of the Vatican Congregation for the Causes of Saints. However, the consultants made some remarks highlighting that the evidence was sometimes poor, that the temperament of Father Damien made him not always easy to get along with, and that his relationships with his superiors were sometimes strained. In any case, the following month the case was officially accepted by the Congregation.

At the Vatican, more research was immediately undertaken. New interrogation missions were done in the years 1956–1957: in Mechelen, Nantes, Honolulu, and Versailles. No more eyewitnesses were found, but many Picpus fathers who had read and written about Father Damien were heard. They all gave very positive testimony. Let us just take, as an example, what Father Gérald De Becker, professor of theology in Louvain, who was born in Tremelo like Damien, testified about how Damien had lived the virtues: "With regard to the exercise of the virtues, he was *supra modum commune humanum* [above the common human norm]. It has to be emphasized that the character of his virtues was enduring (sixteen years in Molokai), strictly supernatural ('I myself became a leper with the lepers to win them all for Jesus Christ'), and universal (he gave his all to everything he did). One can even say, using the doctrine of Saint Alphonsus Liguori, that Father Damien was not merely a hero of charity but a martyr of charity. I am convinced that he practiced all the virtues in a heroic manner because he let himself be guided by his desire for absolute conformity to the will of God. Perhaps he made mistakes, objectively speaking; but subjectively, his intention was certainly pure and correct." [31]

One of the new witnesses heard was Follereau, the French Catholic lawyer who, as we saw above, had done much in the fight against leprosy in the twentieth century. He had been on Molokai twice and testified: "I was immediately struck, in the course of my conversations with the sick, by the very profound attachment they keep of the memory of Father Damien. . . . One can say that there was a sort of presence of Father Damien." [32] And on the still-growing fame of Damien's holiness, he testified: "The proof thereof is provided by the constant pilgrimage of lepers who come to meditate on his empty grave, as if it continued to radiate his charity."

And of Damien's self-gift, Follereau said: "If the greatest testimony of love one can give is to offer one's life for those one loves, it is an even greater testimony to have wanted to be a leper in order to be closer to those whom he wanted to bring to the truth and to life. The life of Father Damien in Molokai, the memory that this once-upon-a-time condemned island keeps of him, and the worldwide renown of his exemplary charity, especially among the lepers of all continents, seem to me so much irrefutable evidence of his sanctity. A man with merely human powers, no matter how generous, could not do what Father Damien has done."

Once the investigations were finished, it took some years for Damien's case to move forward. In November 1964, Franciscan father Ferdinandus Antonelli, the Promoter of the Faith (the "Devil's Advocate"), presented his objections. In the *Animadversiones*, he highlighted some flaws, omissions, and contradictions in the file of eyewitnesses. He especially wanted more information about Damien's relationship with Bishop Koeckemann. Joseph Dutton had testified: "Before his death, I spoke with him and insisted that he should reconcile, but apparently it was without success." [33] No one denied that Father Damien lived a heroic life of charity. But did he also live the virtues in a heroic way? Was he just a zealous, brave missionary, or was he a real saint? The objections that Bishop Koeckemann made against his case were especially serious. Father Juliotte, a Picpus father, remembered Koeckemann answering, when asked why the canonization process had not started: "A saint! Father Damien a saint! . . . To begin the process would first require that all those who knew him would be dead! He was certainly a good priest with many good qualities and faults, like one of us! A saint is another thing." [34]

More doubts were raised regarding Damien's charity (one witness had declared that his mother was pulled by her ear by Damien when she arrived in church with her hair undone) [35] and some witnesses had declared that he was not prudent in his dealings with the lepers, even allowing them to smoke his pipe. Other observations were made regarding his temperament (Koeckemann: "He has an excellent heart, but at the same time, a head that is hard and weak in judgment. His best friends find that he was often very reckless: lacking tact, he made enemies)." [36] Still other objections were made regarding Damien's justice, his fortitude, and his chastity, as well as regarding his obedience and, of course, his humility.

To all these objections, a response was given two years later by the defense: the *Responsio ad animadversiones* was written by Julius Dante and Guillelmus Felici and was deposed in June 1966. [37] In eighty-seven paragraphs it formulated answers to every objection, highlighting the many witnesses in Damien's favor, the problematic nature of his critics, and the exceptional circumstances of the leprosarium of Molokai.

Three years later, in February 1969, a commission of twelve members (the Congregazione antepreparatoria), in the presence of the Irish cardinal Michael Browne, deliberated on Father Damien's case. Although almost every participant insisted on the value of the witness of Father Damien's life, most of them judged that "not all the difficulties that were raised by the Censura were sufficiently addressed." [38] The result of the vote of the Congregazione antepreparatoria was five *affirmative*, seven *sospensive*. As a consequence, the case stalled once again.

However, two months later, Pope Paul VI decided to go forward with the case. Pope Paul knew the case of Father Damien quite well, and he was also aware of the great expectations that existed, even outside of the Catholic world, for his quick beatification. The pope required more research to be done by the Historical-Hagiographic Office of the Congregation (1) on the nature of the biographical sources of Damien's life; (2) on the sociopolitical and religious situation of the Hawaiian Islands; and (3) on Damien's relationship with his superiors.

The Promoter of the Faith also added some questions raised by the Censura. In his *Novae animadversiones*, deposed in September 1971, he required more research to be done on the early adulthood of Joseph De Veuster (before he departed for Hawaii); on his experience during the first years of his apostolate (before he departed for Molokai); on the effects of his temperament (described as strong, rude, vivid, impetuous, and tenacious) and his efforts to control it; and on his mental condition, especially in the years of his illness. Moreover, some consultants of the Censura asked that the reasons be investigated why the cause of Father Damien was initiated only after almost half a century.[39]

The Spanish postulator Angel Lucas, who was tirelessly devoted to the case, traveled to Hawaii to conduct additional investigations into Damien's virtues and relations with others. In 1974 this study, *Disquisitio de quibusdam quaestonibus vitam servi dei spectantibus ex officio concinnata*, written with the help of Picpus fathers Gérald De Becker and Odile Van Gestel and presented by the general reporter (*rapporteur general*) Melchor de Pobladura, was completed. It contained three sections: (1) biographical sources; (2) information on the life of Father Damien as a religious, missionary, and Apostle of the Lepers; and (3) information on his relationships with his superiors and confreres. In the archives of the Congregation of the Sacred Hearts in Hawaii, Louvain, and Rome, interesting materials had been found, notably weakening the credibility of the major critics of Damien, his superiors Bishop Koeckemann and Vice Provincial Fouesnel. The case study of the sanctity of Father Damien turned out rather to highlight the mediocrity, petty feelings, and jealousy of his immediate superiors.

On the basis of this important document, decisive in the canonization process of Father Damien, the defense prepared a well-documented *Responsio ad novas animadversiones*.[40] In the first part, the reasons for the delay in the start of the canonization process were documented. In the rest, every single question raised by the Censura was properly addressed and answered.

In October 1976, more than seven years after the Congregazione antepreparatoria had raised new questions about Damien's heroic virtues, there was a special meeting of five consultants and four prelates of the Congregation for the Causes of Saints, which deliberated on the new material. This time, all nine of them answered *affermative* on the question whether Damien De Veuster had lived the theological and cardinal virtues in a heroic way.

Probably the most difficult issue was that of prudence. The issue had been raised by the Censura, according to whom Damien was often not prudent enough (1) in baptizing and marrying people without proper preparation and investigation; (2) in allowing women to come in and out of his house at any time, so that rumors could easily spread; and (3) in lacking caution in dealing with the lepers in order not to contract the illness himself. Doctor Mouritz had testified: "If Damien was imprudent, it was a holy imprudence. Without it, Father Damien would not be Father Damien.... He was ready to run every risk, if he only could help his lepers—because, if he would have taken all the necessary cautions, the only solution would have been to leave Molokai ... but for others [i.e., visitors, the other workers] he took every necessary precaution."[41]

As one consultant put it: "If there were some flaws, real or alleged, in the course of his life, that was so different from the life of common people; they were burned by the fire of his love, which pushed him always to go further, always to perform better. And this always for spiritual goals: 'I want to give my life, in order to save your soul', he said."[42] The commission agreed, in fact, that prudence is not an absolute value: are the Gospel and Jesus' love not always exaggerated?

In 1977 Pope Paul VI recognized Damien's heroic virtues and declared him "venerable". That was the conclusion of the first phase of the canonization process. It is doubtful whether the process would have had a good outcome without Mother Teresa of Calcutta. She untiringly insisted on this with Pope John Paul II. On May 7, 1984, she asked him explicitly for a saint to enable her congregation to continue its work of love and healing. "Father Damien could be that saint. Holy Father, our lepers and each one throughout the world beg you for this gift—a saint and martyr of charity and a beautiful example of obedience to us religious." [43]

However, a miracle is required for beatification. That was lacking in Damien's case. Mother Teresa had a solution. She saw two miracles that Damien had produced in the twentieth century: "the removal of fear from the hearts of the lepers to acknowledge the disease and proclaim it and ask for medicine—and the birth of the hope of being cured". The second miracle was the altered attitude of people and governments toward victims of leprosy: "greater concern, less fear, and readiness to help—any time and all the time". [44]

The Congregation for the Causes of Saints took a close look at an old story. Simplicia Hue was a French Picpus sister who in 1895 was cured of a life-threatening intestinal illness after the sisters prayed a daily novena to Damien. The required miracle was found. The beatification was scheduled to take place in Brussels on May 10, 1994, Damien's feast day. But shortly before the beatification, the pope fell and broke his hip, and the ceremony was postponed until June 4, 1995, Pentecost Sunday—which gave the event "a note of particular eloquence", in the pope's own words. [45] Mass was celebrated against the backdrop of the National Basilica of the Sacred Heart in Koekelberg. In his homily, Pope John Paul said: "The Apostle of the Lepers is a shining example of how the love of God does not take us away from the world. Far from it: the love of Christ makes us love our brothers and sisters even to the point of giving up our lives for them." [46]

After the beatification a relic of Damien's right hand was returned to Hawaii for reburial in Kalaupapa. The right hand was chosen because it is the one he used to bless and care for the sick. The relic's tour stopped at many of the sites crucial to his life and mission on the islands, including the church where he had heard his bishop speak about Kalaupapa's leprosy patients and had eagerly volunteered to be their priest.

In 2005 Damien was voted "the Greatest Belgian" in the nation's history in polling conducted by the Flemish public broadcasting service. The Jesuit Edourd De Moreau had foreseen it correctly when he wrote in 1945: "He will only grow with the passage of time, and Belgium will always place him in the first row of its most heroic sons."[47]

On June 2, 2008, the Congregation for the Causes of the Saints attributed the inexplicable cure of a Hawaiian woman with terminal cancer, Audrey Toguchi, to her devotion to Damien and voted to recommend raising him to sainthood. A month later, on July 3, Pope Benedict XVI promulgated the decree officially verifying the miracle needed for canonization.

The canonization Mass took place in a packed Saint Peter's Basilica on October 11, 2009. A large delegation from Hawaii attended, including Toguchi and leprosy patients from Molokai. Some forty thousand faithful who could not fit inside the basilica filled Saint Peter's Square, from via della Conciliazione at the entrance to the piazza to the dome, on a warm, sunny morning. The ceremony was moved into the basilica at the last moment due to heavy thunderstorms the night before.

Pope Benedict began his homily by asking the question posed to Christ by the rich young man in that Sunday's Gospel: "What must I do to inherit eternal life?"[48] "The Divine Master looks at him with love", the pope continued,

> and proposes the qualitative leap, he calls him to the heroism of sanctity, he asks him to abandon everything and follow him: "Sell what you own and give the money to the poor ... then come, follow me!" This is the Christian vocation that flows from a proposal of love by the Lord, and that can be realized only thanks to our loving reply. Jesus invites his disciples to the total giving of their lives, without calculation or personal gain, with unfailing trust in God. The saints welcome this demanding invitation.... Their perfection, in the logic of a faith that is humanly incomprehensible at times, consists in no longer placing themselves at the center, but choosing to go against the flow and live according to the Gospel.[49]

Saint Damien, he went on to say, focused on what joins people together; he "opens our eyes to the leprosy that disfigures the humanity of our brothers". After the Mass, the pope delivered a message in Flemish before praying the Angelus together with those gathered in Saint Peter's Square: "May the intercession of Our Lady and the Apostle of the Lepers free the world from leprosy, make us open to the love of God and grant us enthusiasm and joy in the service of our brothers and sisters." [50]

The celebrations did not begin or end with the canonization ceremony. Damien's hometown opened the festivities a week earlier when Belgium's primate, Godfried Cardinal Danneels, presided and preached at Mass in a large white tent across from Damien's childhood home. Among the two thousand in attendance in Tremelo were King Albert II and Queen Paola and many prominent political figures, including the Belgian prime minister, who seven weeks later was elected the first European Council president, and the U.S. ambassador to Belgium. In his homily, Cardinal Danneels expressed gratitude to the many Hawaiians present: "We gave Damien to you as a human being, and you gave him back as a saint." [51] Following Mass, the cardinal presented a new bust of Damien.

On the Saturday after the canonization, an open-air Mass was celebrated in Louvain's Father Damien Square, preceded by a procession through the university town where the new saint had taken the name Damien. The Church in Belgium concluded her celebrations the following day, Mission Sunday, in Brussels with a Mass of Thanksgiving in the Basilica of the Sacred Heart attended by, among others, Belgian Princess Astrid and a U.S. presidential delegation headed by ambassador Howard Gutman.

The Church in America also continued the celebrations. Damien's right heel bone, which was given by Pope Benedict to Hawaii bishop Larry Silva after the canonization Mass, was permanently placed in Honolulu's Cathedral of Our Lady of Peace. Along the way from Rome to Hawaii the relic stopped in Detroit, Oakland, and San Francisco. It then toured the Hawaiian Islands, including Kalawao, where it was welcomed by about a dozen patients still living on the peninsula. Mass was concelebrated in the recently renovated Church of Saint Philomena by Cardinal Danneels, Bishop Silva, and a dozen bishops from California. In his homily, the cardinal called on those assembled to see Damien no longer merely as a hero but also as a saint: "Brethren, it is time that we not only admire Damien but approach him as a saint and an intercessor before God. Damien wants to work, as he always did on Molokai. Maybe he is telling us: You do not give me enough work. I have too little to do. Give me work! Pray to me; ask more of me. There is so much I can do for you. So more requests, please!"[52]

Fittingly, the formal canonization observances ended on All Saints Day with the arrival of Damien's relic at the noon Mass at Honolulu's cathedral, followed by a tribute at Iolani Palace, where his friendship with Hawaiian royalty was recalled and his charity extolled by leaders of other faiths. In his homily, Bishop Silva employed the image of Jesus' saving blood to elucidate Damien's holiness. "The blood of suffering has bleached his soul with glory," he said, "and we rejoice that he has taken his place in that vast throng who cry out forever in a loud voice, 'Salvation come from our God, who is seated on the throne, and from the Lamb.' But this amazing transformation of blood to bleach only takes place if we are willing to plunge our hands into the bloody mess of human suffering, unprotected by latex gloves or sanitized hearts."[53] After the Mass, the relic was carried to the palace grounds, where Princess Abigail Kawananakoa and Belgium's ambassador to the United States, Jan Matthysen, among others, spoke. Prayers were chanted as the relic was taken to the statues of Damien and Queen Liliuokalani on the grounds of the state capitol. Following these ceremonies the relic was carried back to the cathedral for Evening Prayer and its final placement in a new shrine.[54]

Miraculous cure

The inexplicable cure of Audrey Toguchi, born in Honolulu on June 23, 1928, provided the second miracle needed for Father Damien to be declared a saint.[55] A fast-spreading, aggressive form of cancer disappeared in a medically inexplicable way. The cure was attributed to her devotion to Father Damien.

Audrey Toguchi is an elderly woman with strong faith and a ready laugh. She is married, has two grown children, and is known in her neighborhood and parish as a friendly, unassuming woman. She was a high school teacher her entire professional life.

In 1997 a small lump formed on her left hip, which she originally attributed to a fall. When the lump expanded, she consulted Doctor Walter Chang, a renowned Honolulu surgeon.
During an operation at the beginning of 1998, a fist-sized lump
was removed and examined. It turned out to be high-grade ple-
omorphic liposarcoma, an aggressive and rare form of cancer of
the fat tissues. In April, May, and June she received radiation
treatments. On September 3, 1998, she was examined. The cancer had spread to both lungs. Perhaps chemotherapy could bring
some relief, but not for long. The doctors gave her at most six
months to live. Toguchi refused the chemotherapy. "I will turn
to Father Damien", she said. "He will save me."

Like every Hawaiian, Toguchi knew Damien. As a seven-year-
old schoolgirl, she stood on Honolulu's quay to see him off when
his body was transferred to Belgium in 1936. What is more, her
family history is linked with the leprosy settlement of Kalaupapa. Her grandfather was exiled there for a few years but was
allowed, as one of a very few, to leave the settlement in 1940
due to a mistaken diagnosis. But an aunt and an uncle, children
of the man, had to stay behind and died there. Toguchi always
had a great devotion to Damien, as well as to many other saints
and blesseds. Yet it was only in September 1997 that she went
for the first time to pray at his grave, with her two sisters. "For
I was afraid of the operation", she said afterward. A priest friend
recommended that she pray more to Father Damien. He gave
her a prayer card and a medal he had touched to Damien's burial
site.

Doctor Chang did not know what to think when he looked
at X-rays of the patient's lungs on October 2, 1998. The tumors
had begun to shrink. Was Audrey receiving chemotherapy somewhere else? Or undergoing an herbal treatment or acupuncture?
She told him that she had gone to Kalaupapa and prayed to
Damien and that family and friends had also been praying. The
next monthly examinations, on November 2 and December 2,
revealed further shrinkage. "Maybe you should write to the pope",
he said to her. Doctor Chang was not a practicing Catholic, but
this was scientifically inexplicable. X-rays on May 14, 1999, showed

the total disappearance of the cancer. An examination in February 2003 confirmed that the patient remained cancer free. Toguchi was grateful for her cure. Witnesses confirmed that she had never doubted a good outcome. Her confessor, Father Daniel McNichol, regarded it as a typical case of denial of death, as happens often among patients with a terminal disease. She reproached him for having so little faith.

The Vatican reacts with skepticism and caution to the numerous reports of supernatural phenomena. In this case it waited three years before reacting. In 2003 the medical documentation was collected and a series of witnesses was heard, especially the doctors who had treated Toguchi and others from her environs. In 2005 and 2007 additional examinations were carried out before a tribunal of the diocese.

Two things needed clarification. First, could the cure be explained by the phenomenon of spontaneous regression, as does happen exceptionally with cancer? Doctor Chang, who studied the phenomenon, and the other doctors who were consulted considered that entirely unlikely. This type of cancer (liposarcoma) can be cured only by complete surgical removal. In the case of the cancer spreading, such as in Toguchi's case, 80 percent of patients die within six to twelve months. The specialized Memorial Sloan-Kettering Cancer Center in New York reported that out of 135 patients with the same pathology as Toguchi, mortality was 100 percent three years after the diagnosis. The consulted doctors were unanimous: given the present state of medical science, this cure was inexplicable.

Second, to what extent could the cure be attributed to the intervention of Damien De Veuster? The elderly Toguchi was often mistaken regarding the times and order in which events had taken place. Her first pilgrimage to the grave of Damien had taken place in September 1997, before she knew she had cancer, and the second only in May 1999, after the cure had taken place. Besides, she had mentioned in her letter to Pope John Paul II that she had sought help not only from Damien but also from Mother Teresa, Mother Marianne, and Joseph Dutton. The witnesses were heard again. Finally the commission concluded that the patient, in the crucial month between the diagnosis of the spreading of her cancer (September 3, 1998) and the assessment of the regressing of her cancer cells (October 2, 1998), had prayed especially to Damien, even though she had not gone to his grave during that period.

The inexplicable cure could be attributed to Toguchi's special devotion to Damien. On July 3, 2008, Pope Benedict XVI declared that nothing stood in the way of the canonization of Damien De Veuster.

On May 3, 1936, the ship Mercator *sailed into the port of Antwerp with Damien's body. The transfer of his body to Louvain was witnessed by massive crowds unequaled in Belgian history.*

10. Saint Damien

What can the life of a nineteenth-century saint say to our times? Both during and after his life, Damien De Veuster was called a hero, a saint, a martyr. These terms sound overwrought in an era like ours, which seeks especially to be rational and secularized. And yet Damien's life still speaks to us and our contemporaries, as his enduring popularity shows—among Christians as well as among persons of other faiths and of no faith.

Our media age daily serves up heroes from the worlds of sports, cinema, and music, who often tumble from their pedestals as quickly as they were set up on them. Nevertheless, "hero" and "heroism" are terms that today strike many as exaggerated—as if Damien was not an ordinary man, just like us. But in Damien's life there was undeniably an element of heroic fearlessness, apparent in the way in which he dealt with suffering. A famous Jewish rabbi, Hillel, once said: "If you find yourself in a situation where there is a lack of men, then make an effort to be a man." Damien made that effort. He devoted his life to the victims of one of humanity's most horrific diseases. The victims' desperate situation was further aggravated by their segregation from society.

How much suffering, even today, is aggravated by hopelessness and loneliness? That is more the rule than the exception—from stigmatized AIDS patients to cancer patients, the mentally ill, prisoners, the homeless, beggars, and the elderly, all of whom are isolated from day-to-day society. If the contemporary Westerner, so bent on his comfort and entertainment, has a weakness, it is his inability to deal with suffering—that of others and of himself. As much as possible, the sick and the poor are concealed from sight, sometimes even "put out of their misery". Contemporary man wants to run away.

But Damien's witness shows that beauty, joy, and human dignity can be found even in the deepest misery—perhaps precisely there. He did not surrender to hopelessness; by itself, his loving presence brought hope. Our time has a great need for such heroes. It is not enough to protest against injustice or to work for better social structures: a witness becomes genuinely relevant only through loving and selfless presence among the poor.

Mahatma Gandhi was right when he said that it was necessary to search for the source of Damien's heroism. The greatest treasure that Damien bestowed on the lepers was the Gospel and faith in Jesus. "The good news is proclaimed to the poor" is a sign of God's kingdom on earth.[1] Even more than with his words, Damien showed with deeds that genuinely serving God never separates itself from genuinely serving others. Above all, God is served through service to "the least of these [his] brethren".[2] That is the good news that Jesus of Nazareth brought and that Damien lived in his own circumstances. That is why he is a saint. Not in the sense of a perfect person: not everyone liked him, and sometimes his headstrong character caused him trouble. But what ultimately counts in God's eyes is that "I was thirsty and you gave me drink, ... I was naked and you clothed me, I was sick and you visited me."[3] This is exactly what Damien did. Setbacks or uncomprehending superiors could not turn him away from his life's task. The good news is that love compensates for many faults. Although today many people, including some Catholics, think it makes no difference whether Damien is declared a saint, it is to the credit of the Roman Catholic Church that she wanted to make such a life, albeit after many decades, a universal example. The path to holiness can be walked by everyone, regardless of who one is or when one lives.

In the end, through his illness, Damien identified with the suffering Christ. The striking photo of the "martyr of charity" on his deathbed is that of the *ecce homo* who has arrived at the summit of his Calvary. In the school of suffering, Damien was cleansed and attained an unprecedented spiritual depth and purity. He had not sought leprosy, but once he had contracted the disease, it became for him an unexpected gift. That is not a glorification of suffering, of which Christians are so often accused. Only through

Jesus' own self-gift, his suffering and death, did he redeem the world. The servant is not greater than his master, and Damien too traveled this road. Through suffering and death, unsuspected new life is given. There is no Easter without Good Friday. And so we arrive at the heart of the mystery that is Christianity.

NOTES

INTRODUCTION

1. Cardinal Godfried Danneels, "Pater Damiaan op weg naar heiligverklaring—Kardinaal Danneels dankt de paus [Father Damien to be canonized—Cardinal Danneels thanks the pope]", Brussels, July 3, 2008, Press office of the Belgian Bishops Conference.

2. In addition to Father Damien, four other blesseds were canonized at the Eucharistic celebration: Rafael Arnáiz Barón (1911–1938), a Spanish member of the Order of Cistercians of the Strict Observance; Zygmunt Szczęsny Feliński (1822–1895), a Polish archbishop and founder of the Congregation of Franciscan Sisters of the Family of Mary; Francesco Coll y Guitart (1812–1875), Spanish priest of the Order of Friars Preachers and founder of the Congregation of the Dominican Sisters of the Annunciation of the Blessed Virgin Mary; and Marie de la Croix (Jeanne) Jugan (1792–1879), French virgin and founder of the Congregation of the Little Sisters of the Poor.

3. Pope Benedict XVI, homily at the canonization Mass, St. Peter's Basilica, October 11, 2009 (Libreria Editrice Vaticana, 2009).

4. "On the Canonization of 5 Saints", Zenit.org, October 11, 2009, http://www.zenit.org/article-27157?l=english.

1. FROM JEF DE VEUSTER TO DAMIEN

1. He rejoiced in the fact, for example, that news from Europe was reaching the Hawaiian Islands more quickly all the time. "In less than twenty days we know what's going on in Europe. It seems even that soon there will be a telegraphic line coming here, and from here to Japan. Then we will be able to know here in the morning what is going on in Europe at noon—thanks to the sun, which rises here eleven hours later than in your place." See Damien to Pamphile, Kohala, September 22, 1870, in *Le Père Damien De Veuster: Vie et documents*, compiled by Odile Van Gestel, SS.CC., with 212 letters of Father Damien and other documents (Louvain, Belgium: Damiaan Documentatie en Informatiecentrum [Damien Documentation and Information Center]), pp. 206–8 (hereafter cited as *VD*).

2. For a recent study of the revival of Catholicism in this period, see Vincent Viaene, *Belgium and the Holy See from Gregory XVI to Pius IX (1831–1859): Catholic Revival, Society and Politics in 19th-century Europe* (Louvain: Leuven University Press, 2001).

3. Cf. Hilde Eynikel, *Damiaan: De definitieve biografie* (Louvain: Davidsfonds, 1999), pp. 35–36.

4. According to Jean-Pierre Delville (Catholic University of Louvain), it is possible that the De Veuster family had in their home precisely this work of Heribert Rosweyde, which since the seventeenth century was often republished and widely spread. It indeed existed in the middle of the nineteenth century in folio format and was printed in gothic characters.

5. Heribertus Rosweyde, *Generale Legende der Heylighen met het leven Jesu Christi ende Marie: Vergadert wt de H. Schrifture, Oude Vaders ende Registers der H. Kercke door P. Petrus Ribadineira.* First edition, 1619, followed by many reprints and editions.

6. Joseph De Veuster to his parents, Braine-le-Comte, n.d., *VD* 12.

7. Joseph De Veuster to his parents, Braine-le-Comte, July 17, 1858, *VD* 16.

8. This information is found in a letter by Gerard Schellinger, vice rector of the American College in the 1930s, who himself heard it from Jules De Becker, rector of the college from 1898 to 1931, thus four decades after the reported event. De Becker's source is unknown. See Vital Jourdan, *The Heart of Father Damien*, trans. Francis Larkin, SS.CC., and Charles Davenport (Milwaukee: Bruce, 1955), p. 16n1.

9. Cf. Acts 5:29.

10. Joseph De Veuster to his parents, Braine-le-Comte, December 25, 1858, *VD* 19.

11. Cf. Edouard Brion, "La vocation religieuse du père Damien", *Vie consacrée* 61 (1989): 69ff.

12. Cf. Cor Rademaker, "Damiaan, priester-missionaris: Krachtlijnen en ontwikkeling", in *Rond Damiaan* (Louvain: Kadoc, 1989), p. 74.

13. From the testimony of Father Wendelin, *VD* 1053.

2. WHO WILL GO IN MY NAME?

1. Damien to his parents, Paris, January 16, 1861, *VD* 29.

2. Damien to his parents, Paris, April 25, 1861, *VD* 32.

3. Damien to his parents, Paris, August 1861, *VD* 35–36.

4. Ibid.

5. Damien to his parents, Paris, April 25, 1861, *VD* 33.

6. Cf. Is 6:8.

7. *Life and Letters of Father Damien*, edited with introduction by Pamphile De Veuster (London: Catholic Truth Society, 1889), p. 44.

8. Damien to his parents, Bremerhaven, October 30, 1863, *VD* 45.

9. Damien to his parents, Honolulu, March 22, 1864, *VD* 54–57.

10. Ibid.

11. Damien to Pamphile, Hawaii, August 23, 1864, *VD* 70.

12. Damien to superior general, Hawaii, November 1, 1864, *VD* 84.

13. Favens to Euthyme Rouchouze, Honolulu, August 10, 1865, *VD* 100.

14. Damien to his parents, Sandwich, March 1865, *VD* 99.

15. Damien to Pamphile, March 1865, *VD* 93–98.

16. Damien to Pamphile, Kohala, September 22, 1870, *VD* 206.

17. The term *kahuna* covers both healers (who used, e.g., herbal medicines) and sorcerers.

18. Damien to Pamphile, Kohala, September 22, 1870, *VD* 206.

19. Damien to Pamphile, Kohala, October 1867, *VD* 154.

20. Quoted in Gavan Daws, *Holy Man: Father Damien of Molokai* (New York: Harper and Row, 1973), p. 51.

21. Ibid.

22. Damien to Pamphile, Kohala, September 22, 1870, *VD* 206.

23. Damien to Pauline, Kohala, July 14, 1872, *VD* 226.

24. Ibid., *VD* 225.

25. "We learned of the new war between France and Prussia by telegraph.... I hope these political quarrels soon end and that the poor inhabitants of Belgium will be left alone. A vague rumor reached me that papal infallibility has been declared in the Council. That's all I know of Rome. When is the Council going to end?" Damien to Pamphile, September 22, 1870, *VD* 206.

26. Quoted in Daws, *Holy Man*, p. 60.

3. THE LEPERS: TO ISOLATE OR TO TOUCH?

1. Damien to superior general Marcellin Bousquet, Molokai, August 1873, *VD* 256–57.

2. Hilde Eynikel, *Het Zieke paradijs: de biografie van Damiaan* (Antwerp: Standard Uitgeverij, 1993).

3. Quoted in Gavan Daws, *Holy Man: Father Damien of Molokai* (New York: Harper and Row, 1973), p. 83.

4. Damien to Pamphile, Molokai, November 25, 1873, *VD* 272; quoted in *Life and Letters of Father Damien*, edited with introduction by Pamphile De Veuster (London: Catholic Truth Society, 1889), p. 93.

5. Quoted in Daws, *Holy Man*, pp. 63–64.

6. Lev 13:45–46.

7. Lk 5:12–16.

8. Damien to Pamphile, Molokai, November 25, 1873, *VD* 272.

9. Damien to Jan De Veuster and L. Peeters, Kalawao, March 15, 1876, *VD* 355.

10. Daws, *Holy Man*, p. 152.

11. *Testament of St. Francis*, trans. David Burr, http://www2.kenyon.edu/projects/margin/testamen.htm.

12. Mt 25:40.

13. Damien to Favens, Kalawao, May 12, 1873, *VD* 249.

14. *Ka Nupepa Nuhou*, May 13, 1873, quoted in Richard Stewart, *Leper Priest of Moloka'i: The Father Damien Story* (Honolulu: University of Hawaii Press, 2000), p. 98.

15. Daws, *Holy Man*, pp. 135–37.

16. Maigret to P. Germain, Honolulu, June 19, 1873, *VD* 253.

17. Damien to Maigret, July 28, 1873, *VD* 254.

18. Favens to Bousquet, October 8, 1873, *VD* 265.

19. Damien to his parents and brothers, Molokai, November 25, 1873, *VD* 274–75.

20. Ibid.

4. A FATHER MAKES THE DIFFERENCE:
PATERNALISM OR FATHERLINESS?

1. Damien to Bousquet, Molokai, August 1873, *VD* 256–59.

2. Jas 2:15–16.

3. Report on the leprosarium of Molokai, Kalawao, March 17, 1886, in *Disquisitio de quibusdam quaestionibus vitam Servi Dei spectantibus ex officio concinata* (Rome, 1974), pp. 104–18.

4. Ibid., p. 105.

5. Ibid., pp. 109–10.

6. Damien to his family, Molokai, December 8, 1874, *VD* 330–31.

7. Report of March 17, 1886, in *Disquisitio*, p. 110.

8. Ibid.

9. Gavan Daws, *Holy Man: Father Damien of Molokai* (New York: Harper and Row, 1973), p. 134.

10. Report of March 17, 1886, in *Disquisitio*, p. 116.

11. Ambrose Hutchison did not die from the consequences of leprosy and became very old. His unpublished manuscript "In Memoriam of Reverend Father Damien Joseph De Veuster" is dated 1930 and is found in the archives of the Damiaan Documentatie en Informatiecentrum [Damien Documentation and Information Center] in Louvain, Belgium.

12. Ibid.

13. Report of March 17, 1886, in *Disquisitio*, p. 115.

14. Ibid., p. 113.

15. See, e.g., Maigret to Damien, Honolulu, April 4, 1875, *VD* 340: "Leprosy does not break the marital bond; pay good attention to that. You would do better to obtain information from our fathers before consecrating a marriage."

16. Report of March 17, 1886, in *Disquisitio*, p. 112.

17. Ibid.

18. Damien to Pamphile, Molokai, January 31, 1880, *VD* 423–25.

19. Arthur A. Mouritz, *The Path of the Destroyer: A History of Leprosy in the Hawaïian Islands and Thirty Years Research into the Means by Which It Has Been Spread* (Honolulu: Star-Bulletin Press, 1916), p. 76.

20. *Positio super virtutibus* (Rome, 1966), p. 120.

21. Hutchison, "In Memoriam".

22. Ibid.

23. Ibid.

24. Damien to Pamphile, Kalawao, February 1879, *VD* 413. Original in English.

25. Damien to Bousquet, Kalawao, February 4, 1879, *VD* 411–12.

26. Report of March 17, 1886, in *Disquisitio*, p. 117.

27. Ibid., p. 105.

28. Damien to Bousquet, Kalawao, February 4, 1879, *VD* 411–12.

29. Hilde Eynikel, *Damiaan: De definitieve biografie* (Louvain: Davidsfonds, 1999), p. 207. The delivery of Chinese medicines did not take place in 1878 but in the course of 1879.

30. Damien to Father Etienne, Kalawao, November 1879, *VD* 422.

31. Damien to Pamphile, Kalawao, January 31, 1880, *VD* 423.

32. Ibid.

33. Ibid.

34. Damien to Bousquet, Molokai, August 1873, *VD* 258.

35. Damien to Bousquet, Honolulu, April 24, 1877, *VD* 367.

36. Damien to Bousquet, Kalawao, February 4, 1879, *VD* 411.

37. Damien to Bousquet, Honolulu, April 24, 1877, *VD* 367.

38. Acts 20:35.

39. Damien to Bousquet, Kalawao, February 4, 1879, *VD* 411–12.

40. Quoted in John Tayman, *The Colony: The Harrowing True Story of the Exiles of Molokai* (New York: Scribner, 2006), p. 113.

41. Damien to Pamphile, Kalawao, January 31, 1880, *VD* 423–25.

42. Damien to Bousquet, Molokai, February 4, 1879, *VD* 411.

43. *Positio super virtutibus*, p. 123.

44. See the Archivio Generale dei Padri dei Sacri Cuori (SS.CC.) [General Archives of the SS.CC.] in Rome, P. Damien De Veuster, 92 PD-1^E.

45. Ibid.

46. Cf. Lk 22:35.

47. See the Archivio Generale dei Padri dei Sacri Cuori (SS.CC.) [General Archives SS.CC.] in Rome, P. Damien de Veuster, 92 PD-1^E.

5. LOVE OVERCOMES MANY BOUNDARIES

1. "Father Damien, a Progressive Priest: The Reconstruction of His Life (1840–1889)", title of the doctoral dissertation of Hilde Eynikel, presented at the Catholic University of Louvain, 1996.

2. Damien to Bousquet, August 1873, *VD* 257.

3. Quoted in John Tayman, *The Colony: The Harrowing True Story of the Exiles of Molokai* (New York: Scribner, 2006), p. 103.

4. Damien to Bousquet, March 14, 1876, *VD* 348.

5. Report of Koeckemann to the Central Council of the Propagation of the Faith, Honolulu, October 19, 1882, *VD* 499.

6. Damien to Koeckemann, July 12, 1883, *VD* 541.

7. Cf. Richard Stewart, *Leper Priest of Moloka'i: The Father Damien Story* (Honolulu: University of Hawaii Press, 2000), pp. 203ff.

8. Liliuokalani to Damien, *VD* 464. Original in English.

9. Koeckemann to the Associates of the Holy Childhood, Honolulu, October 21, 1881, *VD* 471.

10. Damien to Pamphile, December 13, 1881, *VD* 479.

11. Ibid.

12. From the notes of Ambrose Hutchison, *VD* 472.

13. Charles Warren Stoddard, *The Lepers of Molokai* (Notre Dame, Ind.: Ave Maria Press, 1886), p. 26.

14. *Hawaiian Gazette*, September 21, 1881; quoted in Stewart, *Leper Priest*, p. 206.

15. Cf. Tayman, *The Colony*, pp. 127–28.

16. Quoted in ibid., p. 128.
17. Ibid., p. 128.
18. Regarding Walter Murray Gibson, see, among others, Tayman, *The Colony*, pp. 140ff.
19. Regarding Eduard Arning, see, among others, ibid., p. 136.
20. Quoted in ibid., p. 140.
21. Ibid., p. 155.
22. Quoted in ibid., p. 155.
23. Regarding J. H. Stallard, see Stewart, *Leper Priest*, pp. 238–39.
24. Quoted in Tayman, *The Colony*, p. 149.
25. Damien to Pamphile, February 1879, *VD* 414.
26. Damien to Pamphile, January 31, 1880, *VD* 424.
27. Regarding Charles Warren Stoddard, see, among others, Tayman, *The Colony*, pp. 129–35.
28. Quoted in ibid., p. 126.
29. Ibid., p. 127.
30. Stoddard, *Lepers of Molokai*, pp. 37–38.
31. Quoted in Tayman, *The Colony*, p. 132.
32. Stoddard, *Lepers of Molokai*, p. 71.
33. Ibid., p. 102.
34. Quoted in Tayman, *The Colony*, p. 132.
35. Stoddard, *Lepers of Molokai*, p. 73.
36. Ibid., p. 99.
37. Ibid., pp. 93–94.
38. Quoted in Tayman, *The Colony*, p. 126.
39. Stoddard to Damien, December 4, 1884, *VD* 584.
40. http://www.vatican.va/news_services/liturgy/saints/ns_lit_doc_20050514_molokai_en.html.

6. STUBBORN OBEDIENCE

1. *Disquisitio de quibusdam quaestionibus vitam Servi Dei spectantibus ex officio concinata* (Rome, 1974).
2. Damien to Koeckemann, Kalawao, December 6, 1881, *VD* 477.
3. "Regula generalis est nullum Societatis socium neque sacerdotem neque fratrem solum aliquou mitti aut relinqui in insularum complexu."
4. See Reginald Ijzendoorn, *History of the Catholic Mission in the Hawaiian Islands* (Honolulu: Star-Bulletin Press, 1927), p. 220.
5. Moncany to Bousquet, September 29, 1879, *VD* 420.
6. Moncany to Bousquet, July 5, 1880, *VD* 435.
7. Moncany to Bousquet, April 6, 1880, *VD* 432.
8. Moncany to Bousquet, Honolulu, September 12, 1878, *VD* 297, cited in *Disquisitio*, p. 15.
9. Damien to Bousquet, March 14, 1876, *VD* 348.
10. Ibid.
11. Burgerman to Bousquet, Kaluaaha, September 4, 1875, *VD* 345.
12. *Summarium super virtutibus*, in *Positio super virtutibus* (Rome: 1966), p. 280.

13. Damien to Favens, December 21, 1878, *VD* 397.

14. Ibid.

15. Cf. *Disquisitio*, p. 151.

16. Letter found almost a century after the date on the letter by postulator Angel Lucas in the archives of the Board of Health of Honolulu in 1972, published in *Disquisitio*, p. 180.

17. Moncany to superior general, July 5, 1880, *VD* 435.

18. Moncany to superior general, July 5, 1880, cited in *Disquisitio*, p. 153.

19. Damien to Pamphile, December 13, 1881, *VD* 479–80.

20. See Damien to Koeckemann, December 31, 1881, *VD* 483.

21. Moncany to Bousquet, May 10, 1875; November 23, 1877; February 4, 1878; May 9, 1879; August 20, 1879; and April 21, 1880; *VD* 454–56.

22. Cf. Steven Debroey, *Wij melaatsen* (Apeldoorn: Averbode, 1989), p. 67.

23. Damien to Koeckemann, December 31, 1881, *VD* 483.

24. Damien to Koeckemann, Kalawao, August 31, 1882, *VD* 493.

25. Damien to Pamphile, January 18, 1883, *VD* 515.

26. Damien to Koeckemann, Kalawao, August 31, 1882, *VD* 493.

27. Koeckemann to Damien, Honolulu, September 3, 1882, *VD* 494.

28. Koeckemann to Bousquet, Honolulu, December 15, 1882, *VD* 504.

29. Damien to Pamphile, January 18, 1883, *VD* 512.

30. Damien to Pamphile, Molokai, January 18, 1883, *VD* 515.

31. Ibid., *VD* 516.

32. Montiton to Damien, Kalaupapa, January 3, 1883, *VD* 507.

33. Koeckemann to Bousquet, October 30, 1884, *VD* 580.

34. Quoted in Koeckemann to superior general, March 30, 1885, *VD* 606.

35. The "Notes" that Superior General Bousquet had drafted are located in Archivio Generale dei Padri de Sacri Cuouri (SS.CC.) [General Archives of the SS.CC.] in Rome, section A 47–12. Cited in *Disquisitio*, p. 154.

36. Corneille to superior general, June 30, 1887, quoted in ibid., pp. 154–55.

37. Fouesnel to Bousquet, Honolulu, February 8, 1889, *VD* 1029.

38. Cf. *Disquisitio*, p. 7.

39. Fouesnel to Bousquet, Honolulu, November 16, 1883, *VD* 552.

40. Rom 12:3.

41. Damien to Fouesnel, Kalawao, November 22, 1883, *VD* 553.

42. Ibid.

43. Fouesnel to Damien, Honolulu, November 27, 1883, *VD* 554.

44. Koeckemann to Bousquet, Honolulu, November 15, 1888, *VD* 973.

45. Fouesnel to Bousquet, Honolulu, September 23, 1884, *VD* 575.

46. Damien to Arning, Kalawao, October 31, 1884, *VD* 581. Original in English.

47. Damien to Pamphile, Kalawao, January 31, 1885, *VD* 595–96.

48. Damien to his family, January 31, 1885, *VD* 599.

49. Damien to Koeckemann, Molokai, October 29, 1885, *VD* 642.

50. Damien to Bousquet, Kalawao, August 26, 1886, *VD* 737.

51. So Damien expressed himself in his very last letter: Damien to Clifford, Kalawao, February 28, 1889, *VD* 1035. Original in English.

52. Damien to Koeckemann, Kalawao, December 26, 1884, *VD* 587.

53. Damien to Koeckemann, Kalawao, February 25, 1885, *VD* 601–2.

54. Fouesnel to Damien, September 28, 1885, *VD* 639.

55. Damien to Pamphile, November 26, 1885, *VD* 646–47.

56. Damien to Koeckmann, December 30, 1885, *VD* 649 (emphasis in original).

57. Fouesnel to Damien, February 8, 1886, *VD* 651.

58. The Picpus Fathers Gérald De Becker; Odiel Van Gestel; and Angel Lucas, postulator; and Melchor de Pobladura, Franciscan and author of the report for the Congregation for the Causes of Saints.

59. Ibid.

60. Damien to Koeckemann, June 16, 1886, *VD* 717.

61. Damien to Janvier Weiler [assistant to Bousquet], December 30, 1886, *VD* 766.

62. Quoted in *Disquisitio*, p. 158.

63. Damien to Weiler, Kalawao, December 30, 1886, *VD* 766–67.

64. Quoted in Gavan Daws, *Holy Man: Father Damien of Molokai* (New York: Harper and Row, 1973), p. 186.

65. Damien to Bousquet, August 25, 1886; VD 734–35.

7. WE LEPERS

1. Damien to Koeckemann, Kalawao, October 29, 1885, *VD* 642.

2. Arthur A. Mouritz, *The Path of the Destroyer: A History of Leprosy in the Hawaïian Islands and Thirty Years Research into the Means by Which It Has Been Spread* (Honolulu: Star-Bulletin Press, 1916), p. 285.

3. Quoted in John Tayman, *The Colony: The Harrowing True Story of the Exiles of Molokai* (New York: Scribner, 2006), p. 163.

4. On Dutton, see, among others, Joseph Dutton and Howard Case, *Joseph Dutton: His Memoirs; The Story of Forty-Four Years of Service among the Lepers of Molokai, Hawaii* (Honolulu, 1931); Richard Stewart, *Leper Priest of Moloka'i: The Father Damien Story* (Honolulu: University of Hawaii Press, 2000), pp. 286–90, 399; and John Tayman, *The Colony*, pp. 163–70, 224–25, and passim.

5. Quoted in Tayman, *The Colony*, p. 161.

6. Ibid., p. 162.

7. Quoted in Stewart, *Leper Priest of Moloka'i*, p. 399.

8. Ibid.

9. Koeckemann to Pamphile, Honolulu, July 28, 1886, *VD* 726.

10. Damien to Pamphile, end of August 1886, *VD* 740.

11. Quoted in Gavan Daws, *Holy Man: Father Damien of Molokai* (New York: Harper and Row, 1973), pp. 168–69.

12. Damien to Bousquet, August 26, 1886, *VD* 737.

13. Damien to Hugh B. Chapman, August 26, 1886, *VD* 742. Original in English.

14. Mouritz, *Path of the Destroyer*, pp. 285–86.

15. Charles Warren Stoddard, *The Lepers of Molokai* (Notre Dame, Ind.: Ave Maria Press, 1886).

16. Ibid., pp. 120–21.

17. Damien to Koeckemann, Kalawao, March 31, 1886, *VD* 677.

18. Weiler to Damien, Paris, February 11, 1887, *VD* 810.

19. Chapman to Damien, London, June 4, 1886, quoted in Vital Jourdan, *The Heart of Father Damien* (Milwaukee: Bruce, 1955), p. 273.

20. On Chapman, see Daws, *Holy Man*, p. 169.

21. Ibid.

22. Cf. Mt 23:15.

23. Daws, *Holy Man*, p. 170.

24. Damien to Koeckemann, Kalawao, December 30, 1886, *VD* 768.

25. Stoddard, *Lepers of Molokai*, p. 71.

26. Damien to Koeckemann, Kalawao, January 20, 1887, *VD* 801.

27. Koeckemann to Damien, January 24, 1887, *VD* 802–3 (emphasis in original).

28. This sentence would have been contained in Damien's letter of January 28, 1887, to Koeckemann, of which only the draft, without that sentence, is extant. The sentence is known, however, from Koeckemann's answer of February 5, 1887, *VD* 806. And it is quoted in the letter from Fouesnel to Bousquet of February 8, 1887, *VD* 807.

29. Koeckemann to Damien, February 5, 1887, *VD* 806.

30. Koeckemann to Bousquet, Honolulu, February 11, 1887, *VD* 808–9.

31. Ibid.

32. Ibid.

33. Ibid.

34. Ibid., *VD* 810.

35. *Disquisitio de quibusdam quaestionibus vitam Servi Dei spectantibus ex officio concinata* (Rome, 1974), p. 8.

36. Fouesnel to Bousquet, Honolulu, February 8, 1887, *VD* 807.

37. Ibid.

38. *Summarium super virtutibus*, in *Positio super virtutibus* (Rome, 1966), pp. 142–43, quoted in *Disquisitio*, p. 164.

39. Fouesnel to Damien, Honolulu, February 28, 1887, *VD* 818.

40. Koeckemann to Bousquet, Honolulu, February 15, 1887, *VD* 814–15.

41. Fouesnel to Bousquet, Honolulu, beginning of April 1887, *VD* 823.

42. Weiler to Damien, Paris, February 11, 1887, *VD* 810.

43. Daws, *Holy Man*, pp. 194–95.

44. Koeckemann to Bousquet, Honolulu, June 5, 1887, *VD* 843.

45. Koeckemann to Damien, July 18, 1887, *VD* 849.

46. Meyer to Damien, Kalae, September 3, 1887, *VD* 853.

47. Koeckemann to Damien, Honolulu, October 3, 1887, *VD* 858.

48. Damien to Pamphile, Molokai, November 9, 1887, *VD* 867.

49. Ibid.

50. Ibid., *VD* 868.

51. Fouesnel to Bousquet, beginning of April 1887, *VD* 823.

52. Fouesnel to Bousquet, Honolulu, November 21, 1887, *VD* 870.

53. Fouesnel to Damien, Honolulu, November 21, 1887, *VD* 869.

54. Fouesnel to Damien, Honolulu, December 18, 1887, *VD* 881.

55. Damien to Pamphile, Honolulu, November 9, 1887, *VD* 868.

56. Archambaux to Damien, Kakaako, March 17, 1888, *VD* 910.
57. Conrardy to Damien, Pendleton, Oregon, November 4, 1887, *VD* 873.
58. As Conrardy recalled in a letter from July 19, 1888, *VD* 945.
59. Koeckemann to Damien, Honolulu, January 23, 1888, *VD* 903.
60. Damien to Koeckemann, Kalawao, February 2, 1888, *VD* 904.
61. Koeckemann to Damien, Honolulu, February 13, 1888, *VD* 905.
62. Koeckemann to Bousquet, Honolulu, April 7, 1888, *VD* 916.
63. *Hawaiian Gazette, VD* 924.
64. Koeckemann to Bousquet, April 26, 1888, *VD* 923.
65. Damien to Bousquet, August 26, 1886, *VD* 737–38.
66. Fouesnel to Damien, Honolulu, May 28, 1888, *VD* 926.
67. Koeckemann to Bousquet, Honolulu, June 1, 1888, *VD* 927.
68. This letter is lost; see Koeckemann's note of June 3, 1888, *VD* 928.
69. Koeckemann to Damien, Honolulu, June 10, 1888, *VD* 931.
70. Fouesnel to Damien, Honolulu, June 12, 1888, *VD* 932.
71. Fouesnel to Bousquet, Honolulu, June 28, 1888, *VD* 937–38.
72. Ibid.
73. Conrardy to Imoda, Kalawao, June 27, 1888, *VD* 942.
74. Damien to Chapman, July 19, 1888, *VD* 950.
75. Damien to Weiler, Kalawao, July 26, 1888, *VD* 951–52.
76. Ibid.
77. Koeckemann to Bousquet, Honolulu, July 29, 1888, *VD* 953.
78. Fouesnel to the general chapter, July 30, 1888, *VD* 955.
79. Koeckemann to Weiler, Honolulu, September 19, 1888, *VD* 961.
80. Ibid.
81. Brother Bertrand to Jacques Bund, Honolulu, October 15, 1888, *VD* 964.
82. Koeckemann to Weiler, Honolulu, October 19, 1888, *VD* 965.
83. Report of Corneille to superior general, Waialua, December 1, 1888, *VD* 980.
84. Ibid., *VD* 981.
85. Werner Promper, *Lambert Louis Conrardy: Médecin-prêtre des lépreux, collaborateur et successeur du Père Damien* (Louvain-la-Neuve: Arca, 2009).
86. I take the term *fidei-donum priest* from the 1957 papal encyclical *Fidei Donum* in which Pope Pius XII encouraged bishops to offer some of their priests for temporary service in the Churches of Africa and gave his approval to projects already existing for the purpose. Conrardy's bishops, in sending him to India, Oregon, Molokai, and finally China, anticipated Pope Pius' idea.
87. Letter from Conrardy, December 20, 1905, quoted in Werner Prompter, "Conrardy: de missionaire actie van de seculiere geestelijkheid", in *Rond Damiaan* (Louvain: Leuven University Press, 1989), p. 111.

8. A NEW FAMILY UNDER THE CROSS

1. Conrardy to a friend, Kalawao, November 7, 1888, *VD* 968.
2. Ibid., *VD* 969.

3. Damien to Dr. Kuehn, Kalawao, October 3, 1888, published in Vital Jourdan, *The Heart of Father Damien* (Milwaukee: Bruce, 1955), p. 212.

4. Damien to Clifford, November 11, 1888, *VD* 971. Original in English.

5. Conrardy to Imoda, Kalawao, June 27, 1888, *VD* 944.

6. Meyer to Damien, Kalae, December 10, 1887, *VD* 879.

7. See, e.g., Koeckemann to Weiler, Honolulu, September 19, 1888, *VD* 961.

8. Report of Corneille, December 1, 1988, *VD* 976–85.

9. Ibid., *VD* 984.

10. Edward Clifford, *Father Damien: A Journey from Cashmere to His Home in Hawaii* (London: Macmillan, 1889).

11. Chapman to Damien, London, December 3, 1888, *VD* 986.

12. Fouesnel to Damien, Honolulu, December 3, 1888, *VD* 987.

13. Clifford, *Father Damien*, p. 57.

14. Ibid.

15. Ibid.

16. Ibid.

17. Ibid., p. 79.

18. Quoted in Jourdan, *Heart of Father Damien*, p. 181.

19. Clifford, *Father Damien*, p. 90.

20. Ibid., pp. 94–95.

21. Ibid., pp. 64–65.

22. Ibid., p. 98.

23. Ibid.

24. Mt 25:36.

25. Damien to Chapman, January 1889, *VD* 1022. Original in English.

26. The letter of Damien to which Koeckemann replied on January 28, 1889, is not extant.

27. Fouesnel to Damien, Honolulu, January 28, 1889, *VD* 1024.

28. Meyer to Damien, Kalae, February 5, 1889, *VD* 1028.

29. Koeckemann to Damien, Honolulu, February 11, 1889, *VD* 1030.

30. Koeckemann to Bousquet, Honolulu, February 11, 1889, *VD* 1031.

31. Damien to Pamphile, February 12, 1889, *VD* 1032.

32. Sinnett to Clifford, Kalawao, February 21, 1889, *VD* 1033.

33. Damien to Clifford, Kalawao, February 28, 1889, *VD* 1035. Original in English.

34. Koeckemann to Damien, Honolulu, March 10, 1889, in *VD* 1039.

35. Report of Moellers, *VD* 1053.

36. Fouesnel to Damien, Honolulu, March 25, 1889, *VD* 1049 (emphasis in original).

37. Report of Moellers, *VD* 1053.

38. Ibid.

39. Ibid.

40. Ibid., *VD* 1053–54.

41. Koeckemann to Bousquet, Honolulu, April 10, 1889, *VD* 1051.

42. Report of Moellers, *VD* 1054.

43. Sinnett to Clifford, July 24, 1889, in Damiaan Documentatie en Informatiecentrum [Damien Documentation and Information Center] in Louvain, Belgium.

44. Damien to Swift, *VD* 1050. Original in English.

45. Meyer to Ashley, April 11, 1889, in the Archives of Hawaii in Honolulu.

46. Sinnett to Clifford, Kalawao, April 18, 1889, in Damiaan Documentatie en In-formatiecentrum [Damien Documentation and Information Center] in Louvain, Belgium.

9. DAMIEN AFTER DAMIEN

1. Reprinted in *Great Thoughts*, vol. 2, June 1, 1889, p. 347.

2. Ibid.

3. Quoted in Vital Jourdan, *The Heart of Father Damien* (Milwaukee: Bruce, 1955), p. 377.

4. Koeckemann to Bousquet, Honolulu, December 13, 1889, *VD* 1083.

5. Quoted in Jourdan, *Heart of Father Damien*, pp. 379–80.

6. Quoted in Robert Louis Stevenson, *Travels in Hawaii* (Honolulu: University Press of Hawaii, 1973). This publication contains Stevenson's letters from Hawaii.

7. Robert Louis Stevenson, "An Open Letter to the Reverend Dr. Hyde of Hono-lulu", February 25, 1890, published online by the World Wide School, http://www.worldwideschool.org/library/books/hst/biography/FatherDamien/Chap1.html.

8. Jn 15:13.

9. Quoted in Jourdan, *Heart of Father Damien*, pp. 359–60.

10. Ibid., p. 347; also, see Richard Stewart, *Leper Priest of Moloka'i: The Father Damien Story* (Honolulu: University of Hawaii Press, 2000), pp. 385–86.

11. Quoted in Jourdan, *Heart of Father Damien*, p. 293.

12. Fouesnel to Bousquet, Honolulu, August 12, 1890, *VD* 1100.

13. Wendelin Moellers to Maurice Raepsaet, Molokai, October 6, 1890, *VD* 1106.

14. Obituary of R. P. Pamphile De Veuster in *Annales SS.CC.*, 7 bis1909, pp. 285–88.

15. Ibid., p. 287.

16. Edward Clifford, quoted in Gavan Daws, *Holy Man: Father Damien of Molokai* (New York: Harper and Row, 1973), p. 221.

17. T. N. Jagadisan, *Mahatma Gandhi Answers the Challenge of Leprosy* (Madras, 1965), p. 3.

18. See, among others, Steven Debroey, *Een zonderling advocaat: Levensschetes van Raoul Follereau* (Kasterlee: De Vroente, 1972).

19. Raoul Follereau, *Petitions to Statesmen* (Association suisse Raoul Follereau, n.d.), published online by AIFO (Associazione italiana amici de Raoul Follereau), http://www.aifo.it/english/gen/follereau/petitions-statesmen.pdf (emphasis in original).

20. Ibid.

21. Cf. *L'Osservatore della domenica*, May 7, 1967, p. 7.

22. Cf. Archivio Generale dei Padri dei Sacri Cuori (SS.CC.) [General Archives of the SS.CC.] in Rome, 92PD-E t.e.m. P.

23. "L'udienza del Papa a Raoul Follereau", in *L'avvenire d'Italia* (Bologna), April 26, 1967, p. 2.

24. Interview with Sœur Emmanuelle at http://www.ssccpicpus.fr/article.asp?contenu_ssrub=soeur+emmanuelle+et+le+pere+damien&contenu_rub=Bx+DAMIEN_+DE+MOLOKA%CF.

25. Corneille to Bousquet, Heeia, March 7, 1890, *VD* 1089.

26. Koeckemann to Bousquet, Honolulu, April 10, 1890, *VD* 1091.

27. Quoted in Msgr. Juliotte's notes about Damien, written on Hainan between 1924 and 1930, *VD* 1189.

28. Cf. Edouard De Moreau, S.J., *Les missionnaires belges de 1804 jusqu'à nos jours* (Brussels: Les presses de Belgique, 1944), p. 8.

29. The koa tree is the second most common tree on the Hawaiian Islands. Its name means "brave, bold, fearless, or warrior".

30. Gordon Seeley, "Father Damien's connection," http://www.sfarchdiocese.org/about-us/news/2009/Father-Damiens-connection-1837/.

31. *Summarium super virtutibus*, in *Positio super virtutibus* (Rome, 1966), p. 281.

32. Ibid., pp. 354–56.

33. "Poco prima della sua morte, io gli parlai, premurandolo di riconciliarsi (scil cum Vicario apostolico, Koeckemann), ma apparentemente senza successo", *Animadver siones*, in *Positio super virtutibus*, p. 11.

34. Ibid., p. 14.

35. Ibid., pp. 18–19.

36. Ibid., p. 21.

37. *Responsio ad animadversiones*, in *Positio super virtutibus*.

38. See *Relatio et vota: Congressus peculiaris super virtutibus*, October 19, 1976, p. 7.

39. "Sarebbe curioso sapere perché la Congregazione dei Picpus non si era interessata prima della causa." *Novae animadversiones*, in *Nova positio super virtutibus*, December 19, 1975, p. 45.

40. *Responsio patroni ad novas animadversiones*, in *Nova positio super virtutibus*.

41. *Relatio et vota*, p. 36.

42. Ibid., p. 59.

43. Mother Teresa, "El padre Damian De Veuster y Madre Teresa de Calcuta", note by postulator Angel Lucas, SS.CC., June 24, 1986, in the Archivio Generale dei Padri Sacri Cuori (SS.CC.) [General Archives of the SS.CC.] in Rome, 92PD–13G, 6/9.

44. Ibid.

45. Pope John Paul II, "Blessed Damien De Veuster—Witness to God's Presence in History", message given on June 7, 1995, in *L'Osservatore Romano*, Weekly Edition in English, June 14, 1995, p. 11.

46. Pope John Paul II, homily at Saint Damien's beatification Mass, Brussels, June 4, 1995, in *L'Osservatore Romano*, Weekly Edition in English, June 7, 1995.

47. De Moreau, *Les missionaires belges*, p. 79.

48. Mk 10:17.

49. Pope Benedict XVI, homily at canonization Mass, St. Peter's Basilica, October 11, 2009 (Libreria Editrice Vaticana, 2009).

50. http://www.zenit.org/rssenglish-27157

51. Godfried Cardinal Danneels, homily, Tremelo, October 4, 2009.

52. Godfried Cardinal Danneels, homily at the Church of Saint Philomena, Kalawao, October 31, 2009.

53. Bishop Larry Silva, homily, Cathedral of Our Lady of Peace, Honolulu, November 1, 2009.

54. Patrick Downes, "A royal welcome," http://www.hawaiicatholicherald.com/Home/tabid/256/newsid884/2640/Default.aspx.

55. The complete medical documentation and transcripts of witness interviews are collected in the *Positio super miraculo* (Rome, 2008).

10. SAINT DAMIEN

1. Cf. Lk 4:18.
2. Mt 25:40.
3. Mt 25:35–36.

INDEX